Being Homeless

Being Homeless

Textual and Narrative Constructions

Amir B. Marvasti

LEXINGTON BOOKS
Lanham • Boulder • New York • Oxford

LEXINGTON BOOKS

Published in the United States of America
by Lexington Books
A Member of the Rowman & Littlefield Publishing Group
4501 Forbes Boulevard, Suite 200, Lanham, Maryland 20706

PO Box 317
Oxford
OX2 9RU, UK

British Library Cataloguing in Publication Information Available

Library of Congress Cataloging-in-Publication Data

Marvasti, Amir B., 1966–
    Being Homeless: textual and narrative constructions / Amir B. Marvasti.
        p. cm.
    Includes bibliographical references and index.
    ISBN 0-7391-0619-8 (alk. paper)
    1. Homelessness. 2. Homeless persons. I. Title.

    HV4493.M37   2003
    305.5'69—dc21   2003040038

Printed in the United States of America

⊖™ The paper used in this publication meets the minimum requirements of American
National Standard for Information Sciences—Permanence of Paper for Printed Library
Materials, ANSI/NISO Z39.48–1992.

6816

For Arya, who means home to me

Contents

Acknowledgments

I would like to give thanks to the staff and clients of the Abbot House who generously shared their lives with me. I also owe a debt of gratitude to Jay Gubrium, James Holstein, Joe Feagin, Hernan Vera, and Karyn McKinney for their support and insightful suggestions throughout this project. Finally, I am grateful to Jason Hallman and his editorial staff for their help with completing this manuscript.

Introduction

Fieldwork and the Research Problem

A few years ago, during a presentation on homelessness at the annual meeting of the American Sociological Association in Chicago, I was asked by a young black woman who introduced herself as an activist, "How does your research *help* the homeless?" I took a deep breath and replied, "You mean the intellectual masturbation aside, what does this do for the homeless?" She nodded with a chuckle. I went on, "You know, this is something that I have struggled with since I started working on this project. On the one hand, I feel that I have robbed people of their stories without any compensation, that I exploited them to advance my academic career and get a few publications. That's something that will never go away. . . . On the other hand, to the extent that I have been able to add complexity to our understanding of who the homeless are and what they experience, I feel that my work might have a positive effect." The young woman was obviously less than pleased with my reply.

Later that day, I was walking around the streets of downtown Chicago with a group of colleagues. It was impossible to ignore the shabby characters that boldly competed for attention with the city's Cow Parade Exhibit, consisting of hundreds of wooden cows artistically decorated and displayed throughout the downtown area. One of my companions remarked, referring to the shabby characters, "These guys look a little more mentally ill than the ones we see in our hometown." Rushing to claim my area of study, I embarked on an analytical journey to explain both the causes of homelessness and its regional variations. As I painfully realized the limitations of my substantive knowledge, I spared my friends by confessing, "Not all homeless people are the same."

These anecdotes represent two of the most challenging aspects of this study—the moral obligation to the people I studied, and my struggle to make a substantive contribution to the discipline of sociology by studying the experience of homelessness. Although I gave a great deal of thought to finding a happy marriage between these two goals, I found myself wildly swaying between them. As far as my responsibility to give something back to those I worked with, the advice was plentiful. Most of that advice offered the "objective researcher" position as a safe haven: "As a researcher, it is your job to report the facts. What people do with those facts is not your concern." Unfortunately, I found no solace in the sanctuary of objectivity. Maybe it was all the reading I had done on postmodernism that led me astray, or just the fact that I wanted my work to have more significance than just an objective assessment of the problem. In either case, I went on bemoaning the dilemmas of my research.

During this time, I especially disagreed with those who contended that I had nothing to worry about because I had obtained oral consent from my subjects. In fact, in one professional presentation, I disdainfully announced to the other participants, "A contractual agreement is a poor substitute for morality." I think they were duly impressed by my convictions, but went on wondering, like myself, how I was ever going to resolve the issue. I never did.

As far as the sociological significance of my work is concerned, things were a bit easier. My research seemed to be connected with a wide range of sociological topics. If race was the topic of discussion, my work had racial implications. If gender was the focus, I had something to say about that as well, because I did interviews with women who spoke of being the victims of sexism. Over time, most of my colleagues and peers grew weary of my lofty conjectures and began greeting me in the hallways with, "Are you done yet?" or "What page are you on?" I must admit I always found it easier to talk about my research than to actually write about it.

In the end, as the present text shows, the research was completed and the writing finished. But the personal side of the project lingers on. In many ways, this book reflects the lessons of a personal journey. The cliche "Working with this group of people has taught me a lot" certainly applies to me, with one minor qualification. I had to learn how to learn. I had to find ways of making sense of what I saw, heard, and felt in the context of the particular moral contingencies of this field as well as the circumstances of my own personal life. This will be apparent throughout the book, as I highlight how the learning process coincided with my experiences in the field.

Membership Roles in the Field

In their book *Membership Roles in the Field,* Patricia and Peter Adler[1] discuss three types of membership roles for ethnographers: peripheral, active, and complete. The Adlers argue that membership roles in the field are based on epistemological choices, structural necessities, and personal characteristics and preferences,[2] all of which certainly characterize my own experience. These roles also represent various degrees of "self-involvement" in the field. In the case of peripheral membership, the researcher's self is marginally involved. By contrast, active membership leads to, and requires, a deeper sense of involvement:

> Assuming an active membership role can also have far more profound *effects on the researcher's self* than are generated by peripheral membership involvement. In functioning as a member, researchers get swept up into many of the same experiences as members. While this has the distinct advantage of adding their own selves as data to the research, both as a cross-check against the accounts of others and as a deepened

awareness of how members actually think and feel, it propels researchers through various changes.[3]

The Adlers contend the self undergoes a transformation as a result of the fieldwork.
While the researcher may choose the active role to collect better data, she or he is
transformed in the process. According to the Adlers, this is particularly the case
when the fieldworker becomes completely involved:

> The complete membership role entails the greatest commitment on the
> part of the researcher. Rather than experiencing more participatory
> involvement, complete-member-researchers (CMRs) immerse them-
> selves fully in the group as "natives." They and their subjects relate to
> each other as status equals, dedicated to sharing in a common set of
> experiences, feelings, and goals.[4]

Here self-immersion is both the goal and the consequence of fieldwork. In
essence, the researcher's self does not just enhance the quality of the data, but it
becomes data. In extreme cases, it is the only data being analyzed, as in the recent
turn to intrasubjectivity in fieldwork, often referred to as "autoethnography."[5]

In many respects, my own fieldwork experiences coincided with this insightful
scheme. I, too, grappled with finding a position at my site that represented a happy
medium between my epistemological preferences, personal characteristics, and the
existing structural contingencies of the shelter. In addition, other external
circumstances completely outside the field affected my data collection. For
example, on many occasions, the demands of my home life and other personal
relationships required that I spend less time at the shelter. On other occasions, I had
to completely withdraw from the field due to financial constraints. As a whole,
along with my subjective stance or self, my data collection strategies were heavily
influenced by structural conditions both inside and outside the field, which I
discuss at greater length later in the book.

Actually, I often had to occupy more than one role on any given day in the
field. For example, I might have begun a typical day at the shelter with the
peripheral role of just listening to the clients' conversations in the parking lot while
I smoked a cigarette. I could then go on to the more active role of a volunteer as I
worked more closely with the clients and the staff. The day could have ended with
me assuming the complete participant role of the night manager. Thus the analytical
distinctions among the various types of field membership roles were, in practice,
blurred to say the least. Indeed, if the emphasis should be placed on how the
researcher's self is transformed in the course of fieldwork, as the Adlers[6] suggest,
then my data collection experiences can be better understood using a different
analytical framework.

Fieldwork as Analytic Bracketing

In my view, the working complexity of fieldwork for the fieldworker is better captured by Jaber Gubrium and James Holstein's[7] notion of working self of everyday life, which they argue is constructed through the constant interplay of agency and structure. Gubrium and Holstein use the term *analytic bracketing* to refer to their method of studying the reciprocal action and reaction that gives concrete reality to self in everyday life. In their words:

> This procedure amounts to alternately bracketing the *whats*, then the *hows*, in order to assemble a more complete picture of practice. The objective is to move back and forth between constitutive and substantive resources, alternately describing each, making informative references to the other in the process.[8]

Similarly, fieldwork can be seen as an ongoing process of constructing a research self that is mediated by both personal choices (i.e., agency) and material contingencies internal and external to the field (i.e., structure). Consequently, my methodological approach in this study evolved along the same lines as my theoretical stance. That is to say, much in the same way I view the social construction of the client as a multiperspective and polyphonic discourse, I also approach the data collection process as one that is informed by a complex set of contingencies. In other words, my methodological framework mirrors my theoretical approach in that I constantly shift between my own subjectivity and the external or objective conditions of the field. As the agency/structure dichotomy is the focal point of any sociological project, I argue that the process of collecting data and writing about social phenomena is no exception to this rule.

Accordingly, using the idea of analytical bracketing, both theoretically and methodologically, I examine the various methods by which the category of the homeless client is socially constructed at an emergency shelter. The overall goal is to show the complexity of discourses and practices that constitute the client at this site. In other words, where conventional wisdom holds that there is "homelessness" and it has a story, I take the point of view that the homeless client is a set of stories, drawn from historical, demographic, and lived accounts. Taken together, these construct homelessness.

It should be noted that my fieldwork experiences were instrumental in my conceptualization of the research problem. While my observations enabled me to appreciate the complexity of homelessness, at times they led me to question the conventional academic discourse on the topic. After only a few months of fieldwork, I became aware of, and at times irritated by, the gap between the everyday nuances of being homeless and its textual representations in scholarly publications. The following section briefly highlights the analytical pathway through which this project was developed.

The Research Problem and the Organization of the Book

The academic literature on homelessness typically suggests that the "homeless" are helpless victims of circumstances beyond their control. Homeless people are typically regarded as social misfits who have fallen through the cracks of conventional modes of social control. Little attention is given to their agency. Instead, the homeless are viewed as objects of contempt, fear, or sympathy.

Ironically, the most conscientious attempts at "giving voice" to the homeless may have further concretized their negative identities. Romantic images of the "down-and-out" on the streets of America have in some cases provided the very stock of knowledge[9] that constitutes "homelessness" as a form of pathology. Indeed, the reality of homelessness for most researchers in this area is treated as universal—analytically concretized from the beginning and empirically pursued for social variation.[10] Furthermore, this is set against an implicit model of normality that approaches "the homeless identity" in terms of its deviant shortcomings.

In this context, it is thought that the "homeless" label is to be avoided at all costs, a sentiment expressed in the works of many ethnographers who have attempted to show how the homeless manage to "preserve" or "restore" their humanity.[11] For example, in their article "Identity Construction and Avowal of Personal Identities," David Snow and Leon Anderson write:

> Our primary goal in this paper is [to] . . . further understanding of the manner in which a sense of personal significance and meaning is generated and sustained among individuals who have fallen through the cracks of society and linger at the bottom of the status system.[12]

Having established the homeless at the "bottom" of the status system, the central question for these authors becomes, How do the homeless manage to survive or escape the confines of selves stigmatized by this location?

As empirically sensitive and analytically useful as Snow and Anderson's, Liebow's, and related accounts of homelessness are, there is empirical evidence that homelessness in the course of everyday life is represented in more situationally variable and artful ways. For example, J. W. Spencer[13] shows how homelessness is constructed in accordance with the organizational contingencies of human service providers. He shows how "clients constructed their narratives as rhetorical devices which could accountably cast themselves in ways which would guarantee their reception of services."[14] According to Spencer, clients use various situationally appropriate themes to construct identities that are deemed "service worthy" by social workers. For example, some clients used the theme of "tryin' to make it" to establish that in spite of their best efforts, they are helpless, alone, and consequently in legitimate need of services.[15] These findings suggest that the portrayal and management of the homeless client is both practical and situational.

Jaber Gubrium and James Holstein offer a more precise theoretical foundation of such an approach, arguing that identities, stigmatized or otherwise, are the products of contextually conditioned and goal-oriented practices. As they put it: "In the course of everyday life, individuals adroitly construct selves using locally available and meaningful materials shaped to the specifications and demands of the interpretive task at hand."[16] Specifically, they view identities as matters of "biographical work," the situationally sensitive activity of giving shape to the self through coherent narratives, which are actively composed to reveal a person's identity to others for a practical purpose.[17]

Gubrium and Holstein's framework is especially concerned with the contingencies that shape how narratives are articulated: "Biographical work thus reflects locally promoted ways of interpreting experience and identity so that what is constructed is distinctively crafted, yet assembled from the meaningful categories and vocabularies of settings."[18] For Gubrium and Holstein, "the meaningful categories and vocabularies of settings" constitute "local cultures"—sited, circumscribed meanings that mediate and enter into the production of stories. In their words:

> [L]ocal culture does not so much determine participants' biographical work as it provides circumstantially recognizable and accountable interpretive resources for constructing an understanding of lives.[19]

In short, Gubrium and Holstein put forth an analytical framework that emphasizes both the discursive contingencies and the actors' agency. Narration gives shape to one's identity and the local culture of the setting provides the descriptive resources for, and constraints on, storytelling.[20]

Following this approach, this research aims to empirically examine the social construction of homelessness in two ways. First, homelessness is analyzed in relation to literary and academic texts that give shape to the topic for various practical purposes. I argue that these textual representations are not simply descriptive of the experience; rather, they help to construct the very reality of homelessness.

The second goal of this book is to study the narrative production of homelessness at a specific site. Using ethnographic techniques, I show how the staff and clients at an emergency shelter narratively produce the category of the "homeless client" for the practical purpose at hand. Specifically, the narrative production of homelessness at this site is viewed using data from three sources: interviews with the staff, interviews with the clients, and the social worker's intake interviews.

Accordingly, this work begins with a brief introduction of the problem. Chapter 1 goes on to offer a brief history of the category of "homelessness" in the United States. This chapter presents the argument that the recent debate on the interrelationship between mental illness and poverty can be traced to early colonial America. The main point is that the contemporary methods of dealing with the homeless reflect multiple disciplinary discourses that rose and fell in prominence over the past two hundred years.

Chapters 2, 3, and 4 focus on the textual constructions of homelessness. Specifically, chapter 2 suggests that the often ambiguous demographic characteristics of the homeless population are *used* by various agencies to construct a "typical" profile that is consistent with their particular missions. Chapter 3 looks at the textual constructions of homelessness in literary works to underscore the latter's contribution to scientific discourses on the problem. The last chapter in this series, chapter 4, critically examines the textual constructions of the homeless in various ethnographic idioms and lays down the conceptual framework for this book.

The empirical analysis of homelessness using ethnographic data is put forth in chapters 5 through 9, with each chapter offering a different perspective on the narrative construction of this social problem. In particular, chapters 5 and 6 look at the local practices and policies that help to define homelessness at this particular site. Chapters 7, 8, and 9 respectively detail the narrative production of homelessness based on staff accounts, interactions between the staff and the clients, and clients' individual accounts.

The final section of this book summarizes the overall contribution of this research to the existing body of literature on homelessness.

Notes

1. Patricia A. Adler and Peter Adler, *Membership Roles in Field Research* (Newbury, Calif.: Sage, 1987).

2. Adler and Adler, *Membership Roles*, 52-53.

3. Adler and Adler, *Membership Roles*, 64.

4. Adler and Adler, *Membership Roles*, 67.

5. Carol R. Ronai, "Multiple Reflections of Child Sex Abuse: An Argument for a Layered Account," *Journal of Contemporary Ethnography* 23 (1995): 395-426.

6. Adler and Adler, *Membership Roles*.

7. Jaber Gubrium and James Holstein, *The New Language of Qualitative Method* (New York: Oxford University Press, 1997); James Holstein and Jaber Gubrium, *The Self We Live By: Narrative Identity in a Postmodern World* (New York: Oxford University Press, 2000).

8. Gubrium and Holstein, *The New Language*, 119.

9. Alfred Schutz, *On Phenomenology and Social Relations* (Chicago: University of Chicago Press, 1970).

10. Alice Baum and Donald W. Burnes, *A Nation in Denial: The Truth about Homelessness* (Boulder, Colo.: Westview, 1993); Christopher Jencks, *The Homeless* (Cambridge, Mass.: Harvard University Press, 1994).

11. Benedict Giamo, *On the Bowery: Confronting Homelessness in American Society* (Iowa City, Iowa: University of Iowa Press, 1989); Eliot Liebow, *Tell Them Who I Am: The Lives of Homeless Women* (New York: Free Press, 1993); David A. Snow and Leon Anderson, *Down on Their Luck: A Study of Homeless Street People* (Berkeley, Calif.: University of California Press, 1993).

12. David A. Snow and Leon Anderson, "Identity Work among the Homeless: The Verbal Construction and Avowal of Personal Identities," *American Journal of Sociology* 92 (1987): 1337-38.

13. William J. Spencer, "Homeless in River City: Client Work in Human Service Encounters," in *Perspectives on Social Problems*, vol. 6, ed. James Holstein and Gale Miller (Greenwich, Conn.: JAI Press, 1994), 29-46.

14. Spencer, "Homeless in River City," 39.

15. Spencer, "Homeless in River City," 35-37.

16. Jaber Gubrium and James Holstein, "Individual Agency, the Ordinary, a Postmodern Life," *The Sociological Quarterly* 36 (1994): 557.

17. Jaber Gubrium and James A. Holstein,"Narrative Practice and the Coherence Personal Stories," *Sociological Quarterly* 39 (1998): 163-87.

18. Jaber Gubrium and James Holstein, "Biographical Work and New Ethnograph in *The Narrative Study of Lives,* vol. 3, ed. Amia Lieblich and Ruthelen Josselon (Newbu Park, Calif.: Sage, 1995), 47.

19. Gubrium and Holstein, "Biographical Work," 50-51.

20. Holstein and Gubrium, *The Self We Live By;* Jaber Gubrium and James Holste eds., *Institutional Selves: Troubled Identities in a Postmodern World* (New York: Oxfc University Press, 2000).

Chapter 1

A Brief History of Homelessness

Taking into consideration the complexity of homelessness as a social problem requires paying attention to the various discourses that have shaped this problem over the course of time. In this regard, developments in the discourse of mental illness are of special interest. This chapter examines the discourse of mental illness in the United States as it relates to poverty and the category of "homelessness." Building on the argument that, historically, mental illness has been used as a method of social control for responding to poverty and vagrancy,[1] I suggest that the contemporary dispute regarding the definition and treatment of homelessness is reflective of shifts in official responses to poverty as they coincide with the expansion of the discipline of psychiatry.

Rethinking the Problem

Many researchers in the area of homelessness have cited the deinstitution-alization of the mentally ill as the primary reason for the increase in the number of the homeless;[2] while their opponents argue that mental illness is the consequence rather than the cause of homelessness and poverty.[3] Following Blumer's admonition that "students of social problems ought to study the process by which a society comes to recognize its social problems,"[4] in this section I trace the history of the public debate on the conjunction of poverty and mental illness in the United States. For the purpose of analysis, three distinct periods are examined: pauperism, institutionalization, and deinstitutionalization.

Using Foucault's notion of discursive practices[5] as they figure into the construction of the subject (e.g., the homeless) and the methods of controlling the object (i.e., the body), I argue that the first period in this discussion represents the pre-enlightenment era when the category of mental illness did not exist. During this time, the discourse of state power rather than psychiatry shaped how authorities responded to people they considered to be social outcasts.

The second era represents a period when official control and reaction to the problems of poverty and "insanity" become more differentiated. To a great extent, "troubled people" of this era are dealt with on the basis of the "objective" language of rationality and scientific discourse. As Foucault would argue, during this period, the object of mental illness (i.e., the body) is confined for the purpose of reforming the subject of mental illness (i.e., the individual in question).[6] This period is marked by the growth of the discipline and the "disciplinary" regime of psychiatry, resulting in the belief that mental illness, unlike poverty, is a medical disorder that can be cured within the boundaries of professional and institutional practice.

Finally, the contemporary treatment of mental illness at first glance may seem reminiscent of the pre-enlightenment era in that, once again, the distinction between the poor and the insane has become blurred. But the ideas underpinning the new movement are quite different. I argue that unlike the earlier periods, when one discourse, either explicit state interest or techno-scientific treatment, tended to dominate, the contemporary gaze on undesirables is informed by a multiplicity of discourses that emphasize modern notions such as individual responsibility, treatment, and state welfare, on the one hand, and the more dated notions of pauperism and the unworthy poor, on the other.

Pauperism (1640s-1840s)

Although this story can begin anywhere, I have chosen colonial America through the 1840s as the starting point. The main reason for this is that the history of the United States as a nation begins here. Admittedly, discussions of the treatment of the poor and the mentally ill have a much longer history. For example, it has been suggested that the ecclesiastical system of jurisprudence in medieval Europe (i.e., the canonist law) was radically different from contemporary views on the matter in that it did not associate poverty with any character flaws: "They no more thought of punishing a man for poverty than we think of punishing a man for being afflicted with tuberculosis."[7] In addition, in Europe there were the great witch hunts long before the emergence of the bipolar opposition of reason and insanity,[8] and also in the new world there were some instances of putting social outcasts to death.[9] Nevertheless, such practices, particularly in the early history of this country, were uncommon. Thus, for the telling of historical narrative of the poor and the mentally ill in America, 1640-1840 seems like an appropriate choice.

Having said that, let us examine the general patterns of how what could be regarded as a group of outcasts was defined and treated from the colonial period through the mid 1800s. One of the better discussions of this topic can be found in Albert Deutsch's *The Mentally Ill in America*. Published in 1945, this book is a primary source of data and analysis in this chapter. Deutsch describes how this population was defined in the following passage: "The individual in need of assistance was apt to receive public attention only when his condition was looked upon as a social danger or a public nuisance—and was then 'disposed of' rather than helped."[10] Deutsch goes on to point out that economic class was a decisive factor in whose condition came to public attention. Simply put, the more affluent members of society had the financial resources to keep the manifest signs of mental illness away from official scrutiny. Thus the problem of "disposing of" the insane was from the start closely tied with poverty: poor people, if in any way deviant, were more visible and consequently more likely to be subjected to official scrutiny and formal processing.

The other component of official interest in the problem of outcasts at the time was how their estates were to be handled. As Deutsch puts it: "Significant in this respect is the fact that several of the colonies passed laws regarding the estates of insane persons long before enacting legislation regarding their personal well-being."[11] Clearly, the idea of "treating the mentally ill" was not a primary concern. In fact, the category of mental illness and the very idea of treatment did not exist. This is further supported by the observation that for those mentally disturbed individuals who did come to the attention of the state, incarceration in jail was the most likely method of disposition. With few exceptions, those with apparent mental problems were treated no differently from common criminals.[12] From a Foucauldian perspective, the official gaze on the problem was not informed by the techno-scientific discourse of psychiatry and its division of the body and the mind (the object and the subject). Rather, official concern was guided by the discourse of explicit state power and its maintenance, unmediated by the language of psychiatry, power that was directly stated and practiced, literally in the open, in front of court houses through pillories, whipping posts, and gallows.

Similarly, the intended purpose of some of the earlier "Poor Laws" legislated to control social outcasts was self-evident. Such laws were typically titled "For the Preventing of Poor Persons"[13] and were designed to actively discourage undesirables from settling in places where they were not wanted. In addition, these settlement restrictions made the business of handling this population a local responsibility. The insane were placed in the general category of "paupers" or the undeserving poor (their poverty could not be justified by the moral standards of the time). "Paupers" were often returned to the cities of their origin. In some cases, they were transported to neighboring cities under the cover of darkness. In fact, a similar practice is relatively common to this day where law enforcement officials "run the homeless out of town" or give them a bus ticket to another city, which in the vernacular is sometimes called "Greyhound therapy."

Another official response to the problem of "pauperism" took the form of houses of correction or workhouses, where the missions of charity and penalty were combined under the same roof. In the words of Deutsch:

> [The workhouse] was considered as a penal establishment for rogues and vagabonds, idle and vicious; a means for profitably employing the able-bodied poor; a deterrent to those who might not resist the temptation of pauperism were it not for the threat of forced labor and the stigma of workhouse confinement; and an asylum for the impotent poor and the insane.[14]

During this period, however, there was one official response to the problem of "pauperism" that seems remarkably barbaric by contemporary standards: auctioning the poor to the lowest bidder.[15] According to Deutsch, this practice was relatively common in most states. The poor would be placed on an auctioning block and the bidding would start. Ironically, the mentally disturbed had a unique advantage at these auctions: "The insane and the feeble-minded are often most eagerly sought after, for 'strong backs and weak minds' make good farm laborers—and the bidders are invariably farmers."[16] Thus, the poor were auctioned off into the custody of the *lowest* bidders for weeks or months. The bidders hoped to improve their own economic status by exploiting the free labor of those whom they were paid to take into their care. It is important to note that such practices stand in stark contrast, if not opposition, to the prevailing ideologies of our time. For example, where contemporary theories of poverty emphasize the role of family in providing a stable environment that could prevent poverty and mental illness, the practice of auctioning off the poor weakened the family unit by separating parents from their children.

As a whole, this trend of grouping the poor with the insane continued until approximately the 1840s. Although the Pennsylvania Hospital, the first institution in the United States specifically designed to house and treat the mentally ill, was established in 1752 in Philadelphia, this institution did not become an official mechanism for dealing with the insane until much later in the 1820s, when through legislative acts the "pauper insane" were beginning to be separated from the rest of the poor.[17] It must be noted that the Pennsylvania Hospital, and other asylums of the time, did not necessarily provide a considerable improvement in the living conditions of its residents. In fact, one of its renowned therapists of the time, Benjamin Rush, known as the first American psychiatrist, practiced venesection (bloodletting) as a therapeutic technique and invented the first "tranquilizer," a metal chair to which patients would be strapped for hours, supposedly to help reduce their pulse rate and calm them down.[18]

Institutionalization (1840s-1940s)

The story of the institutionalization period centers on the relatively obscure character of Dorothea Lynde Dix. According to Deutsch,[19] in 1841 "Miss Dix," a retired schoolteacher in her late thirties, was asked by a young man who felt he was "unsuited for the task" to teach a Sunday school class for female inmates at East Cambridge Jail in Boston.[20] While visiting the prison, Dix was agonized by the harsh treatment of the "insane persons locked up in cells." A dramatic epiphany occurred when she demanded from prison officials that the heat be turned on for the "insane inmates," and she was told, "The insane need no heat."[21] Supposedly, this event forever changed her life.

> A rather trivial incident, this, but it marked the beginning of a long crusade without parallel in American annals. It transformed a retired New England school teacher, seemingly fated to go through life silently and unknown into a fiery, world-famous standard bearer in a unique cause. For forty years thereafter she journeyed through the land, this apostle of the insane, spreading the gospel of humane treatment for the mentally ill. She built, instead of churches, hospitals where lost minds might find regeneration.[22]

Dix would go on to champion the cause of helping the mentally ill in the United States and Europe for years to come. Her opponents called her "a self-appointed Lunacy Commissioner,"[23] but apparently undaunted by the opposition, she pressed on. The peak of Dix's moral crusade was when she managed to have a bill passed through the House and the Senate that would declare the mentally insane "wards of the nation." Under this proposed bill, the federal government would direct some of the funds from the sale of public lands to build state hospitals for the mentally ill.[24] In 1854, this was vetoed by President Franklin Pierce on the grounds that such a bill would violate state rights and would increase the responsibility and the power of the federal government beyond the limits of the Constitution. In defense of his decision, Pierce wrote:

> If Congress have power . . . to make provision for the indigent insane . . . , it has the same power to provide for the indigent who are not insane, and thus to transfer to the federal government the charge of *all the poor in all the states*.[25]

This debate marks the beginning of an important but hesitant shift in the way policy makers as well as the general public saw the "indigent insane," as somehow separate from the "indigent who are not insane." It also marks initial opposition to what would later become a welfare policy for taking care of state dependents.

In spite of this setback, Dix and her friends from the fledgling psychiatry establishment managed to open several state mental health hospitals around the country. By the time she died in 1887, Dix was thought responsible for establishing more than thirty mental hospitals in the United States and abroad.[26] Ironically, by the end of her life, patients in many state hospitals she helped establish were not much better off than they were in prisons or poorhouses, and this was a great source of distress for her.

Nevertheless, the idea of state care was well under way and so was the separation of the insane from the poor. In 1855, the resolutions of the New York county commission on the status of the poor and the insane read:

> Whereas it is already conceded, and has been adopted as the policy of this State, that insanity is a disease requiring, in all its forms and stages, special means for treatment and care; therefore, Resolved, that the State should make ample and suitable provision for all its insane not in the condition to reside in private families.
> Resolved, that no insane person should be treated, or in any way taken care of, in any county poorhouse or almshouse, or other receptacle provided for, and in which, paupers are maintained or supported.[27]

This law symbolizes three ways in which, during the period of institutionalization, "insanity" was removed from the category of "pauperism." First, insanity was recognized as a disease that is not just *capable* of being cured, but *requires* a cure. Second, the state was to take on the responsibility of providing such care, particularly for those "not in the condition to reside in private families." Mental illness is of state interest (i.e., a public problem) only to the extent that it is visible and outside the "privacy of the family." Finally, the third resolution legally separates paupers from the insane.

With the legal changes in place, the number of state hospitals and asylums was on the rise. Between 1840 and 1890, the number of insane in asylums and hospitals increased by about 2,400 percent (from 2,561 to 74,028), where during the same time, the U.S. population grew by only about 300 percent (from 17,069,453 to 62,947,714).[28] This disproportional growth of the number of the institutionally confined relative to the general population would continue until the 1950s.

The astounding growth begs the question: Was this increase caused by shifting people from earlier institutions (i.e., poorhouses) to the new institutions of the time (i.e., asylums)? According to some researchers, "asylum growth was too explosive to be explained by a shifting of bodies from one institution to another."[29] Sutton argues that during the early days of growth, the majority of asylum inmates were referred there by their families "who were unable to tolerate or provide care for a troublesome member."[30] What then accounts for the "explosive" growth? The answer for Sutton lies with the "elastic status" of mental illness in its early history. He suggests that the first psychiatrists were administrators rather than medical practitioners. Diagnosis of mental illness was principally based on a moral judgment regarding the patient's background and lifestyle. Similarly, the prevailing therapies of the time consisted of "work and disciplinary routines that contributed to administrative efficiency."[31]

Sutton's explanation is consistent with Deutsch's account of the beginning years of the institutionalization movement. Deutsch, too, points out that the primary function of early psychologists was more custodial than therapeutic:

> [T]he main emphasis in treating the insane during this period was placed on the mechanics of institutional arrangement. . . .The paramount question to the early psychiatrists, then, was to provide state institutions built especially for the insane. It remained for later generations to concentrate on the problems of therapeutic treatment.[32]

From the 1850s to the 1940s, a number of important developments helped further establish psychiatry as a new scientific discipline. First, the status of psychiatrists was elevated from custodial caretakers to scientists,[33] in part due to their affiliation with research universities. Second, a division of labor was under way that would allow psychiatrists to be "specially" concerned with diagnosis and treatment rather than the minutia of dealing with the mentally ill. Specifically, the occupation of social work was growing as the extramural component of psychiatry.[34] Early in their history, social workers took on the responsibility of collecting data on the clients' life histories and socioeconomic backgrounds for diagnostic purposes: "Visits had to be made to the patient's home and to his place of employment, to his relatives or friends, for first hand information concerning the personal and environmental background of the individual's illness."[35]

The division of labor between psychiatry and social work is of particular relevance to social problems work[36] in human service organizations. Simply put, the practice of social work, contrary to its nominal definition, concentrated on the individual as the object of diagnosis and treatment. Thus, the troubled person, not the society at large, was the focus of investigation and intervention.[37] This gaze on the client sometimes referred to as "case work" or "case management" is a foundational bureaucratic practice that constructs recipients of services as subjects whose complexity of life experiences *can* and *should be* reduced to files containing easily accessible and pertinent information for the purpose of intra or inter-organizational decision making. In some ways, case management heralded the beginning of the end for institutionalization as the primary mode of dealing with social outcasts. The discursive practice of psychiatry and its related fields would soon expand outside the walls of institutions and focus on society as a whole.

Deinstitutionalization (1950s - Present)

The circumstances surrounding the end of the era of institutionalization have been the focus of much sociological pondering. On the one hand, what is known is that from the 1950s to the 1980s the number of resident patients in mental hospitals went down by about 81percent, from 512,501 in 1950 to 109,939 in 1985.[38] Explaining this reduction, on the other hand, has proved difficult; namely, there does not appear to be a single cause that can account for the systematic decline of the overall number of confined mental patients.[39]

According to Mechanic and Rochefort,[40] the theories of deinstitutionalization fall into two broad categories. First, there is the "perspective that emphasizes the idealistic and intellectual underpinnings of the community mental health move-ment."[41] Accordingly, researchers from this camp see deinstitutionalization as the fortuitous combination of advancements in the field of psychiatry and raised public awareness brought about by the Civil Rights movement.

The advent of psychotropic drugs in particular was thought to have the potential to radically change the nature of caring for the mentally ill. It was assumed that new drugs would enable patients to be functional and self-sufficient outside the walls of institutions, without the need for constant monitoring. At the same time, the publication of Goffman's *Asylums*, the film *One Flew over the Cuckoo's Nest*, and other portrayals of life in confinement were seen as the impetus for "humanitarian" concern for the plight of people locked up in state hospitals.[42] The coupling of humanitarian concern with scientific advancement is eloquently praised by Deutsch.[43] "Humanitarianism, groping its way forward along the dark corridors of ignorance, can accomplish but little by itself. It becomes truly effective only when its path is lighted by the beacon of science."[44]

Other theoretical explanations for the decline of deinstitutionalization were based on a different set of assumptions. Namely, sociopolitical conditions rather than ideological orientations were thought responsible for the change. To begin with, neo-Marxists argued that deinstitutionalization simply marked the emergence of a new form of "community-based social control," which operated under the auspices of the welfare state.[45] Other researchers regard federal legislation and ensuing programs, such as Medicaid and Supplemental Security Income (SSI), as instrumental in providing financial incentives for the shift from confinement to community mental health.[46]

In support of this line of thinking, it is important to point out that unlike President Pierce, who vetoed Dix's proposal for national welfare in the 1850s, the twentieth century leaders of America took a more active approach toward the problems of poverty and insanity. For example, President Franklin D. Roosevelt through the New Deal program effectively established a national welfare system, and President John F. Kennedy through the Community Mental Health Act of 1963 made caring for the mentally ill a federal responsibility.

Finally, some have asserted that changes in involuntary commitment laws have made it difficult to commit the mentally ill to institutions against their will.[47] However, as Loseke[48] has pointed out, the business of involuntary commitment is reappearing on the legislative agenda as a viable option for responding to the poor.

What is lacking in almost all these accounts of deinstitutionalization is the realization that the first organized movement that took the idea of mental illness outside the walls of asylums dates back to the turn of the twentieth century. Exposés on the conditions of mental institutions were published as early as the 1860s. Perhaps the first exposé was written by "Mrs. E. P. W. Packard" in 1867 describing her own commitment of three years in State Asylum of Jacksonville, Illinois.[49] Packard wrote that "she was committed to and confined in this asylum while perfectly sane, and that other patients she met there were likewise sane."[50] In 1867 Packard helped enact a law in Illinois prohibiting "the commitment of any person to an institution for the insane without trial by jury."[51]

Another set of exposés was written for Joseph Pulitzer's *New York World* in the 1880s. These exposés were based on the experiences of a newspaperwoman who pretended to be mentally ill and had herself committed to mental hospitals. Her accounts were published under such titles as "Ten Days in a Mad-House" and "Feigning Insanity in Order to Reveal Asylum Horrors."[52]

According to Deutsch, the most notable account of this period was published by Clifford Beers under the title *A Mind that Found Itself*. Published in 1908 with an introduction by William James, this book was an autobiographical narrative of Beers's own commitment experiences. Beers was a Yale graduate who reportedly suffered from "delusions of persecution." Supposedly by the end of his commitment, "these delusions vanished quite dramatically, never to reappear, and Beers passed from a state of profound depression into one of extreme exaltation."[53] Nevertheless, his book was an account of the "harsh and stupid treatment" he had suffered at the hands of hospital officials. At the same time, the book *A Mind that Found Itself* promoted the idea that mental illness is treatable through prevention and "mental hygiene." In the following years, the idea of mental hygiene grew as a movement that linked psychiatry with other institutions such as the juvenile justice system, prisons, and many bureaucratic organizations in general.[54]

Thus, it is plausible that deinstitutionalization can also be explained in terms of internal changes in the discipline of psychiatry. As mentioned earlier, institutional psychiatry was in many ways more "custodial than therapeutic,"[53] and its practitioners hoped to gain the status of scientists by downplaying their role as administrators of confinement and highlighting their claims to cure and prevent mental illness. The idea of prevention in particular meant that psychiatry could be applied to the general population as a whole, rather than just a group of undesirables.[55] I argue that to some extent the deinstitutionalization movement of the 1950s was the result of the expansion, not the diminishment, of the discourse of psychiatry. In other words, under the general rubric of mental hygiene, the discourse of psychiatry was becoming more involved in the control and maintenance of normality than the repression of abnormality. As Foucault[56] would argue, the shift here is from "repressive power" to "Bio-power," from confinement to self-control.[57]

What then becomes of the "insane poor" during this period? Well, it may be that they were the beneficiaries, or the victims, of the growth of psychiatry into mainstream America. Although no empirical data is available on the topic, it would seem plausible that the poor were among the last groups to be released from state hospitals. Of course, as Jencks[58] points out, in addition to those who were released, we must also take into consideration the number of people who would have been confined under the previous dominant practice of repressing of the "insane poor."

Conclusion

Embedded in and synonymous with this type of analysis is the tension between help and control. As Loseke[59] puts it:

> Any level of government in the United States can intervene in private lives for only two reasons: intervention must be justified as either necessary to protect the public by *controlling* those who violate social rules, or as *helping* persons requiring assistance.[60]

Building on Loseke's insight, and borrowing from Foucault, I note that the pre-institutionalization period was characterized by discursive practices that explicitly centered on state power. In this context, control and repression of the problem of "pauperism" was at the heart of public policy. By contrast, during institutionalization and postinstitutionalization eras the language of "help" is interfused with that of "control," resembling Foucault's model of power/knowledge.[61]

Notes

1. Gerald N. Grob, *Mental Illness and American Society, 1875-1940* (Princeton, N.J.: Princeton University Press, 1983); John R. Sutton, "The Political Economy of Madness: The Expansion of Asylum in Progressive America," *American Sociological Review* 56 (1991): 665-78.

2. Alice Baum and Donald W. Burnes, *A Nation in Denial: The Truth about*

Homelessness. (Boulder, Colo.: Westview, 1993); Mary L. Durham, "The Impact of Deinstitutionalization on the Current Treatment of the Mentally Ill," *International Journal of Law and Psychiatry* 12 (1989): 117-31; Laurence French, "Victimization of the Mentally Ill: An Unintended Consequence of Deinstitutionalization," *Social Work* (Nov-Dec 1987): 502-05; Torrey E. Fuller, "Thirty Years of Shame: The Scandalous Neglect of the Mentally Ill Homeless," *Policy Review* (Spring 1989): 10-15.

3. James D. Wright, "Poor People, Poor Health: The Health Status of the Homeless," *Journal of Social Issues* 46 (1990): 49-64.

4. Herbert Blumer, "Social Problems as Collective Behavior," *Social Problems* 18 (1971): 298-306

5. Michel Foucault, *Discipline & Punish: The Birth of the Prison* (New York: Vintage, 1979).

6. Hubert L. Dreyfus and Paul Rabinow, *Michele Foucault: Beyond Structuralism and Hermeneutics* (Chicago: University of Chicago Press, 1982).

7. Brian Tierney, *Medieval Poor Law: A Sketch of Canonical Theory and Its Application in England* (Berkeley: University of California Press, 1959).

8. P. L. Currie, "Crimes without Criminals: Witchcraft and Its Control in Renaissance Europe," *Law Society Review* 3 (1968): 7-32.

9. Kai T. Erickson, *Wayward Puritans* (New York: Wiley, 1966).

10. Albert Deutsch, *The Mentally Ill in America: A History of Their Care and Treatment from Colonial Times* (New York: Columbia University Press, 1945).

11. Deutsch, *The Mentally Ill in America*, 40.

12. David J. Rothman, *The Discovery of Asylum* (Boston: Little, Brown, 1971).

13. Deutsch, *The Mentally Ill in America,* 44.

14. Deutsch, *The Mentally Ill in America*, 51-52.

15. Deutsch, *The Mentally Ill in America*, 117.

16. Deutsch, *The Mentally Ill in America*, 118.

17. Deutsch, *The Mentally Ill in America*, 98.

18. Deutsch, *The Mentally Ill in America*.

19. Deutsch, *The Mentally Ill in America*.

20. Deutsch, *The Mentally Ill in America*, 158.

21. Deutsch, *The Mentally Ill in America*, 159.

22. Deutsch, *The Mentally Ill in America*, 159.

23. Deutsch, *The Mentally Ill in America*, 174.

24. Deutsch, *The Mentally Ill in America*, 177.

25. Deutsch, *The Mentally Ill in America*, 178.

26. Deutsch, *The Mentally Ill in America*, 159.

27. Deutsch, *The Mentally Ill in America*, 234.

28. Deutsch, *The Mentally Ill in America*, 232.

29. Sutton, "The Political Economy of Madness," 665-78.

30. Sutton, "The Political Economy of Madness," 667.

31. Sutton, "The Political Economy of Madness," 668.

32. Deutsch, *The Mentally Ill in America*, 187-88.

33. Deutsch, *The Mentally Ill in America*, 274.

34. Deutsch, *The Mentally Ill in America*, 287.

35. Deutsch, *The Mentally Ill in America*, 287.

36. James A. Holstein and Gale Miller, "Social Constructionism and Social Work," *Constructionist Controversies*, ed. G. Miller and J. Holstein (Hawthorne, N.Y.: Aldine De Gruyter, 1993), 131-52.

37. Thomas Bernard, *The Cycle of Juvenile Justice* (New York: Oxford University Press,

1992).

38. David Mechanic and David A. Rochefort, "Deinstitutionalization: An Appraisal of Reform," *Annual Review of Sociology* 16 (1990): 301-27.

39. Willias Gronfein, "Psychotropic Drugs and the Origins of Deinstitutionalization," *Social Problems* 32 (1985): 425-436; Mechanic and Rochefort, "Deinstitutionalization: An Appraisal of Reform," 301-27; Eldon L. Wegner, "Deinsititutionalization and Community-based Treatment for the Chronic Mentally Ill," *Research in Community and Mental Health* 6 (1990): 295-324.

40. Mechanic and Rochefort, "Deinstitutionalization," 301-27.

41. Mechanic and Rochefort, "Deinstitutionalization," 306.

42. Durham, "The Impact of Deinstitutionalization on the Current Treatment of the Mentally Ill," 117-31.

43. Deutsch, *The Mentally Ill in America.*

44. Deutsch, *The Mentally Ill in America,* 189.

45. A. Scull, *Decarceration: Community Treatment and the Deviant—A Radical View* (New Brunswick, N.J.: Rutgers University Press); Mechanic and Rochefort, "Deinstitutionalization," 301-27.

46. Christopher Jencks, *The Homeless* (Cambridge: Harvard University Press, 1994)

47. Jencks, *The Homeless.*

48. Donileen R. Loseke, "Writing Rights: The 'Homeless Mentally Ill' and Involuntary Hospitalization," in *Images of Issues: Typifying Contemporary Social Problems*, ed. J. Best (Hawthorne, N.Y.: Aldine De Gruyter, 1995), 261-85.

49. Deutsch, *The Mentally Ill in America,* 306.

50. Deutsch, *The Mentally Ill in America,* 306.

51. Deutsch, *The Mentally Ill in America,* 307.

52. Deutsch, *The Mentally Ill in America,* 307.

53. Deutsch, *The Mentally Ill in America,* 304.

54. Deutsch, *The Mentally Ill in America,* 323-330.

55. Sutton, "The Political Economy of Madness," 665-78.

56. Fuller E. Torrey, *Nowhere to Go: The Tragic Odyssey of the Homeless Mentally Ill* (New York: Harper and Row, 1988), 147-48.

57. Michel Foucault, *The History of Sexuality* (New York: Vintage, 1978).

58. Foucault, *The History of Sexuality.*

59. Christopher Jencks, *The Homeless* (Cambridge: Harvard University Press, 1994).

60. Loseke, "Writing Rights: The 'Homeless Mentally Ill.'"

61. Loseke, "Writing Rights: The 'Homeless Mentally Ill.'"

62. Michel Foucault, *The Archaeology of Knowledge* (New York: Pantheon, 1972).

Chapter 2

The Constructive Demography
of Homelessness

In his seminal work "'Good' Organizational Reasons for 'Bad' Clinic Records,"[1] Garfinkel emphasizes the importance of institutionalized practice in producing official data. In his words, "Which documents will be used, how they will be used, and what meanings their contents will assume, wait upon the particular occasions, purposes, interests, and questions that a particular member may use in addressing them."[2]

Thus, Garfinkel lays the groundwork for what I refer to here as "constructive demography," or the social construction of problem populations through institutionally grounded demographic data.

In the area of homelessness, constructive demography is of particular relevance, given the remarkable lack of consensus among researchers on the number and causes of homelessness in the United States. In the following discussion, I begin by pointing out some problems with defining homelessness and then move to a more abstract epistemological analysis that shows how definitional quandaries guide the *constructive* nature of the problem, creating and shaping homeless demographics.

Early Sociological Studies

Studies of these various populations in the field of sociology are plentiful. The first sociological treatise on the problem that contained the word "homeless" in its title was Alice Solenberger's *One Thousand Homeless Men* published in 1911. Based on her interviews with a thousand homeless men in Chicago, Solenberger developed demographic profiles and typologies for the study of this population. She concluded that the majority of her respondents suffered physical and mental problems ranging from "feeble-mindedness" to "heart disease."[3]

Complementing her work was another notable study by Nels Anderson simply titled *The Hobo*. Published in 1923 by the University of Chicago Press, this book is recognized as one of the first in-depth qualitative studies of life on the streets. Based on a sample of the inhabitants of an area of Chicago known as "Hobohemia," the project was primarily aimed at providing policy makers with a better understanding of the problem. From the onset, Anderson was confronted with all the problems that would plague researchers in this area for years to come: the complications of defining, counting, and causally assessing the status of homelessness. Namely, Anderson had to tackle the questions: Who are the homeless? How many are there? and Why are they homeless?

Although his research was conducted nearly seven decades ago, his general approach to the problem parallels the most sophisticated research designs of contemporary sociology. For example, note the care with which he classifies the different types of "homeless" men:

> Although we cannot draw lines closely, it seems clear that there are at least five types of homeless men: (a) the seasonal worker, (b) the transient or occasional worker or hobo, (c) the tramp who "dreams and wonders" and works only when it is convenient, (d) the bum who seldom wonders and seldom works, and (e) the home guard who lives in Hobohemia and does not leave town.[4]

Following Anderson's work, sociological interest in the topic of homelessness shifted to the broader issues of poverty and the underclass for several decades. But by the mid 1980s, there was a renewed interest in the topic and a vast body of literature was devoted to the "scientific" study of "homelessness." The remaining sections offer a critical examination of this literature, particularly as it applies to the constructive demography of homelessness.

What Is "Homelessness?"

A casual read of hundreds of books containing the word "homeless" in the title reveals the steadfastness with which the question, "What is the homeless?" is posed. Some approach the question directly and with conceptual rigor: "Where it is apparent that we need to define a phenomenon before we can study or understand it, defining homelessness has proved to be a sticky business."[5] Others, on the other hand, tend to bypass methodological hygiene and rush to romanticized literary descriptions that signal large numbers.

> Everyday, in cities and towns across the country, men and women dressed in rags walk the streets aimlessly, oftentimes talking to visions, and frequently begging for money. They are often carrying plastic bags or pushing shopping carts filled with their possessions. . . . These people are called the homeless, but they are obviously more than just people without homes. They are dirty and sometimes frail; when they talk to visions, they show signs of mental illness or drug addiction, and the smell of alcohol that infuses their clothing reveals their drunkenness.[6]

The vast majority of the researchers, however, err on the side of caution, citing the problems of defining the population and moving on to establish a conceptual definition for the purposes of their projects. For example, one definition begins: "Homelessness can be simply defined as the inability to secure regular housing when such housing is desired."[7] Realizing the potential shortcomings of this definition (e.g., Are people who *choose* to be without "regular housing" homeless?), the same authors are quick to make the following disclaimer: "In the final analysis, social policies and programs that seek to lessen the problem of homelessness must be informed by a larger vision that rejects simplistic solutions and constraining definitions."[8]

Consequently, the various attempts to objectively define the homeless can be viewed as strategies for the constructive demography of the homeless. For example, consider the list of general typifications put forth by Breakey et al.: [9] (1) people who have no roofs over their heads (e.g., people who sleep in the streets, woods, subways, abandoned buildings); (2) people in shelters and other transitional housing programs; and (3) people with marginal housing (single-room occupancy in hotels, or doubling up with relatives or friends). As the authors point out, such definitions are empirically weak because they fail to take into consideration the frequent shifts in the status and geographical position of this population. Nevertheless, these methods of approaching the problem can be regarded as circumstantially valid constructions in the sense that they fulfill the sociopolitical agenda of the research project.

The idea that people shift from being homeless to being domiciled has led some researchers to examine homelessness from a longitudinal perspective. They contend that homelessness may better be understood in terms of shifts in and out of residential stability and offers the term "residential instability" as an alternative.[10]

Another researcher suggests that the definitions of homelessness fall into two general categories of "place-based" and "theory-based."[11] Accordingly, definitions of homelessness either emphasize a person's physical location (e.g., a shelter or transitional housing) or his or her reason for being there (e.g., social disaffiliation or mental illness). Jaheil argues that most government programs define homelessness from a place-based perspective. For example, the Stuart B. McKinney Act of 1987 primarily defines a homeless person as "an individual who lacks a fixed, regular and adequate nighttime residence."[12]

Theory-based definitions of the problem broaden the focus to include those who are not necessarily without a home, but have the potential to become homeless. Thus, housing- and poverty-oriented theories may refer to those who have "doubled-up" with their families or friends as the "hidden homeless" (as opposed to what is referred to in the literature as "literal homelessness") —presumably since they could become homeless at anytime. These texts expand the demography of homelessness by blurring the distinction between demographic reality and demographic potential.

> There are also "medicalized" definitions of the problem dividing homelessness into such categories as *benign* and *malignant:*
> Benign homelessness . . . [refers to] the state of homelessness that causes relatively little hardship, lasts for a relatively short time, and does not recur soon, and it is relatively easy to gain back a home and a stable tenure of that home. Malignant homelessness means that the state of homelessness is associated with considerable hardship or even

permanent damage to the person who is homeless.[13]

As a definition, this is no more lucid than any of the ones previously discussed in this section since the core of the distinction has to do with the highly subjective notions of "relative" versus "considerable" hardship, which the author assumes to be self-evident. In addition, this definition is a poignant illustration of the theme of "medicalization of deviance"[14] in that it compares homelessness to a tumor with various stages of progression, in this instance underscoring the medical construction of the category.

As a whole, it seems that there is very little consensus on the definition of what is commonly referred to as "homelessness" by both researchers and activists. This, however, by no means has stopped the flood of academic literature on the prevention and treatment of the vaguely defined phenomenon.

How Many Are They?

Compounding the problem of definition is the issue of enumeration. The first national attempt to count the homeless was conducted by the Department of Housing and Urban Development in 1984, which estimated the number of the homeless to be between 250,000 and 350,000 individuals. This figure ignited a good deal of controversy fueled by accusations that the conservative Reagan administration was deliberately downplaying the level of poverty in the country to justify further cutbacks of welfare programs.

The controversy was reignited by the Census Bureau's so-called S-night enumeration of March 1990 (the "S" stands for shelter and street).[15] The plan was deceptively simple. Census takers were instructed to go to shelters between 6:00 p.m. and midnight and count the people who were sleeping there. Between 2:00 and 4:00 a.m. on the following morning, they attempted to count people who *appeared* homeless on streets. These counts estimated less than a quarter of a million homeless people across the country (178,683 in shelters and 49,734 on streets).

Many homeless advocacy organizations were quick to dismiss this figure as government propaganda designed to downplay the severity of the problem, which they projected to affect millions, not thousands. Social scientists found the S-night enumeration equally problematic. Specifically, Wright and Devine[16] argue that the fact that the census data show over three times as many homeless people stayed in shelters than on the streets contradicts all conventional as well as academic wisdom.

In explaining the inadequacies of the S-night count, Wright and Devine begin with the observation that many people living on the streets have developed elaborate strategies to stay out of sight. The authors call this group the *uncounted*. Subsequently, they designate another group of homeless people as *uncountable* since they move in and out of the status of homelessness. A number of follow-up experiments on the validity of the S-night enumeration have supported Wright and Devine's conjectures by showing that the S-night procedure was highly valid (90 percent) in regard to people staying in shelters, but seriously undercounted street people.[17]

The advocates of the S-night enumeration, in contrast, have argued that the whole endeavor was not intended to specifically count the homeless but simply to improve the quality of the census data,[18] thus lending support to the notion that demographies are purposely constructed to meet the local demands of a specific organization or political entity, as apparent in the following disclaimer from the Census Bureau:

> S-night was not intended to, and did not, produce a count of the "homeless" population of the country. . . . S-night was designed to augment traditional census procedures to ensure the fullest possible count of America's population. Even if that [counting the homeless population] had been our objective, the absence of a generally agreed-upon definition of homelessness would have made that task impossible.[19]

Clearly this line of reasoning raises the issue of whether the practical purpose of a research project can and should be separated from its findings. In this instance, it is ironic that the Census Bureau, the most quantitatively driven government agency, declares that it is impossible to count this problem population and places the term in quotes in an "ethnomethodological-like" style of bracketing reality.[20]

The upshot of the debate is that counting the homeless brings us back full circle to the "definitional quandaries" discussed above, splitting researchers into two camps. One side sees the dilemma as solvable through emphasizing the purpose of the research from the outset and developing better methodological techniques.[21] The other side raises more fundamental questions about this matter: "[I]t may well be time to rethink the question of what it means to measure homelessness in America. It's the categories as much as the counts that have us hamstrung."[22] This, of course, strikes at the heart of the constructive demography, which argues that the so-called facts cannot be separated from the practical concerns of the fact-finding agencies.

Why Are They Homeless?

By pointing to the presumably at risk or compromised populations, causal theories of homelessness play an important role in the constructive demography of the problem. Such theories fall into two general categories: structural theories and individual categories.[23] Structural theories emphasize such factors as unemployment, lack of low income housing, and cutbacks in social welfare programs. The individualistic factors fall into two broad categories: disabilities and choice. Accordingly, people become homeless either because they suffer from drug abuse or simply because they choose to live without permanent housing. The following discussion first examines a number of structural factors, then turns to the individualistic theories, and concludes with the potential for the convergence of the two.

Chief among the structural factors that have been associated with homelessness is the lack of low-income housing. Proponents of this theory stress the lack of affordable housing as the primary force behind the increasing number of homeless in the 1980s. Simply put, homelessness is examined in terms of "low-income housing ratios": when there are more low-income families than available low-income housing, homelessness increases.[24] They propose such measures as rent control, housing vouchers and subsidies, and various other forms of government and community intervention as the solution to the problem.[25]

Another important structural theory of homelessness is more directly focused on government policies as they relate to reduced incomes, unemployment, and cutbacks in welfare and social security programs.[26] Particularly under attack were the policies of the Reagan and Bush era of government during the 1980s. These administrations were thought responsible for failing to create jobs while at the same time reducing the much needed welfare programs that would help support low-income families and individuals through the crisis of unemployment.[27]

The last and perhaps most controversial structural factor that has been offered as a cause of homelessness is the policy of deinstitutionalizing the mentally ill, as mentioned in chapter 1. According to the critics of deinstitutionalization,[28] the release of mental patients from asylums and hospitals beginning in 1955 through 1985 can account for a considerable portion (one-third) of the homeless in the United States. The general argument is that the promises of the Community Mental Health Center Act of 1963 were not fulfilled since the majority of patients released from institutions were not absorbed into community-based mental health services that would support and monitor them. Rather, these individuals were left to their own devices in the streets, where their conditions were exacerbated.

The other side of the debate about the explanation of homelessness emphasizes the role that personal disabilities and tendencies play in its demography. The basic idea here is that people become homeless due to individual pathology or choice. Thus homelessness is viewed as the manifestation of individual failure or personal flaw. The most obvious pathology of this kind is mental illness. As stated earlier, it has been estimated that about one third of the homeless are the mentally ill whose afflictions are prominently displayed on the streets thanks to the supposedly well-intentioned but ill-informed policy of deinstitutionalization.[29]

However, two issues complicate the task of attributing mental illness as the cause of homelessness.[30] First, there is the issue of how street survival strategies may be labeled as antisocial or pathological by inadequately trained researchers and poorly designed research projects:

> It may be that because we lack an understanding of homeless individu-
> als and the exigencies of their life, we are more liable to misinterpret
> their behavior and to brand as psychotic or as signs of mental illness
> behavior that would make complete sense if viewed in the context of
> their current existence—that, indeed, may be adaptive.[31]

Second, the critics of the mental illness approach have pointed out the issue of causal order, questioning which came first: homelessness or mental illness. That is to say, to causally identify mental pathology as the reason people live on the streets, it must first be established that the condition of living on the streets does not in its own right cause a person to become mentally ill.

Another increasingly prevalent textual construction centers on the causal effect of drug abuse. Specifically, alcoholism and crack use have been cited as important causes of homelessness.[32] For example, it has been estimated that the homeless constitute about 5 percent of the overall alcoholic population in the United States.[33] However, as in the case of mental illness, the drug abuse explanation is also susceptible to the problems of contextual understanding and constructive causal ordering. For example, one can argue that socially constructed "drug scares" historically have been used as a convenient method for dealing with problem populations.[34] In the case of homelessness, it can be said that the image of street people as drug users is a rhetorical justification for criminalizing poverty.

Finally, some have argued that research on homelessness has been overly focused on individual factors rather than structural factors. They assert that more research is needed on how individual problems are both the cause and the consequence of homelessness. In addition, they highlight the fact that the findings on the portion of the homeless who are mentally ill are inconclusive, with estimates ranging from 20 to 35 percent for single adults to 4 to 5 percent for adults in families.[35] The source of this variation is attributed to regional differences and the type of population surveyed (e.g., shelter users versus applicants versus the street homeless).

Similarly, Wright[36] has suggested that poor health is both the cause and the consequence of homelessness. Wright's definition of poor health is not limited to poor mental health, but it includes a wide range of physical ailments and disabilities that may be linked to homelessness both as a cause and a consequence. Accordingly, the problem is further exacerbated by the fact that health care delivery is particularly challenging in this context, making the homeless especially vulnerable to conditions such as hypertension, gastrointestinal disorders, and infectious diseases (tuberculosis and AIDS) due to their living conditions.

The emerging positivist agenda aims to incorporate the various dimensions of the problem into a complex multicausal model, as in the following equation put forth by Schutt and Garrett,[37] transforming textual debate into arithmetic objectivity:

$$\text{Homelessness} = f(\text{poverty/housing, disability/supports})$$

This "homeless equation" is intended to capture the complexity of the phenomenon so that no single factor is left out, ostensibly "de-constructing" the issue. Ironically, such an effort concisely conceals the many issues that indirectly construct the problem in the first place. The unanswered questions are hidden in an array of numbers.

Similarly, other grand positivistic formulations of homelessness gloss over its complexities by attributing the problem to a common symptom. This is illustrated through an examination of the fairly well-known theory of *institutional disaffiliation*, which states: "homelessness is a condition of disengagement from ordinary society—from family, friends, neighborhood, church, and community; perhaps most important, it is a loss of self."[38] Here, taken-for-granted notions, such as "family" and "community," are pieced together in an ideological assertion that textually privileges "ordinary society" and casts the homeless individual as a pathological self.

Some researchers have opted for an alternative that does not necessarily include an all-encompassing "homeless equation," theory, or definition for that matter. Specifically, a number of researchers in the area of homelessness have called for more ethnographic studies on the topic. For example, Koegel[39] lists the following under the heading "Existing Distortions and the Ethnographic Corrective"

> 1. Individual characteristics, not the ecology in which homeless individuals find themselves, have been the almost exclusive focus of the attention of those concerned with homeless people. . . .
> 2. The search community's understandings of homelessness are based on static, rather than processual, perspectives. . . .
> 3. The behavior of homeless people has been looked at almost exclusively from an outsider's perspective.[40]

Koegel's criticism effectively lays out an agenda for a methodological shift in the way the problem has been investigated, which will be considered in chapter 4.

This sentiment is reiterated by other investigators who see qualitative research as being best suited to deal with the "definitional quandaries" discussed above. For example, Salo and Campanelli[41] argue that overreliance on survey research and its design may be ill suited for the study of homelessness since homeless people "may not be familiar with, and may balk at, the norms and behaviors associated with survey research."[42] By contrast, the authors praise ethnographic methods for their potential to privilege the natives' expertise and definitions, a task that would be next to impossible in the context of survey research. They conclude that "ethnographic techniques do not have to be merely supplemental to survey research, but can play an integral part in shaping the entire procedure."[43]

Epistemology versus Epidemiology

The question remains: Why is it that in spite of the lack of consensus on the most rudimentary part of the project (that is, how to define "homelessness"), as well as the overwhelming problems surrounding the enumeration of this population, the academic discourse in this area continues to be dominated by quantitative studies? This is especially the case among those who focus on the individualistic causes of the problem.

Throughout much of the 1980s, very few researchers, if any, were interested in this question. In recent years, a number of academics have focused on the *epistemology* of homelessness rather than its *epidemiology*. For example, Blasi[44] criticizes early research in this area by stating: "[E]arly research on homelessness tended to define homelessness fairly narrowly, and then to look at it only in static terms: 'The homeless' were a group defined as people lacking a place to stay, who were differentiated by individual characteristics."[45]

Blasi is particularly concerned with the emphasis placed on the individualistic aspect of the discourse on homelessness, suggesting that "this simple-minded reasoning, however, has more to do with strong currents in our culture to blame individuals for their situations than it does with scientific explanation."[46] In a manner of speaking, cultural proclivities construct the homeless problem and its demography. Blasi ends his critique by proposing a new agenda for research on homelessness that would underscore the role that public perception plays in defining and responding to the problem of homelessness. Specifically, he asks, "What are the aspects of poverty and homelessness that touch the nonpoor, the voting public, opinion leaders?"[47]

By the mid 1990s, the issues raised by Blasi were beginning to become the focal point of a number of research projects. For example, in a constructively oriented text, Lee et al.[48] examine the correspondence between "causal beliefs" and "policy attitudes" using a national survey. They conclude, as we might expect, that people who think of homelessness as having been caused by structural factors are more likely to support government intervention, and those who frame homelessness individualistically are more laissez faire, each with their respective demographic intonations.

In a similar vein, Bunis et al.[49] studied patterns of sympathy toward the homeless in England and the United States. Based on a content analysis of newspaper articles, as well as an analysis of the rate of "voluntarism" in both countries, they found seasonal variation in sympathy toward the homeless. In particular, they noted an increase in sympathy during holiday seasons in late November and December. Based on these findings, the authors argue that public interest in the topic of homelessness follows seasonal and cultural patterns, rhythmically heightening and diminishing its demographics.

Finally, Loseke[50] shows how policies are informed by certain images or types: "My major argument is that images of what people *should* do depends on our images of *types* of people."[51] In the case of homelessness, she argues that in the last decade the public image of the street person has shifted from one who could be normalized through deinstitutionalization to one whose best interest lies in involuntary commitment and hospitalization. Loseke goes on to point out the inevitable discrepancy between images of homelessness and the experience of homelessness: "*[A]ny* particular image will *never* encompass the heterogeneity of practical experience."[52]

More comprehensive analyses of the political economy of homelessness can be found in a number of texts published in recent years. Perhaps the best known work of this kind is David Wagner's *Checkerboard Square*. In the introductory pages of his ethnography, Wagner[53] critically examines the status of the bulk of contemporary research on the topic of homeless. Specifically, he offers three reasons for the emphasis placed on the "pathological behavior" of the homeless.

First, Wagner challenges the methodology of most studies in this area.

He argues that since most studies are cross-sectional (i.e., "one-time") surveys or interviews conducted at emergency shelters, it is not unexpected that the majority of the people interviewed in these situations show signs of stress.[54] In his words: "[S]ocial workers, social scientists, and others observing or working in homeless shelters or in crisis centers are in a sense caught in an ecological fallacy by dealing with the poor only at their point of greatest vulnerability."[55]

The second reason Wagner offers for the individualistic emphasis on the problem is "the self-interest and professional training of researchers, advocates, and social service providers."[56] He argue that experts in this area are not likely to risk their career interests and expectations by proposing structural or revolutionary solutions to the problem, signaling the political undertone of homeless demographics.

It is . . . extremely rare for even the most radical social worker or psychiatrist to urge street people to foment revolution. In a parallel fashion, social scientists—whose livelihood is reliant on government and foundation funding, university largess, and outlets for publication, are unlikely to either say that the problem is intractable or simply write a tract on the need for revolution.[57]

Wagner's third and final reason has to do with the reformist and liberal ideology of the academic establishment, which he sees as being more interested in democratic victories" than "radical transformations." Accordingly, pathologizing life on the streets would be more consistent with a reformist agenda than proposing and implementing structural changes.[58]

Another book that addresses similar issues is Wright's[59] *Out of Place*. In a section titled "Academic Segmentation of Homeless Bodies"[60] he argues that the academic discourse on the topic has been driven by the forces of funding, job security, and moral entrepreneurship. According to Wright, researchers in this area gravitate toward pathological issues because: (1) funding is plentiful if the spotlight is on the individual; (2) focusing on individual pathology is safe in that it would be accepted by the mainstream; and (3) pathologizing the homeless body is consistent with the moral tone of a mainstream sociology that divides the poor into the *deserving* and *undeserving*.[61] The net result of this framework is that "'homeless' persons were treated as passive subjects, subordinate to the intentions of the researchers, policy analysts, advocates, and shelter providers, not unlike the previous debates over the 'underclass.'"[62] Borrowing from Hoch and Slayton's[63] "languages of disability" and the "politics of compassion," Wright contends the pathological model of homelessness "enabled policy makers to understand homelessness through a client model that portrayed homeless persons as passive victims deserving of charity."[64]

The demography of homelessness has thus been critiqued by a number of researchers. Skepticism about the objective definition and causes of homelessness are no longer easily dismissed as "measurement problems." Instead, an emerging body of research is asking foundational questions about how the category of "homelessness" is rhetorically and interactionally constructed as a social problem.

Notes

1. Harold Garfinkel, *Studies in Ethnomethodology* (Englewood Cliffs, N.J.: Prentice Hall, 1967).

2. Garfinkel, *Studies in Ethnomethodology*, 203.

3. Alice W. Solenberger, *One Thousand Homeless Men: A Study of Original Records* (New York: Charities Publication, 1911).

4. Nels Anderson, *The Hobo: The Sociology of Homeless Men* (Chicago: University of Chicago Press, 1923).

5. James D. Wright, *Address Unknown: The Homeless in America* (Hawthorne, N.Y.: Aldine de Gruyter, 1989), 19.

6. Alice Baum and Donald W. Burnes, *A Nation in Denial: The Truth about Homelessness* (Boulder, Colo.: Westview, 1993), 11.

7. Russell K. Schutt and Gerald Garrett, "The Homeless Alcoholic: Past and Present," in *Homelessness: A National Perspective*, ed. M. Robertson and M Greenblatt (New York: Plenum, 1992), 177-86.

8. Russel K. Schutt and Gerald Garrett, *Responding to the Homeless: Policy and Practice* (New York: Plenum Press, 1992), 3.

9. William R. Breakey and Pamela J. Fischer, "Homelessness: The Extent of the Problem," *Journal of Social Issues* 46, no. 4 (1990): 31-47.

10. Michael Sosin, Irving Piliavin, and Herb Westerfelt,"Toward a Longitudinal Analysis of Homelessness," *Journal of Social Issues* 46, no. 4 (1990): 157-74.

11. Rene I. Jahiel, "The Definition and Significance of Homelessness in the United States," in *Homelessness: A Prevention-oriented Approach*, ed. R. I. Jahiel (Baltimore, Md.: Johns Hopkins University Press, 1992), 1-10.

12. Jahiel, "The Definition and Significance of Homelessness," 2.

13. Jahiel, "The Definition and Significance of Homelessness," 100.

14. Peter Conrad and J. W. Schneider, *Deviance and Medicalization* (St. Louis: Mosby, 1980).

15. James D. Wright, "Housing Dynamics of the Homeless: Implications for a Count," *American Journal of Orthopsychiatry* 65, no. 3 (1995): 320-29.

16. Wright, "Housing Dynamics of the Homeless," 320-29.

17. Wright, "Housing Dynamics of the Homeless," 323.

18. Roger Straw, "Looking behind the Numbers in Counting the Homeless: An Invited Commentary," *American Journal of Orthopsychiatry* 65, no. 3 (1995): 330-33.

19. Census Bureau, "Census Bureau Releases 1990 Decennial Counts for Persons Enumerated in Emergency Shelters and Observed on the Streets," (Press Release), U.S. Department of Commerce News. Cited in Sraw, April 12 "Looking behind the Numbers," 330-33.

20. Garfinkel, *Studies in Ethnomethodology*.

21. Martha R. Burt, "Critical Factors in Counting the Homeless: An Invited Commentary," *American Journal of Orthopsychiatry* 65, no. 3 (1995): 334-39.

22. Kim Hopper, "Definitional Quandaries and Other Hazards in Counting the Homeless: An Invited Commentary," *American Journal of Orthopsychiatry* 65, (3) 1995: 340-46.

23. Ronald W. Fagan, "Homelessness in America: Causes, Consequences and Solutions," *Journal of Interdisciplinary Studies* 7 no. 1-2 (1995): 101-18; Anne B. Shlay and P. H. Rossi,"Social Science Research and Contemporary Studies of Homelessness," *Annual Review of Sociology* 18 (1995): 129-60.

24. Kay Y. McChesney, "Family Homelessness: A Systematic Problem," *Journal of Social Issues* 46, no. 4 (1990): 191-205.

25. Peter Dreier and John Atlas, "Grassroots Strategies for Housing Crisis: A National Agenda," *Social Policy* 19, no. 3 (1989): 25-38.

26. Shlay and Rossi. "Social Science Research and Contemporary Studies of Homelessness," 129-60.

27. Shlay and Rossi, "Social Science Research and Contemporary Studies of Homelessness," 148.

28. Baum and Burnes, *A Nation in Denial*.

29. Shlay and Rossi, "Social Science Research and Contemporary Studies of Homelessness," 138.

30. Paul Koegel and M. Audrey Barnum. "Problems in the Assessment of Mental Illness among the Homeless," in *Homelessness: A National Perspective*, ed. M. Robertson and M. Greenblatt, 77-99.

31. Koegel and Barnum, "Problems in the Assessment of Mental Illness," 80.

32. Christopher Jencks, *The Homeless* (Cambridge: Harvard University Press, 1994), 41-42.

33. Russell K. Schutt and Gerald Garrett, "The Homeless Alcoholic: Past and Present," in *Homelessness: A National Perspective*, ed. M. Robertson and M. Greenblatt, 177-86.

34. Craig Reinarman and Harry Gene Levine, "Crack in Context: Politics and Media in the Making of a Drug Scare," *Contemporary Drug Problems* 16 (1989): 535-77.

35. Marybeth Shinn and Beth C. Weitzman, "Research on Homelessness: An Introduction," *Journal of Social Issues* 46, no. 4 (1990): 1-11.

36. James D. Wright, "Poor People, Poor Health: The Health Status of the Homeless," *Journal of Social Issues* 46 (1990): 49-64.

37. Russell K. Schutt and Gerald Garrett, *Responding to the Homeless: Policy and Practice* (New York: Plenum Press, 1992), 3.

38. Baum and Burnes, *A Nation in Denial*.

39. Paul Koegel, "Understanding Homelessness: An Ethnographic Approach," in *Homelessness: A Prevention-oriented Approach*, ed. R. Jahiel (Baltimore, Md.: Johns Hopkins University Press, 1992), 127-38.

40. Koegel, "Understanding Homelessness," 128-33.

41. Matt T. Salo and Pamela C. Campanelli, "Ethnographic Methods in the Development of Census Procedures for Enumerating the Homeless," *Urban Anthropology* 20, no. 2 (1991) 127-39.

42. Salo and Campanelli, "Ethnographic Methods," 135.

43. Salo and Campanelli, "Ethnographic Methods," 127.

44. Gary Blasi, "Social Policy and Social Science Research on Homelessness," *Journal of Social Issues* 46, no. 4 (1990): 207-19.

45. Blasi, "Social Policy and Social Science," 209.

46. Blasi, "Social Policy and Social Science," 210.

47. Blasi, "Social Policy and Social Science," 217.

48. Barrett A. Lee, D. W. Lewis, and S. H. Jones, "Are the Homeless to Blame? A Test of Two Theories," *The Sociological Quarterly* 33, no. 4 (1992): 535-52.

49. William K. Bunis, A. Yanik, and D. Snow, "The Cultural Patterns of Sympathy

toward the Homeless and Other Victims of Misfortune," *Social Problems* 43, no. 4 (1996): 387-402.

50. Donileen R. Loseke, "Writing Rights: The 'Homeless Mentally Ill' and Involuntary Hospitalization," in *Images of Issues: Typifying Contemporary Social Problems*, ed. J. Best (Hawthorne, N.Y.: Aldine De Gruyter, 1995), 261-85.

51. Loseke, "Writing Rights," 278.

52. Loseke, "Writing Rights," 279.

53. David Wagner, *Checkerboard Square: Culture and Resistance in a Homeless Community* (Boulder, Colo.: Westview, 1993).

54. Wagner, *Checkerboard Square*, 7.

55. Wagner, *Checkerboard Square*, 8.

56. Wagner, *Checkerboard Square*, 8.

57. Wagner, *Checkerboard Square*, 8-9.

58. Wagner, *Checkerboard Square*, 9.

59. Talmadge Wright, *Out of Place: Homeless Mobilizations, Subcities, and Contested Landscapes* (Albany: State University of New York Press, 1997).

60. Wright, *Out of Place*, 20.

61. Wright, *Out of Place*.

62. Wright, *Out of Place*.

63. Charles Hoch and R. A. Slayton, *New Homeless and Old: Community and the Skid Row Hotel* (Philadelphia: Temple University Press, 1989).

64. Hoch and Slayton, *New Homeless and Old*, 27.

Chapter 3

Literary Constructions of Homelessness

The significance of examining literary texts on poverty and homelessness is grounded in recent debate in qualitative research on the difference between science and literature. On the one hand, it has been suggested that the modern distinction between scientific facts and literary fictions in this area is dubious and based on the assumption that *facts* are self-evident truths and *fictions* are contrived. Challenging this polar opposition, a number of social scientists such as James Clifford have proposed that all ethnographies are fictional in that they are "made or fashioned."[1] The emphasis on the constructed nature of ethnographic work has resulted in much debate about the concepts of text and authorship, blurring the line between science and literature.

> On the other hand, the process of writing as a whole has been reexamined. This is particularly evident in the field of anthropology:
> No longer a marginal, or occulted, dimension, writing has emerged as central to what anthropologists do both in the field and thereafter. The fact that it has not until recently been portrayed or seriously discussed reflects the persistence of an ideology claiming transparency of representation and immediacy of experience. Writing is reduced to method: keeping good field notes, making accurate maps, "writing up" results.[2]

Following this, some researchers have tried to consider the stylistic and textual qualities of ethnographies while at the same time deconstructing the author as the benevolent and neutral arbiter of truth.[3] What is of particular significance here is the fact that questioning the division between social science and literature makes it possible to examine literary prose in a new light. We can now reasonably ask the question: To what extent have literary works on homelessness influenced sociological writing, constructing the very reality social scientists then turn to in their research objects?

Literary accounts form an important dimension of the polyphonic discourse of homelessness. Indeed, when social actors and social scientists speak of homelessness, they often borrow from literary themes on the subject matter to construct their accounts. Thus, a homeless man may describe his life in terms of romantic themes found in a particular literary genre. In a similar manner, researchers may construct sympathetic accounts of street people. Thus, at least a passing familiarity with the vast body of fictional texts on homelessness will help to better understand how the homeless are more broadly culturally constructed.

Firsthand Accounts

Long before sociology turned its attention to the topic of homelessness, and perhaps long before the inception of sociology as a discipline, various authors had been writing about the experiences of poverty and life on the streets. In fact, few topics have captured the imagination and interest of literary scholars as has "life on the street." Some of these works are written in a reportage style and include detailed descriptions of everyday life, with the intended goal of educating policy makers and ordinary people about homelessness and street life.

Interestingly enough, one of the first such efforts was written in a somewhat humorous tone by Nels Anderson (the sociologist who is credited with writing the first ethnography on homelessness) under the pseudonym Dean Stiff. In the introduction, under his real name Anderson writes: "I have never asked Dean Stiff his real name. I understand very well that in the world of which he writes names are of little import."[4] Dean Stiff is thus introduced as a homeless man who went around the country asking college professors if he could lecture on "The Methods of Panhandling" to their classes. He supposedly approaches Anderson with the idea of writing a book on the topic, telling him:

> What with professors like you doing researches and the novelists with their human interest stuff, the rest of the world is getting to think of the hobo game as a lot of cheap comedy. I say it's a grand art and it's about time somebody stepped in and saved it from the hitch-hikers.[5]

The book is assessed in Stiff's own voice in an equally self-confident tone:

> This book is not only my protest against all such puny peripheral efforts, but my attempt to present, out of the fullness of experience, the true picture. This is meant to be a guide for the curious, and so valid in its content that beside it all the cheap patter of mountebanks and eavesdroppers will pale like a candle before the sun.[6]

From very early on literature mediates the history of sociology; the literary firsthand account can compete with the academic discourse for recognition by claiming to be based on experiential knowledge.

Jack London's *The Road*[7] represents one of the earliest accounts of homelessness in the United States at the turn of the twentieth century. Based on London's own experiences and written in an autobiographical style, the book tells the story of his life as a "tramp." Although some may dismiss this work as being "subjective" and therefore void of sociological content, a closer examination of London's masterful tale reveals the depth of his insights into the complexity of human interactions that give life to the problem of homelessness. Consider, for example, how he describes the importance of storytelling in the life of a "hobo":

> The successful hobo must be an artist. He must create spontaneously and instantaneously—and not upon a theme selected from the plenitude of his own imagination, but upon the theme he reads in the face of the person who opens the door, be it man, woman, or child, sweet or crabbed, generous or miserly. . . . I have often thought that to this training of my tramp days is due my success as a story-writer. In order to get the food whereby I lived, I was compelled to tell tales that rang true.[8]

Decades before Erving Goffman[9] introduced the notion of *dramaturgy* into the analysis of social problems, London wrote keenly about how the interpretation of context enters into deciding what *front* to present. Undoubtedly, this theme of site-specific storytelling continues to be of great relevance in understanding the interactions between the needy and contemporary service providers.

Similarly, in his book *The People of the Abyss*, apparently published posthumously in 1967, London writes about his "explorations" of the city of London's "under-world" in the summer of 1902. His methodological approach in studying the topic can roughly be called participant observation. He "descends" into the "East End of London" incognito and conducts his observations while living in the area. The result is a rich study of the poverty and homelessness that parallels some of the best ethnographies on the topic both in terms of its scope and its sophistication. Naturally, his literary license allowed him to infuse his descriptions with an unsurpassed esthetic quality, as evident in this account of a homeless man:

> Home life he had never known. The word "home" aroused nothing but unpleasant associations. In the low wages of his father, and of other men in the same walk of life, he found sufficient reason for branding wife and children as encumbrances and causes of masculine misery.[10]

Mixed in with the style-conscious prose are insightful *data* about the experience of homelessness. For example, the idea that some people live on the streets in their opposition and resistance to the notion of *home* and its practical and ideological implications is adroitly implied in the previous excerpt. Thus, London provides the reader with astute observations without sacrificing esthetic quality, suggesting that homelessness may be a form of *resolution* to a social problem, not a problem in its own right.

In addition, reportage such as London's may be theoretically rich and informative. Consider, for example, how the author struggles with the problem of representing the "depth" of the experience to his readers:

> But, O dear, soft people, full of meat and blood, with white beds and airy rooms waiting you each night, how can I make you know what it is to suffer as you would suffer if you spent a weary night on London's streets? Believe me you would think a thousand centuries had come and

gone before the east paled into dawn; you would shiver till you were ready to cry aloud with the pain of each aching muscle; and you would wonder that you could endure so much and live. . . .

But when the dawn came, the nightmare over, and you would hale you home to refresh yourself, and until you died, you would tell the story of your adventures to groups of admiring friends. It would grow into a mighty story. Your little eight-hour night would become an Odyssey and you a Homer. . . . Not so with these homeless ones who walked . . with me.[11]

Clearly, the author is tackling the problems of representation, which decades later would be underscored by so-called postmodernists. But London is not just posing abstract problems; rather, much like a good ethnographer, he is actively engaging his readers in the complexity of the problem by telling them about its mundane aspects. From a more theoretical point of view, his efforts bring to mind the recent emphasis placed on reflexivity and authorship in sociological writing.[12]

Another important work that provides a rich account of being poor and without a home is George Orwell's *Down and Out in Paris and London*. Published in 1933 as the author's first book, this work tells the story of Orwell's troubles as a young man living in Paris and London. Packed with penetrating insight and wit and written in a nonchalant and almost humorous style, *Down and Out in Paris and London* offers page after page of the daily routines of poor and street people. What makes the book particularly powerful is Orwell's ability to nonchalantly critique his interactions and surroundings, as in the following passage:

I stayed in the streets till late at night, keeping on the move all the time. Dressed as I was, I was half afraid that the police might arrest me as a vagabond, and I dared not speak to anyone, imagining that they must notice a disparity between my accent and my clothes. (Later I discovered that this never happened.) My new clothes had put me instantly into a new world. Everyone's demeanour seemed to have changed abruptly. I helped a hawker pick up a barrow that he had upset. "Thanks, mate," he said with a grin. No one had called me mate before in my life—it was the clothes that had done it. For the first time I noticed, too, how the attitude of women varies with a man's clothes. When a badly dressed man passes them they shudder away from him with a frank movement of disgust, as though he were a dead cat. Clothes are powerful things. Dressed in a tramp's clothes it is very difficult, at any rate for the first day, not to feel that you are genuinely degraded. You might feel the same shame, irrational but very real, your first night in prison.[13]

Like a trained participant observer, Orwell constructs his presence in the setting with the reaction of those around him. His self-presentation strategies figure heavily into his account, as well as his mental state during any given experience, but, unlike some of the more contemporary attempts at foregrounding subjectivity,[14] Orwell's descriptions do not privilege an *emotional* vantage point that runs the risk of becoming self-absorbed or narcissistic. The author's own modest assessment of his effort in the final paragraphs of the book admirably reflects his methodology and his mission:

> My story ends here. It is a fairly trivial story, and I can only hope that it has been interesting in the same way as a travel diary is interesting. I can at least say, Here is the world that awaits you if you were ever penniless. . . . Still I can point to one or two things I have definitely learned by being hard up. I shall never again think that all tramps are drunken scoundrels, nor expect a beggar to be grateful when I give him a penny, nor subscribe to the Salvation Army, nor pawn my clothes, nor refuse a handbill, nor enjoy a meal at a smart restaurant. That is a beginning.[15]

Nevertheless, like London's work, Orwell's descriptions of the various characters he encounters are equally potent. Consider, for instance, how he describes a beggar he encountered:

> He had faced his position, and made a philosophy for himself. Being a beggar he said was not his fault, and he refused either to have any compunction about it or to let it trouble him. He was the enemy of society, and quite ready to take to crime if he saw a good opportunity. He refused on principle to be thrifty. . . . He was ready to extract every penny he could from charity provided that he was not expected to say thank you for it. He avoided religious charities, however, for he said that it stuck in his throat to sing hymns for buns. He had various other points of honour; for instance, it was his boast that never in his life, even when starving, had he picked up a cigarette end. He considered himself in a class above the ordinary run of beggars who, he said, were an abject lot, without even the decency to be ungrateful.[16]

Here we can see how Orwell gives life to his observations in a fluid and concise matter without sacrificing the aesthetic quality of his prose. Perhaps, the most outstanding quality of the work, as compared to recent contemporary sociological efforts in this vein, is the fact that *subjectivity* is assumed and deftly utilized without losing sight of the empirical project. Nor does Orwell resort to devising elaborate textual devices to remind the reader where his voice as the author ends and the objective analysis begins. Where the recent emotionalist preoccupation with *self* in sociology has resulted in some deliberately disjointed qualitative studies that literally demarcate the grand entrances and exits of the author in the text,[17] in Orwell's work we can rest assured that the author is *always* in the text without losing sight of the content or the coherence of what is being presented.

It is also important to point out that Orwell does not portray the people he encounters as either "helpless victims," "pure souls," or "degenerate others," themes that often dominate the so-called objective and scientific discussions on the topic. Instead, he opts for a *subjective* style of description that is empirically rich, descriptively colorful, and analytically insightful, as demonstrated in the following passage:

[T]here is no *essential* difference between a beggar's livelihood and that
of numberless respectable people. Beggars do not work, it is said; but,
then, what is *work*? A navvy works by swinging a pick. An accountant
works by adding up figures. A beggar works by standing out of doors
in all weathers and getting varicose veins, chronic bronchitis, etc. It is
a trade like any other; quite useless, of course—but, then, many
reputable trades are quite useless. . . . I do not think there is anything
about a beggar that sets him in a different class from other people, or
gives most modern men the right to despise him. . . . A beggar, looked
at realistically, is simply a businessman, getting his living, like other
businessmen, in the way that comes to hand. He has not, more than
most modern people, sold his honour; he has merely made the mistake
of choosing a trade at which it is impossible to grow rich.[18]

By raising the question, "What is work?" Orwell enters into a deep
phenomenological analysis that questions conventional views of street people and
their lives, offering his readers the brand of constructionist analysis of deviance that
would, years later, be associated with the likes of sociologist Howard Becker.[19] As
a whole, these examples help support the notion that literary texts are sociologically
insightful. The works of London and Orwell are presented, too, to show how
sociology emerged to study a homelessness that was *pre-constructed*, not
empirically pristine. Perusing literary accounts especially provides sociologists with
epistemological insight into the data that they otherwise insist stand on one side of
the division between "facts" and "fiction." Furthermore, by examining the stylistic
features of these works, sociologists can observe the rhetorical character of their
own, ostensibly "separate and distinct" scientific presentation.

Romanticized Accounts

Perhaps the most common textual construction of homelessness takes the form
of romantic accounts. Here, homelessness is represented as exotic and as the last
bastion of authenticity in modern life, as illustrated in the following:

[T]he cozy warmth of the camp-fire, with its many-colored dancing
flames and its red glow painting everything a delicate fire-tint, the
silvery stars twinkling above us in the dark firmament, the nearby
brooklet gurgling soft cadences through the stillness of the night; while
cooling breezes wafted from the high mountain peaks, were faintly
sighing through the tree tops—this coffee, brewed and served in
castaway tomato cans, had a right royal flavor. We were strangers and
yet companions in misery who, as the narcota of the strong coffee began
to circulate through our hunger-gnawed frames, laughed at the "other"
world with its wealth, its family trees, and its endless chain of fibs and
foibles, which polite society only too often applies to tear reputations,
homes, and even lives into shreds.[20]

This is an excerpt from a series of books published at the turn of the century by Leon Ray Levingston,[21] who wrote under the pseudonym "The Rambler," which he explains was his moniker or road name. On the first page of every book the phrase "written by himself" appears in large capital letters, and the preface informs the reader that "this book will be especially entertaining to the adult reader because it gives a vivid insight into the daily life and character of the average tramp." Yet, just before promoting the book in this fashion, another page warns:

To Restless Young Men and Boys

Who Read this Book, the Author, who Has Led for Over a Quarter of a Century the Pitiful and Dangerous Life of a Tramp, gives this Well-meant Advice:

DO NOT

Jump on Moving Trains or Street Cars, even if only to ride to the next street crossing, because this might arouse the "Wanderlust," besides endangering needlessly your life and limbs.
Wandering, once it becomes a habit, is almost incurable, so never run away but stay at home as a roving lad usually ends in becoming a confirmed tramp.

The reference to awakening the "wanderlust" (i.e., the irresistible urge to travel) is both a warning and an invitation; it puts the narratives contained in the book in the context of an adventure that takes one on a journey "away from home." Here the idea of being away from home or being homeless is the consequence of a deliberate act and not solely caused by unfortunate circumstances such as poverty. The "young men and boys" have to be told to fight the urge to leave home. Although this idea is rarely discussed in the academic text, in many literary accounts, leaving home in search of an adventure is portrayed as the primary reason for the increase in the number of "tramps" at the turn of the century.

Admittedly, "homelessness" had a different meaning in the early 1900s—an acknowledgment that is consistent with the notion advanced in previous chapters that "homelessness," as any other social problem, does not occur in a vacuum, but is constructed out of a specific sociohistorical context. However, for the purpose of the discussion at hand, it can be said that the representation of the experience of being away from home as a "tramp's" romantic adventure is part of a larger literary discourse, which thrives to this day in an endless list of novels, as well as in the texts and narratives of homelessness in everyday life.

Another line of romantic representations of homelessness in literary prose carries the broader message of social justice and uses homelessness as a metaphor for the plight of humanity in a modern (or postmodern) age, as seen in this poem by the existentialist Hermann Hesse:[22]

I walk so often, late, along the streets,

Lower my gaze, and hurry full of dread,
Suddenly, silently, you still might rise
And I would have to gaze on all your grief
With my own eyes,
While you demand your happiness, that's dead.
I know, you walk beyond me, every night,
With a coy footfall, in a wretched dress
And walk for money, looking miserable!
Your shoes gather God knows what ugly mess,
The wind plays in your hair with lewd delight—
You walk, and walk, and find no home at all.[23]

Home in this context is not just a physical place but an idea—one that symbolizes serenity, peace, and perhaps more than anything a sense of belonging. Its ideological opposite, homelessness, by contrast represents displacement and alienation. The importance of this for the study of the everyday experience of clients at a shelter lies in the realization that the ideology of home and the assumed consequences of its absence may figure into the daily operations and policies of human service agencies. For example, they may view a homeless person as one who is suffering from more than just lack of physical housing, as someone who is besieged by the mental anguish associated with being without a home.

By the same token, clients may not view themselves as "homeless" in that they may adopt the view, for example, that "home is where I put my head down." Consequently, those clients who emphasize the metaphysical connotation of "being at home" may be adamant in their position that they are not actually "homeless"; rather, they simply need temporary shelter and food.

Finally, in addition to literary accounts, homelessness has been represented symbolically in the visual media to signify something other than itself. For example, many Hollywood productions use homelessness as a metaphor for the supernatural, be it demonic or angelical. This topic, which is not as concretely textual, is outside the immediate scope of this piece, but it is also worthy of further investigation. Norm Denzin,[24] for example, has used film as a setting for conducting cinematic ethnographies in which the visual production is treated as a site for fieldwork.

Notes

1. James Clifford, "Introduction: Partial Truths," in *Writing Culture: The Poetics and Politics of Ethnography*, ed. J. Clifford and G. E. Marcus (Berkeley: University of California Press, 1986), 6.

2. Clifford, "Introduction: Partial Truths," 2.

3. Clifford and Marcus, *Writing Culture: The Poetics and Politics of Ethnography*; Carolyn Ellis and Michael E. Flaherty, *Investigating Subjectivity: Research on Lived Experience* (Newbury Park, Calif.: Sage, 1992); Paul Beson, *Anthropology and Literature* (Urbana, Ill.: University of Illinois Press, 1993).

4. Nels Anderson, *The Hobo: The Sociology of Homeless Men* (Chicago: University of Chicago Press, 1923), xi.

5. Anderson, *The Hobo: The Sociology of Homeless Men,* xii.

6. Anderson, *The Hobo: The Sociology of Homeless Men,* viii-xii.

7. Jack London, *The Road* (New York: Macmillan, 1907).

8. London, *The Road,* 9-10.

9. Erving Goffman, *The Presentation of Self in Everyday Life* (Garden City, N.Y.: Doubleday, 1959).

10. Goffman, *The Presentation of Self in Everyday Life,* 35.

11. London, *The Road,* 53-54.

12. John Heritage, *Garfinkel and Ethnomethodology* (Cambridge: Polity, 1984); Paul Atkinson, *Understanding Ethnographic Texts* (Newbury Park, Calif.: Sage, 1992).

13. George Orwell, *Down and Out in Paris and London* (San Diego: Harcourt Brace, 1933), 120.

14. Ellis and Flaherty, *Investigating Subjectivity.*

15. Ellis and Flaherty, *Investigating Subjectivity,* 213.

16. Orwell, *Down and Out in Paris and London,* 166-67.

17. Carol R. Ronai, "Multiple Reflections of Child Sex Abuse: An Argument for a Layered Account," *Journal of Contemporary Ethnography* 23 (1995): 395-426.

18. Orwell, *Down and Out in Paris and London,* 173-74.

19. Howard Becker, *Outsiders: Studies in the Sociology of Deviance* (New York: Free Press, 1963); John I. Kitsuse, "Societal Reaction to Deviant Behavior: Problems of Theory and Method," *Social Problems* 9 (1962): 247-56.

20. Leon Ray Levingston, *Hobo-Camp-Fire-Tales* (Cambridge Springs, Pa.: A-No.1, 1911), 20-21.

21. Levingston, *Hobo-Camp-Fire-Tales.*

22. Hermann Hesse, *Hermann Hesse: Poems Selected and Translated by James Wright* (New York: Noonday, 1970), 3.

23. Hesse, *Hermann Hesse, Poems,* 3.

24. Norman K. Denzin, *Images of Postmodern Society* (London: Sage, 1991).

Chapter 4

Ethnographic Constructions
of Homelessness

The main argument advanced so far is that the boundary between what is considered literary versus scientific can and should be questioned in the context of this work for three reasons. First, there is much sociology to be learned from so-called works of fiction on the topic of homelessness. Second, it has been suggested that ethnographies can be analyzed in terms of their textual qualities, which raises the question of the degree literary genres and styles enter into ethnographic text. Finally, literary genres form an important, but often neglected, part of the polyphonic, prescientific discourses on the experience of being without permanent housing. This chapter presents an overview of various ethnographies on homelessness with these points in mind.

The traditional understanding of ethnographic work, as the systematic and participatory observation of *facts*, has been challenged by both its critics and its practitioners. A number of social movements and historical changes have helped trigger or at least catalyze this "paradigm shift."[1] Chief among these forces are the growth of the feminist movement and postcolonial developments in the field of anthropology. These and many other factors are often referred to as the postmodern trend in the social sciences.[2]

Unfortunately, in many instances, postmodernism has gradually become nothing more than a catch-all buzzword that offers no analytical framework for guiding research projects. Instead of trying to grapple with the "undefinable" terrain of postmodernism, I turn my attention to a more modest but systematic and coherent effort to analyze ethnographic work as a mode of textually constructing empirical data with the use of Gubrium and Holstein's[3] recent framework.

Qualitative Research as Representational Idioms

In their book *The New Language of Qualitative Method*, Gubrium and Holstein[4] offer a critique of qualitative research by grounding their analysis in what they refer to as "method talk." As they put it:

> Our strategy for understanding the diversity of qualitative research is to treat each variant as an enterprise that develops, and is conducted in, a language or idiom of its own. Accordingly, each idiom represents a distinctive reality, virtually constituting its empirical horizon.[5]

At the heart of their analysis is the division between what they refer to as the "whats" and the "hows" of research. The gist of their argument is that qualitative inquiries vary in terms of their emphasis on either the object of study or the process of its production and representation. Thus, the reader is provided with four "idioms" that represent the range of this tension between *what* is to be studied and *how* it is represented.

The first approach discussed in the book is naturalism. Briefly stated, naturalism is defined as an idiom that is primarily concerned with the object of study, constructing the object of inquiry naturalistically. The topic—the thing to be studied—is given epistemological primacy and the process of its representation is relegated to a discussion of technical dos and don'ts. Thus, by situating himself or herself in the "right place," the researcher obtains an "accurate" and "objective" slice of reality to be passed on to the readers. The major shortcoming of this approach according to Gubrium and Holstein is:

> Because they view the border [between the whats and the hows] as a mere *technical* hurdle that can be overcome through methodological skill and rigor, they lose sight of the border as a region where reality is constituted within representation.[6]

By assuming that reality is self-evident, naturalists ignore important analytical issues regarding both the representational strategies that inform their findings and members' constructive practices.

The second idiom of qualitative inquiry discussed by the authors is emotionalism. This idiom is equally concerned with the *whats*, or the object under study, but it locates it in the emotional life of the researcher, and not in the "natural" setting. As the authors put it, "Emotionalist method talk virtually takes naturalism to heart."[7] The result is method talk that is preoccupied with issues of *authenticity* and "deeper truths." Given that these notions are thought to have been neglected or downright suffocated in traditional modes of ethnographic writing, emotionalists draw on rather innovative means to represent their "true feelings." In particular, they use the language of *romanticism* with all its literary connotations (e.g., the lure of the exotic, the primacy of nature, and the authenticity of the subjective).

The shortcoming of this idiom, according to Gubrium and Holstein, is that "by peering so intently into subject's interior lives and inner realms, emotionalists can blind themselves to the ways that subjects shape these spheres by way of their own interpretive actions."[8] This means that emotionalists also make the error of undermining the importance of the process of reality production (the *hows*) by simply assuming that inward self-reflection is synonymous with deep, self-evident truths. By giving primacy to inner feelings and self-reflective confessions, emotionalist method talk fosters a level of self-absorption that threatens to supplant the topic of analysis.

The third idiom discussed in the book is ethnomethodology. Unlike the other two approaches, ethnomethodology is very much concerned with the *hows* of everyday experience. Ethnomethodologists focus strictly on the process of reality production and its nuances, but in doing so they run the risk of being morally vacuous and presumptuously non-self-reflective. That is to say, ethnomethodology's sole preoccupation with constitutive activity leaves no room for substantive experience itself as something that takes place within a larger sociopolitical structure governed by relations of power and discursive practices that mediate reality production and its representation.[9]

Gubrium and Holstein point out that ethnomethodologists run the risk of reducing the topic of analysis to yet another process:

> Ethnomethodology risks reality's melting into representation as it focuses on the *hows* of reality construction at the expense of the *whats* of lived experience. . . . As the substantively meaningful aspects of local culture are shunted aside in order to concentrate on constitutive interactional activity, the content of lived experience becomes almost incidental.[10]

The net result is that by focusing almost exclusively on the processes of reality construction, ethnomethodology moves to the other extreme of the polar opposition between the *whats* and the *hows*.

The last idiom discussed in the book is that of postmodernism. The central concerns of postmodernism revolve around questions of authority and authorship. Although the terrain of postmodernism is undoubtedly vast, and according to some, "undefinable," Gubrium and Holstein assert that the common theme of this idiom is the practice of representation.[11] Where ethnomethodologists study the processes through which members construct their reality, postmodernists question the power relations and the political rhetoric embedded in these representational strategies of both members and researchers. In doing so, some postmodernists offer alternative modes of representing social reality, while others fundamentally challenge or deprecate all forms of representation to the point of nihilism.[12] Gubrium and Holstein's critique of postmodernism is best illustrated by these ominous words:

> Postmodernism in the guise of qualitative inquiry is very risky business. Rhetorical ubiquity notwithstanding, at the lived border, reality is always on the verge of collapsing into representation, taking with it the substantively distinct parameters of experience whose "qualities" are qualitative method's unique subject matter. Trying to capture that which is not there, or to describe the inexpressible, using mere rhetoric that begs its own deconstruction, is hazardous indeed. Qualitative inquiry is surely in peril as it gambles with empirical nihilism.[13]

The second half of Gubrium and Holstein's presentation is devoted to outlining what they call the new language of qualitative work, which aims to find a middle ground between the *whats* and the *hows* of lived experience. The authors offer detailed procedures and concepts for conducting this type of ethnography, which aims to "keep the constructed *whats* of 'their world' in focus without totalizing the constitutive *hows*."[14] This approach, the authors contend, creates a balanced analytical framework that is equally concerned with the process of reality construction and the substance of what is being constructed. At the heart of this new language is what the authors refer to as *analytic bracketing:* "alternately bracketing the *whats*, then the *hows*, in order to assemble a more complete picture of practice."[15]

Authorship and Responsibility

An alternative method of organizing ethnographic text is offered by Horwitz.[16] He begins his analysis of ethnographic writing this way:

> Fieldwork for a scholar in anthropology, sociology, or folklore can greatly resemble everyday life for most everyone else. In many ways, it is a simple matter. You visit a setting, register surprises, venture generalizations, contrast them with others you have read or recall, and write it up. You tell a story.[17]

Horwitz goes on to discuss two general approaches to writing ethnographies: theoretical and ethical. The theoretical position is said to be primarily concerned with issues of authority and responsibility. Accordingly, theorists ask the question: "[H]ow can I conduct ethnography and write it up so as to fulfill my responsibilities to informants, readers, and myself?"[18] The author argues that feminist scholars have been particularly instrumental in foregrounding these matters. The essence of the theoretical approach is stated below:

> [T]heorists suggest . . . ethnography should be offered as a negotiated agreement, play, polyphony, or dialogue among the ethnographer, the subjects, and the readers. Or the aim should be an unabashed mono-logue by an ethnographer/narrator who challenges the readers to beware of authorial edifice. Or the narrator, amid punctuating confessions, should fill pages with elegant, evocative raw stuff, everyday talk and events. By some accounts the result is a representation that empowers its subjects; by others one that deconstructs itself.[19]

According to Horwitz, the ethical school, in contrast, takes a more rule-oriented approach to the problem. Matters of authority and responsibility are dealt with through administrative and instructional devices. Informed consents and "professional responsibility" replace the tortuous theorizing over such matters as whose voice should/is heard in the text. Horwitz points out, however, that the author does not disappear in the ethical framework. As he puts it, in the context of the ethical framework: "Although, ideally decentered in theory, authors are powerfully centered in the literature and jurisprudence of the field."[20]

These differences notwithstanding, there are points of commonality: they are both concerned with the practice of authority. Thus, the two approaches differ mainly in terms of their positions on the same set of concerns:

Theorists, then, aim to unmask the tricks so that readers and writers will not be so easily duped by hegemonic discourse. Codes of ethics, on the other hand, tend to treat authority in more modernist terms. Authority is earned in the closing of a standard, implied contract between ethnographers, subjects, and readers.[21]

The danger in going to either extreme is that the theorist risks losing sight of the object of the study altogether, while the ethicist transforms substantial theoretical and moral responsibilities into a set of contractual agreements.

As a whole, the two analyses presented above[22] shed considerable light on how to read and classify ethnographic material. This "theoretically self-conscious"[23] trend is as much concerned with the subject matter (i.e., the *whats*) as it is with its mode of representation and production (i.e., the *hows*). In the following section, I present a number of prominent ethnographies of homelessness using the analytical frameworks put forth by Gubrium and Holstein to frame my discussion of ethnographic constructions.

Ethnographic Texts of Homelessness

Looking at the stack of ethnographies on my desk, I realize what must be common knowledge for many: a title speaks a thousand words. Titles of books tell the mission and direction of the book; they set the tone for what is to come. Thus, *Tell Them Who I Am*[24] signifies the presumably untold story of homeless people. *Down on Their Luck*[25] presents a story of misfortunes. *On the Bowery*[26] is about the particular location of the homeless experience, as much as it is about its quality. *Something Left to Lose*[27] tells a story of the struggle for dignity amid harsh conditions.

What these books have in common, of course, is the subject matter—homelessness. But, as argued in the previous section, a focus on the language or "idiom" of qualitative inquiry, especially its textual constructions, would lead to the question: How is homelessness represented in these works? Analytical frameworks, such as Gubrium and Holstein's, are useful tools for classifying and understanding these works in the context of their respective "method talks," while at the same time being sensitive to the topic under consideration.

The following discussion primarily draws on Gubrium and Holstein's[28] analytical vocabulary to highlight the strengths and weaknesses of ethnographic texts on the topic of homelessness. Admittedly, many of the studies presented here do not consistently adhere to one idiom of qualitative inquiry, but rather shift in their orientation depending on the organization of the book and the dimension of the problem being emphasized.

The Researcher Self and the Homeless Other

The Hobo

One cannot begin a review of ethnographies on homelessness without paying homage to the first endeavor of this kind, namely, Nels Anderson's *The Hobo,*[29] a study of homelessness in Chicago's "Hobohemia." In addition to being pioneering, Anderson's work stands out in other ways. What is most striking is Anderson's comments in the introduction to the 1965 edition of his book. Here we find revealing insights about the genesis of his project:

> In 1882 my father migrated to the United States after a boyhood in Sweden and some twelve years in Germany. . . . My father found himself moving about through the Middle West, a real hobo worker: farm hand, minor, lumberjack, building worker, and for a while coachman in Chicago.[30]

Anderson goes on to tell the story of his family, how they moved from Chicago to the West in search of the elusive American dream, and eventually returned to Chicago to continue to live in poverty "on the edge of Hobohemia."[31] Anderson reports that, like his father, he became a hobo. He "rode the freight train" across the country looking for jobs. Eventually he settled in Utah and managed to obtain his undergraduate degree. He was persuaded by one of his professors to pursue graduate work in sociology. Following this advice, he returned home to attend the University of Chicago. Here he latched on to a familiar topic:

> In each class I had to prepare a term paper, which meant field research and reading. I knew the hobo, and his urban habitat, and was permitted in two classes to do papers about that world so little known to most professors.[32]

Note that Anderson "knew" the hobo before he started his research. This is further supported by the remarks of his committee members who reluctantly approved his master's degree. He is told by one of his advisors: "You know your sociology out there better than we do, but you don't know it in here. We have decided to take a chance and approve you for your Master's degree."[33] Anderson's experiential knowledge of "out there" (the natural social world) is signaled by his mentors and contrasted with the formal academic discourse "in here."

Anderson himself points out that, although some have cited his work as a prime example of participant observation, he had never heard of the term when he published his work. In response to a colleague who praised him for his ability to "identify" with "the life of the hobo" and gain "insights into the inner life," he modestly states:

> I did not descend into the pit, assume a role there, and later ascend and brush off the dust. I was in the process of moving out of the hobo world. To use a hobo expression, preparing the book was a way of "getting

by," earning a living while the exit was under way. The role was familiar before the research began. In the realm of sociology and university life I was moving into a new role.[34]

This confession begs the question of the extent that Anderson's representational strategies were influenced by his experiential knowledge of the topic. Specifically, it is clear that there was a personal context in which the work was produced. Indeed, Anderson relies on the "familiar" personal experience as a way of earning a place in the unfamiliar world of the academy.

Not surprisingly, however, these remarks appear in the second edition of the book some forty years after it was originally published, and even then only in the introduction. Anderson's remarks, as Gubrium and Holstein would suggest, are crucial in understanding how homelessness is constructed in the text. This assertion does not imply the substance of the book is irrelevant; rather, it merely points out that it is in the context of Anderson's experiential knowledge of "out there" that we can better understand his findings. For example, his insistence on classifying homeless people into the categories of hobos (those who work and wander) and bums (hedonistic social parasites who don't work) can be better understood in light of the fact that Anderson regarded his father as a hobo, and he placed himself in the same category. He has this to say about hobos in the introduction of the 1965 edition: "Since the hobo has moved on, this Introduction is my tribute to him. Whatever his weakness, and I knew them full well, I present him as one of the heroic figures of the frontier."[35] The point of this discussion is not to highlight the subjective "flaws" of Anderson's work, but to show the nexus between the subject and the object: between the *hows* and the *whats* as they textually construct the homeless.

Down on Their Luck

In a similar vein, in reading the preface to Snow and Anderson's *Down on Their Luck*,[36] we find the authors' acknowledgment that: "in looking back over the genesis of the book, we have been struck by how it originated largely out of situational circumstances and our particular life experiences rather than as the result of studied, conscious formulation."[37] The fact that such admissions appear only in the introductions of ethnographic studies may shed some light on why ethnographers are often accused of being descriptive and journalistic. How can we, as social scientists, acknowledge the subjective contours of our field experience in introductions and nothing more? A systematic analysis of the relationship between what is being presented and who is presenting it is all but absent in such works. This indicates not just a methodological oversight but an empirical omission. It can also be said the shift in "method talk" from the casual first-person voice in the preface, introduction, or appendix, to the detached and formal tone in the body of the text may be seen as the forerunner of the disjointed voice articulated in the emotionalist multilayered accounts.[38]

Again, it is not my intention to throw away the baby with the bathwater. Snow and Anderson's work is truly insightful. The subject matter is well illustrated through a substantial amount of empirical data, but the process of its textual construction is given scant attention. For example, in a decidedly theoretically self-conscious moment in the book the authors state:

> It is our book, not our homeless informants'. We are the choreographers or narrators, so to speak. . . . But we do believe that our descriptions and interpretations are reasonable approximations of what we were privy to, and in that they are restrained both empirically and methodologically. . . . We did not create the settings, the characters, the behaviors, or the life histories and experiences that constitute the empirical basis for the book. . . . We can only hope, then, that the subsequent chapters prove to be effective mediators in the sense that they are not overladen with distortions and that they form a meaningful bridge between the world of the homeless and that of our readers.[39]

Snow and Anderson are aware of the tension between the hows and the whats. Unfortunately, they resolve the tension prematurely through the simplistic disclaimer: "it is our book," not theirs. Rather than offering the reader a convincing and systematic analysis of the dialectical relationship between the content and its representation, the subjective and the objective, the authors simply "hope" that their descriptions are not distorted.

The subjects' representational methods are equally neglected. For Snow and Anderson, the subjects' "artful practices of everyday life"[40] are reduced to and are synonymous with survival strategies:

> [W]hat has impressed us most about the homeless we came to know and whose stories we have endeavored to tell is their resourcefulness and their resilience. Confronted with minimal resources, often stigmatized by broader society, frequently harassed by community members and by law enforcement officials, and repeatedly frustrated by their attempts to claim the most modest part of the American dream, they nonetheless continue to struggle to survive materially, to develop friendships, however tenuous, with their street peers, and to carve out a sense of meaning and personal identity.[41]

There is no question that Snow and Anderson are sympathetic to the plight of the homeless, but the question is: How is this sympathy articulated? Underlying their admiration for the resiliency and resourcefulness of the homeless is the assumption that they "struggle" to be like us. Where "meaning" and "personal identity" are purported to be characteristic features of normal society, the homeless must be praised for struggling "to carve out" what normal society takes for granted. Thus, it is not the *experience* of "homelessness" itself that is the object of investigation, but the *struggle* to get out of it—or perhaps the experience is viewed as nothing more than the impeded desire to be part of normal society or the "American Dream." To define homelessness, as Snow and Anderson have, in terms of residential stability, familial relations, and "the degree of dignity and moral worth"[42] is to reduce the complexity of the experience to how street people come to terms with what they don't have. This would be tantamount to saying that the African American experience is about not being white and black people should be praised for their struggle to be white. (A similar critique of a universal model of normality can be found in Edward Said's[43] discussion of "Orientalism.")

The universal model of normality implied in Snow and Anderson's work can also be found in the writings of another famed ethnographer, Eliot Liebow, who describes the homeless this way:

> At the first sight, one wonders why more homeless people do not kill themselves. How do they manage to slog through day after day, with no end in sight? How in the world of unremitting grimness, do they manage to laugh, love, enjoy friends, even dance and play the fool? How in short do they stay fully human while body and soul are under continuous and grievous assault?[44]

Sympathy is articulated by observing failed expectations of normality. The assumed importance of being part of mainstream society is so great in Liebow's text that he is astonished that more homeless people do not take their own lives. Inverting this assumption of a universal sense of normality involves viewing the status of homelessness from the subjects' point of view. For example, it may be that some homeless people find it astonishing that members of mainstream society are so attached to their status—or as I once heard a homeless man say, "It sucks to be a citizen."

Something Left to Lose

A recent ethnography by Gwendolyn Dordick titled *Something Left to Lose*[45] takes a slightly different tack. Filled with eloquent, comprehensive, and detailed descriptions, the work offers an in-depth account of the lives of New York City's homeless people in four different sites: a bus terminal, a shantytown, a public shelter, and a private shelter. Dordick approaches these settings in terms of the ways in which their inhabitants "socially construct" a sense of home or shelter in relatively public arenas by establishing and maintaining personal relationships. As she explains: "[H]omelessness encourages a process in which personal relationships are mobilized in the production of what the physical environment fails to provide: a safe and secure place to live."[46] Episodes of street life and narratives of her encounters with street people illustrate the quality of life "out there," conveying a naturalistic tone. Dordick shows how homeless people form relationships, construct rules and enforce them, and share resources, all of which supports the notion that they are not fundamentally different from us, but they, too, have "something to lose."

> The conditions in which they live are hard for many to even contemplate. They still have something left to lose, however. The lives they have improvised in the empty spaces of our public world are meaningful, complicated, and consuming. The relationships they engage in are sources of satisfaction and anguish, of security and uncertainty.[47]

Dordick's analysis is thus geared toward showing "what they have, not what they lack."[48] Undoubtedly, the author accomplishes this task admirably. Through her powerful and at times passionate prose, Dordick, in the best tradition of naturalistic inquiry, takes the reader into the world of the other to both "show us what life there is really like" and to "correct our misconceptions." Unfortunately, it seems the author is somewhat oblivious to what Gubrium and Holstein call the *hows* of representation. Although she is very interested in the processes through which her subjects "construct" a sense of shelter through personal relationships, her own representational strategies are rarely questioned. On rare occasion, Dordick allows the reader to get a passing glimpse of her struggle with her status as a white, middle-class Jewish woman doing research in a field where the subjects are predominantly poor people of color, but these self-reflections fall short of a systematic critique of the author's own voice and text.

The depth of the personal information offered throughout calls for a more systematic analysis. For example, we know from reading the book that: (1) the author is a woman who was frequently mistaken for a prostitute or was asked for sexual favors;[49] (2) she is Jewish;[50] (3) she is "built like a football player;"[51] and (4) she was at times "embarrassed" and "angry" with herself.[52] Yet, are we to assume that the only way any of this enters the analysis is to improve the quality of the data and give her better rapport with the natives?

In fact, about the only place in the book Dordick offers any analysis of her presence in the field is where she recounts how her status as a woman helped her establish rapport with her informants at a public shelter. She states, "[M]y authenticity as a female afforded me some security while my ability to stand up for myself earned me some very important respect."[53] Even here, it is not clear if the author takes her "authenticity" for granted as an essential part of her being, or if she is telling us how she may have been perceived by others.

Unfortunately, the overall effect of neglecting the *hows* of her own representational strategies is to reduce the complexity of her voice and research practices to anecdotal accounts of encounters with the exotic. Without an explicit discussion of *how* the researcher's status may have influenced the project, the impressive insights and findings can be dismissed as yet another example of "othering" street people, albeit in this case it is a sophisticated and seemingly benevolent one.

Without explaining to her readers how the author's self-references provide a context for the interpretation of her observations, their very presence may invite the sinister interpretation that the sole purpose of their inclusion in the main body of the text was to portray Dordick as an adventurist who dove into the depths of the unknown, encountered the exotic untamed other, and returned unscathed with stories of her bravery in the face of danger.

A less cynical reading, however, could encourage interest in the conceptual and practical problems encountered by women who wish to study topics that have been traditionally dominated by male researchers. But in the absence of a "self-conscious" analysis, the piece may be regarded as amusing and insightful at best, and cultural tourism at worst.[54]

What is needed, then, is not just colorful confessions and dramatic accounts of how the author confronted danger. Rather, we need to ask what, if anything, does this tell us about the construction of homelessness in her text? Again, a cynical reader might place her in the category of early anthropologists who braved the unknown to explore "other" cultures, and invariably returned "home" with bizarre and unfathomable tales. This brand of research has undergone much criticism in anthropology,[55] and it may behoove us as sociologists to be equally critical and self-reflective when "domestic others" are the subjects of study.

Checkerboard Square

Fortunately, a new sense of direction is beginning to emerge in the study of homelessness. In Wagner's *Checkerboard Square*, for example, we find a shift in both the object of the study and the "method talk." Wagner's work is explicitly concerned with matters of representation and how they affect the findings. By showing how the underlying theme of characterizations of homelessness is an intense and often misplaced preoccupation with individualism, the author criticizes the dominant constructions of homeless people as hostile, dysfunctional, or worthy of charity.[56] Wagner argues that the particular brand of individualism that has dominated the American political landscape obscures the agency and sense of community that he contends is prevalent among homeless people.

The book's central theme is how homeless people actively resist mainstream culture and communities through their collective efforts. The author describes his project in the following:

> I support the perspective that poor people are not just acted upon or just passive victims of society, and I show how street people develop their own self-consciousness, culture, and alternative community. My focus represents a radical departure from other accounts of the homeless.[57]

Indeed, the author's focus does represent a shift away from "survival strategies" of the "down-and-out" and a move in the direction of appreciating their agency, serving to highlight the *hows* of their agency as much as the *whats* of their lives.

Wagner is equally theoretically self-conscious about his methodology. In a section titled "Questions of 'Representativeness' and Interpretation," he voices his reservations about his status as an author: "The ethnographer's authority is almost scary. He or she always translates the lives of others from a vast number of spoken words and visual cues into an organized reality to be presented to others who have no personal experience of the subjects."[58] But he resolves this issue, perhaps somewhat hastily, by stating his mission as one of showing how his subjects remain "human" in spite of being victims of circumstances beyond their control. In his words: "[D]espite all the pain, their lives reflect essential human ingenuity including organizing their communal lives in innovative ways."[59]

Consequently, unlike the other ethnographers discussed thus far, Wagner's self-consciousness about the *hows* and the *whats* of his subjects' world results in a somewhat different conceptualization of the problem of homelessness. "Survival

strategies" are replaced with a "culture of resistance." The experience of homelessness is cast not in terms of a constant pursuit of "housing" and "personal dignity,"
as Snow and Anderson would suggest; rather, it becomes part of a set of complex
relationships and acts of agency that may constitute a rejection of the universal
notion of normality.

Wagner's account, however, fails to directly examine the interactional
activities through which the reality of homelessness is concretely achieved.
Although the ethnography is far more sensitive to the members' practices and the
contingencies of their experience than any text discussed so far, the account
remains grounded in a humanistic discourse that is excessively preoccupied with
allowing the natives to speak for themselves. He is told by his research subjects,
"Tell them who we really are."[60] Faithfully, he accepts his commission and tries to
show us their "essential human ingenuity." Although an admirable goal, this tour
de force falls short of remaining faithful to the lived complexity of agency and runs
the risk of becoming another attempt to show how the homeless are really no
different from the rest of us.

The challenge is to escape the self-imposed limitations of this humanistic
discourse that is founded on the polar opposition between the normal self and the
deviant other, and to subvert the goals of showing *us* how *they*—"courageous
survivalists who are simply the victims of circumstances beyond their control"—are
"no different and still have something left to lose." We begin this task by returning
to the phenomenon of homelessness itself as the starting point of analysis. The first
and foremost task is to abandon the comparative evaluation of how homelessness
is or is not any different from life in mainstream society. This shift in focus implies
an understanding of *how* contextually and discursively circumscribed everyday
practices of the homeless and researchers give shape and meaning to "homelessness" as a contemporary social problem.

Recently, a few researchers have embarked on exactly such as task. For
example, Jack Spencer[61] shows how homelessness is constructed in accordance with
the organizational contingencies of human service organizations. He explains how
clients construct "their narratives as rhetorical devices which could accountably cast
themselves in ways which would guarantee their reception of services."[62] According
to Spencer, clients use various situationally appropriate themes to construct
identities that are deemed "service worthy" by their social workers. For example,
some clients use the theme of "tryin' to make it" to show that in spite of their best
efforts, they are helpless, alone, and consequently in legitimate need of services.[63]
These findings suggest that the portrayal and management of the "homeless" is
practically constructive, not situationally homogeneous.

In a similar study, I[64] show how "homelessness" is narratively assembled, again
for immediate practical purposes. Using public testimonials from a national
conference on the topic, I argue that homelessness can be *used* as a descriptive
resource in the production of a situated identity. I build on Gubrium and Holstein's
concepts of "narrative practice" and "biographical work" to emphasize how
members *use* "homelessness" as a narrative resource to construct needed site-
specific identities.

The notion of members using or manipulating the stigma of homelessness is also advanced in Susan Ruddick's[65] *Young and Homeless in Hollywood*. Using a study of street people in California, the author shows how "homeless people, through the use of space, challenge preconceptions about themselves."[66] At the core of her analysis is the notion that space is a "social resource" that can be used in the "constitution of systems of interaction."[67] Accordingly, by manipulating their location and activity in public spaces, homeless people actively participate in how they are viewed by others, as shown in the following example:

> [T]wo formerly homeless couples performed their wedding ceremonies on the street directly adjacent to a park which was a well-known hangout of the homeless. If the deviance of the homeless could be exposed to the horrified eye of the public, so too could their normalcy.[68]

What is important here is that Ruddick is not interested in why homeless people end up in public places, or how they try to get out of those public spaces. Instead, she shows how the use of public space constitutes an act of agency that can destabilize taken-for-granted statuses.

This recent shift in textual perspective sets a new horizon for the study of homelessness. As Gubrium and Holstein[69] would suggest, these works attempt to reach a balance between the *hows* and the *whats* of research: they examine the topic of homelessness without losing sight of the practices (*hows*) through which service recipients, service providers, and researchers come to understand the topic (*whats*) of homelessness in the course of everyday life. What is lacking is an overall framework that would guide these efforts both methodologically and conceptually, which Gubrium and Holstein begin to provide.

Setting a Different Course

In their book *The New Language of Qualitative Method*,[70] Gubrium and Holstein call for a new "analytic procedure" for bridging the gap between "constitutive activity and substantive resources."[71] In their words:

> [W]e need an analytic procedure that dialectically acknowledges, accommodates, and explicates both sides of the process, while remaining sensitive to the ways in which the two sides are inseparable. Moreover, given the reflexivity of constructive activity and contextual resources, it would be futile and pointless to establish the primacy of one over the other. . . . The trick is to accept and balance the tension derived from the competing sides (and their reflexive relationship), assembling descriptions that intelligibly convey a practical sense of the phenomenon under study.[72]

Accordingly, such an approach overcomes the misplaced emphasis on either the substantive issues or the process of their production. "Reflexivity" here implies a dialectical relationship between the two emphases so that one cannot be studied independent of the other. The authors term this orientation "reflexive bracketing," as noted earlier. In their words, the essence of this approach "is to move back and forth between constitutive activity and substantive resources."[73]

Borrowing from this approach and its analytical vocabulary (e.g., narrative practice, biographical work, horizons of meaning, local culture, etc.), I now turn to an empirical appreciation of the complexity of the experience of homelessness within the context of the constructive practices and the contingencies that give it shape and meaning. My goal in the next four chapters is to demonstrate *how* "homelessness" is produced in and around an emergency shelter through a set of practices and discourses that embody clients and service providers, while also attending to *what* is at stake in the work and lives of those concerned.

I take a narrative perspective to study the construction of homelessness. By this I mean the everyday talk and interaction of those concerned—both staff members and clients themselves—will be center stage. I argue that their narratives of everyday work and life in and about the shelter help to construct the very clients the shelter is otherwise founded to serve.

Notes

1. Thomas S. Kuhn, *The Structure of Scientific Revolutions* (Chicago: University of Chicago Press, 1962).

2. Pauline Rosenau, *Post-Modernism and the Social Sciences: Insights, Inroads, and Intrusions* (Princeton, N.J.: Princeton University Press, 1992).

3. Jaber F. Gubrium and James Holstein, *The New Language of Qualitative Method* (New York: Oxford University Press, 1997).

4. Gubrium and Holstein, *The New Language of Qualitative Method*.

5. Gubrium and Holstein, *The New Language of Qualitative Method*, 5.

6. Gubrium and Holstein, *The New Language of Qualitative Method*, 106.

7. Gubrium and Holstein, *The New Language of Qualitative Method*, 59.

8. Gubrium and Holstein, *The New Language of Qualitative Method*, 108.

9. Michel Foucault, *The Archaeology of Knowledge* (New York: Pantheon, 1972).

10. Gubrium and Holstein, *The New Language of Qualitative Method*, 7.

11. Gubrium and Holstein, *The New Language of Qualitative Method*, 104.

12. Rosenau, *Post-Modernism and the Social Sciences*.

13. Gubrium and Holstein, *The New Language of Qualitative Method*, 109.

14. Gubrium and Holstein, *The New Language of Qualitative Method*, 113.

15. Gubrium and Holstein, *The New Language of Qualitative Method*, 119.

16. Richard P. Horwitz, "Just Stories of Ethnographic Authority," in *When They Read What We Write: The Politics of Ethnography*, ed. C. Bretell. (London: Bergin & Garvey, 1993), 131-44.

17. Horwitz, "Just Stories of Ethnographic Authority," 131.

18. Horwitz, "Just Stories of Ethnographic Authority," 132.

19. Horwitz, "Just Stories of Ethnographic Authority," 133.

20. Horwitz, "Just Stories of Ethnographic Authority," 134.

21. Horwitz, "Just Stories of Ethnographic Authority," 134.

22. Gubrium and Holstein, *The New Language of Qualitative Method*; Horwitz, "Just Stories of Ethnographic Authority."

23. Gubrium and Holstein, *The New Language of Qualitative Method*.

24. Eliot Liebow, *Tell Them Who I Am: The Lives of Homeless Women* (New York: Free Press, 1993).

25. David A. Snow and Leon Anderson, *Down on Their Luck: A Study of Homeless Street People* (Berkeley, Calif.: University of California Press, 1993).

26. Benedict Giamo, *On the Bowery: Confronting Homelessness in American Society* (Iowa City: University of Iowa Press, 1989).

27. Gwendolyn A. Dordick, *Something Left to Lose: Personal Relations and Survival among New York's Homeless* (Philadelphia: Temple University Press, 1998).

28. Gubrium and Holstein, *The New Language of Qualitative Method*.

29. Nels Anderson, *The Hobo: The Sociology of Homeless Men* (Chicago: University of Chicago Press, 1923).

30. Anderson, *The Hobo: The Sociology of Homeless Men*.

31. Anderson, *The Hobo: The Sociology of Homeless Men*.

32. Anderson, *The Hobo: The Sociology of Homeless Men*.

33. Anderson, *The Hobo: The Sociology of Homeless Men*.

34. Anderson, *The Hobo: The Sociology of Homeless Men*.

35. Anderson, *The Hobo: The Sociology of Homeless Men*.

36. Snow and Anderson, *Down on Their Luck*.

37. Snow and Anderson, *Down on Their Luck*.

38. Carol R. Ronai, "Multiple Reflections of Child Sex Abuse: An Argument for a Layered Account," *Journal of Contemporary Ethnography* 23 (1995): 395-426.

39. Snow and Anderson, *Down on Their Luck,* 35.

40. Gubrium and Holstein, *The New Language of Qualitative Method*.

41. Gubrium and Holstein, *The New Language of Qualitative Method*, 316.

42. Snow and Anderson, *Down on Their Luck*, 7-9.

43. Edward W. Said, *Orientalism* (New York: Pantheon, 1978).

44. Liebow, *Tell Them Who I Am*.

45. Dordick, *Something Left to Lose: Personal Relations*.

46. Dordick, *Something Left to Lose: Personal Relations*, 193.

47. Dordick, *Something Left to Lose: Personal Relations*, 200-201.

48. Dordick, *Something Left to Lose: Personal Relations*, 201.

49. Dordick, *Something Left to Lose: Personal Relations*, 11, 111.

50. Dordick, *Something Left to Lose: Personal Relations*, 170.

51. Dordick, *Something Left to Lose: Personal Relations*, 171.

52. Dordick, *Something Left to Lose: Personal Relations*, 72.

53. Dordick, *Something Left to Lose: Personal Relations*, 119.

54. Bell Hooks, *Black Looks: Race and Representation* (Boston, Mass.: South End Press, 1992).

55. James Clifford and George E. Marcus, eds., *Writing Culture: The Poetics and Politics of Ethnography* (Berkeley: University of California Press, 1986).

56. David Wagner, *Checkerboard Square: Culture and Resistance in a Homeless Community* (Boulder, Colo.: Westview, 1993), 175-76.

57. Wagner, *Checkerboard Square: Culture and Resistance*, 18.

58. Wagner, *Checkerboard Square: Culture and Resistance*, 40.

59. Wagner, *Checkerboard Square: Culture and Resistance*, 41.

60. Wagner, *Checkerboard Square: Culture and Resistance*, 40.

61. William J. Spencer, "Homeless in River City: Client Work in Human Service

Encounters," in *Perspectives on Social Problems*, vol. 6, ed. J. Holstein and G. Miller (Greenwich, Conn.: JAI Press, 1994), 29-46.

62. Spencer, "Homeless in River City," 39.

63. Spencer, "Homeless in River City," 35-37.

64. Amir Marvasti, "'Homelessness' as Narrative Redemption." in *Perspectives on Social Problems*, vol. 10, ed. J. Holstein and G. Miller (Greenwich, Conn.: JAI, 1998), 167-82.

65. Susan M. Ruddick, *Young and Homeless in Hollywood: Mapping Social Identities* (New York: Routledge, 1996).

66. Ruddick, *Young and Homeless in Hollywood*, 6.

67. Ruddick, *Young and Homeless in Hollywood*, 34-35.

68. Ruddick, *Young and Homeless in Hollywood*, 65.

69. Gubrium and Holstein, *The New Language of Qualitative Method.*

70. Gubrium and Holstein, *The New Language of Qualitative Method.*

71. Gubrium and Holstein, *The New Language of Qualitative Method*, 118.

72. Gubrium and Holstein, *The New Language of Qualitative Method*, 118.

73. Gubrium and Holstein, *The New Language of Qualitative Method*, 119.

Chapter 5

Abbot House and Its Clients

This chapter describes the setting, clients, and rules and regulations in a homeless shelter I call "Abbot House." My aim is to illustrate how Abbot House policies help construct various types of clients not solely based on their needs, but also in relation to organizational contingencies and necessities. Specifically, I show how clients are divided into two categories (*guests* and *nonguests*) to justify the unequal distribution of limited supplies and services and to promote compliance and conformity among service recipients.

The Setting

On a typical day during my three-year fieldwork experience and later employment at the shelter, I drove from my apartment across town to the Abbot House. Along the way, the landscape slowly changed from serene looking, redbrick buildings, to the sorority row across the campus, with Greek letters flashing on the buildings, to the blood bank about halfway to the shelter, with its clients smoking outside waiting to donate blood in exchange for about thirty-five dollars. Finally, I reached Main Street with its reckless characters in shabby clothes dashing in front of traffic back and forth between a convenience store and the shelter. The sound of power locks from other cars as the light at the shelter's intersection changed to red was a subtle reminder that some drivers had been caught off guard by the scene.

Placed between a funeral home and a fire station, Abbot House, with its six-foot-high stone walls, had the odd appearance of being a cross between a church and a fortress. The occasional sound of a fire truck rushing to an emergency combined with the smell of human flesh burning in the funeral home's crematorium completed the gloomy picture of poverty amid the modern urban landscape.

Across the street, a convenience store owned and operated by an immigrant family displayed a flashing neon sign advertising beer to the presumably vulnerable residents of the shelter. Finally, the nearby city park provided a suitable location for the inconspicuous consumption of alcohol, bought with the generous contributions of university students, who during their weekend escapades in the nearby entertainment district were either too drunk or too scared to turn down a street person asking for change.

The Shelter

The front entrance of the shelter is located on a main city street, but it is used more as an emergency exit than an entrance for fear that the comings and goings of street people might create a spectacle. Turning left from Main Street into the parking lot, I would be greeted by some of the regulars, who would ask me, "Hey buddy, can I have a cigarette?" I would nod nonchalantly, flip open my Marlboro box, and carefully tap it till a few cigarettes slid out far enough to be picked up without touching the filter. I am not sure if my hygiene etiquette was ever noticed or appreciated. I would hand over the cigarette and in my best Dirty Harry imitation follow up with, "You wanna light?"

After this little ritual, I usually walked around the corner and into a scene of apparent leisurely idleness, except that I knew for many of these people idleness was more of a nuisance than a luxury. I had been told by my informants that spending "a day with nothing to do" was their worst nightmare and that some "fell into a bottle" as a way of passing time.

By now the familiar smell of homelessness (a pungent blend of smoke, sweat, and urine) reminded my senses that I was at my research site. Scanning the parking lot, I could see how some had turned the aluminum benches at the back of the shelter into card tables. Others, wrapped in thin blankets with plastic bags holding their belongings within a foot of their heads, slept on the cold aluminum benches. Still others feasted on leftovers from their last soup kitchen meal.

The gathering at the back of the shelter occasionally included local philanthropists, researchers, and even evangelical preachers. For example, it was not uncommon to see university students sitting on benches conducting interviews. They stood out because they were typically younger, cleaner, and better dressed than the rest. Of course, the fact that most held tape recorders or notebooks in their hands and appeared earnestly attentive also helped set them apart.

Getting In

To enter the shelter, one has to ring the bell by the back door and wait for a volunteer behind the front desk to buzz open the electric lock. After a few steps down a wide corridor with client bathrooms and showers to the left, you would be standing immediately under the front desk. The front desk area is elevated about two feet above the floor of the corridor, so the people behind the counter are positioned to look down at those who enter the building. At the end of the corridor, after turning to the right and going up three stairs, one would be standing in the main lobby, a fairly large room furnished by old love seats and couches donated by local businesses and residents. The main lobby is surrounded by nine rooms and two storage closets. Each room holds anywhere from two to four clients, depending on its size and the number of beds placed within it.

In the center of the building, the front desk stands out prominently with its four-foot counter. Anyone behind the counter and facing the lobby could easily see the front door to his left, the back door to his right, and the entire lobby and all its surrounding rooms in front of him. Directly behind the front desk a large glass window provides a clear view of the dining hall, which acts as a soup kitchen between the hours of 12:00 and 1:00 p.m.

The offices of the social worker, the shelter director, and the house manager are all relatively out of sight from the vantage point of the front desk. Thus, the front desk provides a panoptic view of clients anywhere in the building, except for when they are inside their rooms. Like a nurse's station in a hospital, it both separates the clients from the staff and serves as the center of daily routines.

Various policy manuals are kept behind the front desk to instruct volunteers in excruciating detail as to how to provide services and to whom. At the same time, logbooks are used to record service recipients' names and to document cases that involve "the abuse of services." Behind the front desk, some of the drawers store clients' mail, phone messages, medication, and even their cash, while a few others are always full of soap, toothbrushes, and other personal hygiene supplies.

Guests and Nonguests

As a charity organization, the Abbot House provides free services and goods to "needy" clients, but given its limited supplies and staff, rules and policies have been established to regulate the "fair" and "efficient" distribution of these resources. Volunteers and staff have to determine which clients will get what, when, and how often. This screening process is guided by the organizational ideology that Abbot House should discourage chronic dependency and promote discipline and self-control. The board of directors, which is made up of a number of fairly affluent residents of the city, feel so strongly about the concept of "independence" that they recently incorporated it into the mission statement, which now reads:

> The overall mission of Abbot House is to provide temporary emergency food and shelter for people in [local] county, who for whatever reason, find themselves hungry and homeless. . . . Abbot House provides these services in the context of a supportive environment where people in crisis can begin to manage their problems effectively and reestablish themselves as independent members of community.

The goal of becoming an "independent member of community" was echoed by a board member who cautioned others during an annual meeting that: "If we make the shelter too comfortable, they would never want to leave." This theme is also manifested in the following excerpt from staff meeting minutes: "The overall goal is to assist our clients, not to just fulfill their need for a razor. We are here to address the bigger picture of homelessness." The "bigger picture" for shelter staff implies correcting "poor social skills" or other individual problems that staff think are causes of homelessness, as indicated in the following excerpt from staff meeting minutes concerning a client's situation:

> Again we discussed the chronic situation with Pamela. Some of the night managers are still going over capacity to accommodate her. She desperately needs financial and mental assistance, but she is not doing anything to help herself and she is becoming very manipulative. She is too dependent on Abbot House. We should be empowering her, not enabling her.

Accordingly, Abbots's emphasis on independence and self-help borrows from a broader psychiatric discourse that casts clients' troubles in the language of individual responsibility and finds the solution in "independence."

Altogether, the emphasis on self-reliance justifies discriminating between "legitimate needs" and "abuse of services." Over the years, a fairly elaborate and ever growing set of rules and policies has been developed to, first, divide clients into two categories, guests and nonguests, and then regulate access to various resources based on these assignments.

It should be noted that these terms are not consistently used by the staff, their precise meaning often debated during staff meetings. One point of contention about calling service recipients "guests" is that it might create the impression of the shelter being like a hotel and cause clients to think they are not expected to do any chores or participate in "programs." The term *program participant* was suggested as an alternative at one point, but it was rejected for a number of reasons including the fact that "it sounded too formal."

Generally, guests are clients who are formally admitted into the shelter and provided with a bed for a length of time varying from a few days to a few months, depending on the social worker's assessment of their situation. The category nonguest, on the other hand, is used to refer to those shelter users who are not given bed assignments and have limited access to the amenities of the house, such as shower and laundry. The distinction between the two is established and enforced through a long, and often confusing, list of rules that controls three basic facets of shelter life: supplies, space, and behavior.

Policies on the Distribution of Supplies

The primary source of material goods at the shelter is donations from citizens, businesses, and community organizations. The items donated to the shelter cover a wide range. Generally, people donate what they think homeless people need, as well as what they themselves no longer have use for. For the most part, the actual needs of shelter clients coincide with people's assumptions. So, donations of soap and other hygiene items are frequent and welcomed. But in some cases the donated items do not seem to correspond to an immediate need. For example, as a volunteer I was never sure where to place such luxury items as shower caps and shoehorns. Fortunately, the drawer labeled miscellaneous was always available as a last resort.

People who want to donate clothes and furniture are referred to other charity organizations that specialize in distributing goods to the needy. There are exceptions to this policy, however. For example, in the colder months, donations of winter clothes are rarely turned down. Another item of clothing always in high demand is socks. The socks drawer offers an interesting array of colors and designs, with a pair of underwear occasionally squeezed between the layers of socks. Organizing this drawer and reaching into it for me was like a game of Russian roulette, since I worried about running my hands against soiled underwear or something equally repugnant.

The time I spent organizing donations was not a complete waste of time. Particularly, handling the clothing donations, whenever we accepted them, gave me insight into the appearance of street people. The clothes brought to the shelter are often out of style, even if they appear new. Bell-bottom jeans, garish sweaters, and large-collared dress shirts are among some of the garments fashion-conscious citizens cast out of their closets and leave at the doorstep of the shelter. Thus, through acts of charity, some are able to make amends for their fashion faux pas. Of course, most clients are not especially selective about what protects their bodies against the elements. As one of my informants commented, "the loss of vanity" is perhaps one of the most visible and, in his mind, severe consequences of life on the streets. In a way, the seemingly bizarre appearance of street people may simply mirror the fashion excesses of their well-wishers.

In any event, from the time they are checked in at 5:00 p.m. until they leave the next morning by 8:00, guests have relatively unrestricted access to all the material resources in the shelter. This includes food, laundry, showers, and the telephone. Specifically, under a section subtitled "Meals," the shelter policy manual states:

- Supper is provided nightly, either brought in by volunteers or the kitchen/pantry is opened so you can cook your own
- Food in refrigerators, if not identified as belonging to a specific individual, is available for guest use

In contrast, for nonguests, access to anything inside the shelter is heavily regulated. First, nonguest requests are limited to specific times during which volunteers are available to respond to them. This time frame is typically between 10:00 a.m. and 9:00 p.m. Second, every fulfilled request is documented and could potentially be used as grounds for establishing "dependency" and the denial of services. For example, a nonguest who makes a second request for a bar of soap on the same day has to account for the status of the first one. So, it was not uncommon for me as a volunteer to question grown men about the whereabouts of a bar of soap or a toothbrush they had received earlier.

The practical absurdity of such procedures is most evident where blankets are concerned. Nonguests are issued one blanket per year upon availability. This means they should either carry the blanket around with them during the day or stash it away till it is needed again. Needless to say, many nonguests refuse to do the former and are unable to do the latter. Consequently, volunteers are put in a position to turn down blanket requests on many cold nights, even if the storage closet is full of donated blankets. The staff's justification for this and other related policies is very simply stated in the policy manual: "Goal: To empower them to find other resources for themselves; we cannot contribute to their chronic status." This supports the idea that the organizational ideology, not the clients' immediate needs, is the basis for the classification and processing of service recipients.

The following policy further highlights the division of the clients at the shelter: "OBJECTIVE: To accommodate emergency needs of nonguests if appropriate without interrupting services to house guests. Our primary responsibility is to provide for guests of the house." The staff's commitment to separating these two types of clients is also illustrated in this house rule, made known to all incoming guests: "Guests are not allowed to serve nonguests any food or supply from the house. Violation of this rule could result in the loss of your bed!!"

Policies on Living Space

One of the most valued services that a homeless shelter offers is living space. In fact, it can be argued that the use and distribution of space are at the core of the issue of homelessness (as the term itself would indicate). Ironically, with a few exceptions,[1] very few studies have focused on how homelessness is intricately tied with the notion of living space. My research site, the Abbot House, provides some insights into this topic, particularly in regard to how the use and distribution of living space distinguishes guests from nonguests.

Guests are provided access to the following spaces: a bedroom (which they may have to share with up to three other people), bathrooms, showers, the lobby, and the dining area. In a sense, what makes the shelter "homelike" in comparison with the streets is the fact that the space inside the shelter is strictly defined by its use. Accordingly, the bedrooms are where clients sleep and store their belongings, the dining area is where they eat, the lobby where they socialize, and the bathrooms where they take care of bodily functions.

For nonguests, however, outside space is not differentiated by its use. The nonguests who were not banned from the property use the parking lot, the outside bathroom, and the back porch for a variety of purposes. For example, the back porch, a screened room with lockers and a few benches, is used for sleeping, socializing, and storing personal belongings. In the winter months, a line of plastic mattresses is laid on the back porch for the nonguests. Upon availability and with the approval of the staff, lockers are assigned to nonguests to store their possessions.

During cold nights, sleeping space in the back porch becomes a valued commodity. For a time, back porch sleeping accommodations were arbitrarily controlled by a few African American self-appointed outside leaders, who were later accused of discriminating against white clients. This, coupled with reports of drinking and illicit drug use in the back porch, led the staff to establish the position of "porch monitor." The porch monitors were nonguests selected by the shelter director, and they received special privileges, such as late-night dinners, in return for their services. They were expected to report any improper activity to the shelter staff, and distribute the space in the back porch on a first come, first served basis.

Another example of nonguests' use of undifferentiated space is the outside bathroom located by the back entrance. In addition to being a place for completing bodily functions, this bathroom also served as a barbershop. One of the street people would plug his electrical clippers into the bathroom outlet and offer haircuts to others for whatever price they could afford. His customers lined up outside the bathroom and watched clumps of hair fall to the floor as they waited their turns. On other occasions the bathroom would provide enclosure and privacy for sexual activity—the sight of a couple entering the small bathroom late at night was not uncommon. Finally, it was no secret that the bathroom was also an ideal space for illicit drug use.

With respect to both inside and outside, the staff maintains control over space by the use of signs. Signs serve two important functions. First, they act as surrogate authority figures in situations where the constant monitoring of space is impossible. This is illustrated in the following excerpt from staff meeting minutes:

> No one is supposed to be on property (especially those on restriction) except during lunch hours of 11:30 a.m. to 1:00 p.m. . . . Signs are being made to assist with this. This tightening of control over the backyard became necessary after giving them [nonguests] an opportunity to police themselves—and they didn't. Since we can't control drinking and littering we'll have to ask everyone to leave. We realize too that allowing living in our backyard, sitting there all day, etc. is "enabling" their homelessness.

Second, signs provide justifications for future rule enforcement. Posted signs put staff in a better position to reinforce policies and made their intervention seem more rule oriented and less arbitrary. The following excerpt from staff meeting minutes is an example of this function of signs:

> [We] still need a sign for the backyard. Enforcement is the key factor. Thus, we decided that the night manager should go out there every night and morning to remind them they should not be loitering in the backyard. The sign will help to back up the argument.

As a result, nearly every wall both outside and inside the shelter contains signs that are intended to regulate the use of space by clients. Two issues complicate the reliance on signs as a way of controlling space. First, many clients do not read the signs. This is not necessarily due to illiteracy; rather, the notion of reading and following signs does not seem to be part of the cultural repertoire of most street people. My observations at the shelter suggest that the effectiveness of written signs as a method of controlling space does not just depend on clients' reading comprehension, but also on the clients' willingness to take notice of signs and follow them. Contrary to the staff's expectations, many do not consult posted signs before embarking on a course of action, a situation that often resulted in staff members groaning, "Didn't you read the *sign?*"

Another related problem is the fact that some clients, especially nonguests, dispose of or vandalize signs, thus challenging the authority represented by them. By destroying or modifying written signs, clients in a sense transform them into "signs of contested space" (pun intended). Staff members, in turn, respond to these challenges by laminating signs, posting them out of reach, or in some cases making them out of wood or other less destructible materials.

I should point out that the space both inside and immediately outside the shelter is also used by other organizations. For example, sometimes the police in their search for a suspect, with staff's permission, inconspicuously observe clients through the behind-the-counter window during soup kitchen hours. Similarly, the parking lot is used by various organizations as their recruiting ground. In fact, during my study, a couple of social workers from another agency regularly appeared outside the shelter. Working on behalf of a newly established, city-funded program that was geared toward providing stable housing and job training for a small group of homeless people for up to two years, they had essentially established a field office in the parking lot. Their sales pitch included a little yellow pamphlet that introduced them as "housing specialists."

The stated goal of the program was to eventually help clients move out on their own and become self-sufficient. Since the project's future funding was contingent on its success rate at the end of the two-year period, its coordinators were determined "not to waste time on those who can't be helped," and they focused their efforts on carefully screening "eligible" candidates for their program. Naturally, the presence of experts from another agency in their backyard did not go unnoticed by shelter staff, who expressed mixed feelings about such projects. While they generally approved of anything that would help the homeless "get back on their feet," they approached the efforts of "the characters" in charge of a new project with an air of suspicion and mistrust, questioning their expertise in recognizing and dealing with the problems of homeless people.

In short, the most valuable asset at Abbot House is living space. Its distribution and use—the simple practical process of allocation—play a significant part in the typification of clients. On one hand, guests' access to inside space brings them under close scrutiny by the staff, while at the same time sheltering them from agencies that target street homelessness. On the other hand, nonguests' use of outside space affords them relative independence from the shelter, but makes them more visible. Based on these observations, one can offer a new working definition of homelessness that challenges the conventional understanding of the problem as the absence of a given space (i.e., home) and, instead, focuses on how the unauthorized use of public space for private purposes is key in the social construction of homelessness as a social problem.

Policies on Behavior

Another way in which the staff maintains the distinction between guests and nonguests is through the differential enforcement of rules. Consider, for example, the "rules of the house for the guests":

-Cooperate with staff and volunteers
-Be courteous to other guests
-No smoking in the house at any time
-No foul or abusive language
-No weapons, dangerous items, or threatening behavior
-No stealing
-No fighting
-No switching of beds without approval of staff
-Maintain personal hygiene
-Maintain general housekeeping

These rules, which are intended to control clients' behavior inside the shelter, reveal three important dimensions of what constitutes a guest. First, guests are clients who are subjected to the rules. That is, the fact that they stay inside the shelter makes them easier targets for a wider net of social control. Unlike nonguests, who are for the most part outside the physical range of the shelter's social control apparatus, insiders can be instructed and monitored much more closely and consistently.

Second, not only are guests subjected to more control, but they can be guests only as long as they follow the rules. Rule violations rarely raise questions about the underlying ideology of shelter policies; instead, they are merely grounds for downgrading clients from guests to nonguests. Thus, the duality between guest and nonguest makes it possible to shift attention from the legitimacy of rules, or their fairness, to how the clients' actions determine their fates. This is evident in the following excerpt from a staff meeting minutes:

New Business: Need a "Code of Behavior" or Code of Ethics for the guests; need to encourage them to be aware of how their personal behavior affects their reentry into the community as productive citizens. The issue is "standards" to follow.

And, third, the very wording of the house rules is indicative of the staff's perceptions of their clients. For example, what type of person needs to be reminded not to steal, to maintain proper hygiene, and to be courteous? It is doubtful that a Hilton Hotel would warn its guests that they would be thrown out on the street if they did not maintain proper hygiene. Pointing attention to the fact that a homeless shelter is not a Hilton may be a statement of the obvious; what is less obvious is how the difference between the two is interactionally accomplished.

Most private organizations provide services in exchange for a fee, thus being in a position to turn down some clients based on their inability to pay. In contrast, as a charity organization catering to the poor, Abbot House must determine eligibility for goods and services in a manner that is completely independent of the client's ability to pay. House rules then are not just local norms whose violation is grounds for expulsion, but they also actively assist staff in constructing a "rational" duality between their clients, which would justify treating some as serviceworthy and others as unworthy.

Consequently, the staff may label nonguests as "treatment resistant" and approach them with a sense of abandonment, as evident in the following: "Discussed the distinction between a guest (who must follow certain standards) and nonguests. A nonguest receives certain services but they are not required to follow any standards." As seen below, the rules and procedures for handling nonguest requests are primarily designed to screen and limit services:

> Rules and Procedures [for Nonguests]
> 1. Determine if the need is appropriate.
> 2. Get the full name and birth date of person requesting the service.
> 3. Look up name in nonguest note book to determine eligibility.
> Eligibility factors include:
> a) not restricted
> b) no trespassing warrants
> c) no obvious abuse of services
> 4. Only one nonguest can be allowed in the house at a time and only if they are receiving services at the time. Once they are served, they must leave.

As a result, preventing the "abuse of services" is a primary concern in regard to nonguests. This is accomplished by documenting every request in the logbook. This point can be best illustrated in the context of a typical encounter between clients and the front-desk workers, who are mostly student volunteers from the nearby campus. After a very brief orientation, these volunteers are trusted with the tasks of answering the phone, filling out initial intake forms, and responding to client service requests.

After ringing the doorbell, the nonguest is allowed inside the building by a volunteer who buzzes them in. The volunteer is expected to follow the nonguest with his eyes the entire time the nonguest is in the shelter to make sure "they don't disappear into one of the guest bedrooms." (Nonguests often complained about feeling they were being watched all the time.) The nonguest eventually reaches the front counter, where he or she might be asked in a formal tone, "Can we help you?"

The uncertainty associated with the response to this simple question is the source of much anxiety among the volunteers. Specifically, some volunteers find it difficult to deal with the fact that nonguests may ask for things they are not allowed to receive, such as a cup of coffee. Since the average volunteer donates his or her time to the shelter to "give something to the poor," the idea of turning down such simple requests is unfathomable to many.

Of course, the staff repeatedly remind them that to "help" the homeless, it is necessary to follow the rules. Some volunteers take this to mean that they should assume a cold, authoritarian attitude toward the clients. In turn, nonguests who encounter a person who appears to be unsympathetic to their plight can become "abusive" and "hostile." Through this bizarre twist of intentions, the nonguest may end up being placed on "restriction" and denied food and services for up to ninety days. Ironically, rules and regulations, in their application, can deny services to the very people who need them.

Assuming the request from a nonguest is acceptable, the next step is to record the client's name and date of birth in the logbook. But before providing the item, the volunteer is also expected to ascertain the nonguest is not on the restriction list. Finally, he or she would have to look up the name on the nonguest logbook to verify the request is "appropriate" (e.g., the client is not asking for a second blanket in the same year or a second toothbrush on the same day).

The volunteers are particularly encouraged to use the logbooks as a way to make sure the entire process is fair, as indicated in the following note from a staff memo:

> We would like to remind all staff and volunteers to use the Nonguest Notebook when making decisions on special requests (such as blankets, groceries, showers in the evening, and other out-of-the-ordinary requests). It would alleviate some of your agonizing over whether to grant the request if you looked at their page. The notebook could provide you with information on their background, whether or not they are restricted from certain services, or if they just asked for this service yesterday. Pay special attention to the "Comments" section and the information on the back of their page. There is too much reliance on just listing the name and service on the clipboard.

Thus, the logbook serves as a moral guide for deciding if a person should go hungry for the night or be denied a blanket that might protect him from below-freezing temperatures. What is particularly illuminating is how the process of creating the document is detached from its consequences for the client. For the staff, the document's creation is simply a matter of "accurately recording information in the logbook." Each client is assigned a sheet in the logbook with dates and codes for various services (e.g., "bl" for blanket). However, a conscious effort is made to balance the codes with more in-depth information in the form of written comments, which are used to either inform volunteers about a client's extenuating circumstances or to warn them about the negative characteristics of the client.

Altogether, the rules on the three facets (services, space, and behavior) outlined up to this point show how shelter policies are used as resources for classifying two types of clients, guests and nonguests. The next question is: What happens when rules are violated?

Violations and Restrictions

Abbot House uses an elaborate restriction policy as a way of punishing those who refuse to abide by the rules. Generally, guests who violate house rules are "evicted," meaning that they lose their beds, but they are not denied other services. The nonguests, on the other hand, are much more likely to be the targets of restrictions. Although, over the years, the policy has gone through many revisions, the basic premise remains the same. A client who has violated a house rule, according to the staff's opinion, is denied food, supplies, and services for 90 days. If the client re-offends, the restriction is extended to 180 days. Finally, for third-time offenders, the restriction can become permanent, as indicated in this excerpt from staff meeting minutes:

> [T]he policy states that each offense incurs a 90-day restriction. . . . If they need to be put on restriction for the second time, it will last for 180 days. If they need to be put on restriction for a third time, they might be denied services permanently.

At the end of the ninety-day period a client can request that his case be reviewed and the restriction lifted. In the absence of such a request the restriction is indefinite. The process is outlined in a staff memo as follows: "(1) Person requests a review, (2) Check to see if past 90 days, (3) Discussion and decision at next staff meeting, (4) Tom [the shelter director] explains the results to the person."

Abbot House's restriction policy is modeled after some of the most conservative "tough-on-crime" legislation in the country (i.e., "Three strikes and you're out"). This suggests the shelter's methods of punishment and enforcement borrow from a broader discourse that transforms matters of social inequality into individual responsibility and rule violation. A quick glance at the review decisions on whether to keep clients (names fictionalized) under restrictions, as indicated in staff meeting minutes, reveals that the underlying issue in many cases is defiance of authority or unacceptable life style, rather than a specific transgression. The following are a series of specific decisions taken from a staff meeting minutes.

> Tim Phillips: Decided against lifting restriction due to drinking and causing minor disturbances; he is not acting responsibly.
>
> William Johns: Decided against lifting restriction due to long-term problems with him.
>
> Brandon Jones: Decided against lifting restriction due to drinking and causing minor disturbances; he is not acting responsibly.
>
> Arthur Johnson: Restricted 12/7/93 for forcibly entering the house to get food. We decided not to lift the restriction due to his violent and mentally ill behavior since that time (including being intimidating and profane when asking for review). The chances of his behavior changing are slim.

<u>Angie Watson</u>: No way. Dangerous, drunk, and cursing all the time.

<u>Joe Williams</u>: No. Numerous verbal harassment, uses an alias, belligerent.

<u>Angie White</u>: No, due to multiple violations (treatment resistant).

What the staff consider a restriction offense is rarely the type of behavior that would result in a formal arrest or prosecution. Nevertheless, the consequences for the offenders are very severe: they are denied food and other basic necessities. In other words, shelter policies enable the staff to apply what might be regarded as cruel and unusual punishment in other institutional settings.

Some offenses, however, do involve more specific and substantial rule violations. Typically, these fall in the category of theft or assault against other clients, as shown in these examples taken from staff meeting minutes.

<u>Jim Smith</u>: 3/13/94: stealing a bike off Tom's [the shelter director's] truck— no violations in the past 90 days but he has never apologized or recognized that what he did was wrong. He also intercepted a donation in the parking lot last week. No lift.

<u>Joe Perry</u>: Did not have info on his original restriction but we decided not to lift restriction because just this morning he came by asking for coffee and then tried to steal someone's bike. We decided to extend restriction for another 180 days.

<u>Betty Hooke</u>: Originally put on restriction for stealing and inappropriate behavior in the backyard [Betty is a street prostitute who performed sex acts on her clients in the backyard]. In October of this year there is a violation on her log page and in November she was fighting with Julie Ross [another client] in the yard. We denied lifting her restriction.

<u>Terry Banks</u>: Background—April 92 theft, broke into storeroom, stealing garbage bags, using 4 aliases. No December violations but on 1/26/94 he asked the guests to pass food through the back window. These offenses are considered serious, so we denied lifting his restriction at this time. Will review in another 90 days if he requests and if no further violations.

Although this second set of offenses may seem more serious than the first, it is doubtful, for example, that Terry Banks would be arrested for "stealing garbage bags" or receiving "food through the back window." The point is that the severity of an offense is designated in relation to the local culture of the organizational setting[2] and may seem ludicrous or unjust to outsiders.

In fact, at least in one case, the restriction process was criticized by a person outside the organization. This "formerly homeless" person wrote a letter to the shelter director detailing his objections to Abbot's disciplinary practices. Staff's response to his complaint appears in the following meeting minutes excerpt:

> Tom [the shelter director] informed us about a letter from a Coalition [most likely the Coalition against Homelessness] member who was formerly homeless. This person expressed the "injustices" he found in the appeals process at some homeless shelters for disciplinary actions. He felt that homeless clients should be able to immediately appeal the decision to discipline. Our system of a 90-day review period seems to satisfy HUD [Department of Housing and Urban Development] requirements and seems to be adequate for our program. Any grievances can be forwarded to Tom and he will evaluate the discipline if necessary.

The challenge to the authority of the staff is dismissed by linking shelter policies to the guidelines of another larger and more powerful organization (i.e., HUD). Rather than addressing the issue of "injustice," the organization established the legitimacy of its practices by appealing to a higher authority. In this case the local relevance of the rules is discerned in the phrase "adequate for our program."

Thus, the social construction of clients at the Abbot House is aided by both the rules and the relations of power that make their enforcement possible. The rules themselves are grounded in multiple discourses, ranging from self-help psychology and its emphasis on independence to the criminal justice system and its obsession with individual responsibility and punishment.

The homeless client at Abbot House is neither a transparent truth nor the product of whimsical minds that respond to him. Instead, the reality of being a client is produced in the context of a set of rules and policies that are very real in their consequences for both staff and service recipients. By regulating such mundane matters as supplies, behavior, and living space, staff members construct the locally relevant reality of the client, often at the cost of excluding other explanations and possibilities for social action. The masses of destitute bodies are divided into the polar opposition of *guests* and *nonguests* and their common plight is presented in terms of the dichotomy of "treatment resistance" and "treatment responsiveness." The competition between guests and nonguests in the context of a rule-oriented status system stifles the possibility of fundamentally questioning the nature of social inequality, bifurcating a potentially unified group into segmented bodies who, ironically, live at the conscientious mercy of their "rational" hosts.

Notes

1. Susan M. Ruddick, *Young and Homeless in Hollywood: Mapping Social Identities* (New York: Routledge, 1996); Talmadge Wright, *Out of Place: Homeless Mobilizations, Subcities, and Contested Landscapes* (Albany: State University of New York Press, 1997).

2. Jaber F. Gubrium and James Holstein, *The New Language of Qualitative Method* (New York: Oxford University Press, 1997).

Chapter 6

The Local Demography of Homeless Clients

Like any other organization, Abbot House produces official records to guide its internal policies and for purposes of accountability to outside funding agencies. This chapter examines the demographic characteristics of clients at the Abbot House, using official records, with two goals in mind. First, the local data will be compared with national data as a way of assessing the degree to which Abbot clients are representative of homeless people in the general U.S. population. Second, the local data are used to show how the construction of the client is organizationally embedded in the numerical artifacts of the shelter.[1]

As reviewed in chapter 2, the current state of knowledge on the characteristics and numbers of homeless people is far from conclusive. However, this does not preclude discussion of the way staff members and the shelter's funding agencies make rhetorical *use* of national numbers, as unreliable as they might otherwise be. Since my analysis in the coming chapters treats staff and clients' use of such "objective data" as narrative resources pulled from a broader discourse, it is important to examine the local contours of these "facts" in relation to the rest of the nation, as well as in relation to how they are locally applied.

National Trends

Ostensibly, one of the more reliable estimates of the demographics of the U.S. homeless can be found in *Homelessness in the United States*.[2] Although published over a decade ago, this edited volume remains one of the more detailed and comprehensive references on homelessness in this country. Table 1, which is based on a sample of twenty U.S. cities of 100,000 or more, appears in a section of the book titled "A Sociodemographic Profile of the Service-Using Homeless: Findings from a National Survey."[3]

As seen in this table, 81 percent of homeless people who go to soup kitchens or shelters are men. Blacks form a disproportionate 41 percent of this population. Finally, the majority (51 percent) of these service users are between the ages of 31 and 50.

Other data from this study show that 40 percent of the service-using homeless have been without shelter for six months or less, with those who have been homeless for over four years comprising only 19 percent of this population.[4] This suggests that the so-called chronically homeless make up less than one-fifth of the overall homeless population in the United States.

Table 1. Sex, Race, and Age of Homeless Service Users

	Percentage of Homeless Individuals Who:			
	Use Only Soup Kitchens (N=223)[1]	Use Only Shelters (N=670)	Use Both Shelters & Soup Kitchens (N=811)	Total Sample (N=1704)
Totals	24	36	40	100
Characteristics				
Sex				
Male	93	68	84	81
Female	7	32	16	19
Race				
Black	40	35	47	41
White[2]	43	51	43	46
Hispanic	13	12	3	3
Other	0	2	3	3
Age				
18-30	20	32	35	30
31-50	65	47	48	51
51-65	11	17	17	16
66+	4	3	0	3

1. N refers to unweighted data. All percentages are based on weighted data.
2. White non-Hispanic.

Local Trends

Table 2 shows the demographic characteristics of Abbot House clients using data from intake forms and logbooks. As seen in this table, in an average year Abbot House provides shelter for over 1,000 clients, who either receive emergency shelter or other services. The demographic characteristics of these clients closely parallel the national trends shown in table 1. The key difference is that where the national data cited in table 1 do not include people under the age of eighteen in their analysis, my data show that between September 1996 and September 1997 nearly 12 percent of shelter guests were minors and over half (53.8 percent) of these younger clients were below the age of seven.

Since Abbot House does not provide shelter for runaways or unattached minors, we must conclude that almost all of these younger clients were accompanied by a parent. Further analysis of the data reveals that about 90 percent of these parents are single women. During the course of my fieldwork I encountered many of these mothers who cited an abusive husband as their reason for leaving their homes. In fact, shelter policies required that people who answered the phone not answer specific questions about certain female clients, fearing that their enraged husbands might be attempting to locate them. The staff at the Abbot House were particularly sensitive to the needs of these single mothers and families in general. Whenever "families" made up a substantial percentage of housed clients, the shelter director would boastfully announce the news to the staff.

Table 2. Sex, Race, and Age of Abbot House Clients

| | Homeless Individuals Who: | | | |
| | Stayed Inside the Shelter[1] (N=444)[3] | | Used Other Shelter Resources[2] (N=839) | |
	Number	%	Number	%
Characteristics				
Sex				
Male	276	62.2	651	81.9
Female	168	37.8	144	18.1
Race				
Black	164	36.9	357	56.8
White	249	56.1	260	41.4
Other	30	6.8	11	1.8
Age				
0-17	52	11.7	1	.1
18-30	109	24.5	129	16.2
31-50	232	52.3	553	69.6
51-65	39	8.8	97	12.2
66+	12	2.7	14	1.8

1. Based on data from all the intake forms between September 1996 and September 1997.
2. Based on data from current logbooks in January 1999.
3. Column percentages do not include the missing cases.

It should be noted, however, that the staff used the term "family" somewhat loosely. For example, couples were not required to show copies of their marriage certificates to be considered a family. In many ways, "family" applied to any couple that chose to claim that designation, regardless of whether they had children. In this context, the notion of family served both the clients and the staff in the following ways. For the staff members, serving families gave credence to their cause and enabled them to rebut the accusation that they simply served "lazy men" who refused to work. Clients, on the other hand, knew that having the appearance of a family unit increased their chances of being admitted and also increased their length of stay. Here, the sanctimony of the family becomes both a cultural capital and a narrative resource. That is to say, the represented family and the need to protect its unity provide organizationally appropriate narrative linkages for clients' stories while at the same time the desire to have a family and maintain its unity signifies to the staff the clients' investment in mainstream society and thereby their treatment worthiness.[5] In terms of the length of the current period of homelessness, an astonishing 97 percent of my sample of sheltered guests reported in their intake interviews that they had been homeless less than two months, where only 14 percent of the national sample reported similar results.[6] There are two explanations for this discrepancy. First, many researchers have pointed out that homelessness is not a permanent state but a point of transition (see chapter 2). In the case of Abbot House, when clients are asked how long they have been homeless, they tend to respond in terms of how long they have literally been on the streets and not the accumulative sum of being without a home over the course of their lives. In fact, while coding the data for this sample using the intake forms, I came across several marginal comments that support this hypothesis. Specifically, some of the responses to the question, "How long have you been homeless?" were supplemented with the following information: "2 weeks (4 years off and on)," "electricity was turned off 6/13/96," "migrant worker," or simply "on & off." These responses indeed support the notion that for many clients homelessness is not a final destination but a respite, or an "on and off" experience. This period, it turns out, is relatively short for the majority of people who sought shelter at the Abbot House.

The second explanation for why the current length of homelessness for Abbot House residents is considerably shorter compared to the national average has to do with implicit or explicit shelter policies that direct shelter resources away from those who are known to be "chronically homeless." Operating as an "emergency" shelter, Abbot House limits the number of stays inside the shelter to one per year. That is, the average client is not admitted as a regular guest into the house for more than once annually. (After their first annual stay, clients may be readmitted on "one-night-at-a-time" status based on availability of beds.) This policy in effect prevents the chronically homeless from being assigned a bed in the shelter—especially if they live in the area. In addition, many people who are chronically homeless also suffer from severe mental problems. In most cases such clients are unable or unwilling to effectively understand and follow shelter admission requirements. Even if they demonstrate the willingness to cooperate, depending on the perceived severity of their mental conditions (e.g., apparent hallucinations or intoxications), they may be denied admission and referred to other agencies such as the police, Crisis Stabilization Units, or detoxification tanks. As a whole, the implication of this finding is that shelter clients represent a specific type of homelessness—just in the same way hobo camp dwellers may be different from street people.[7]

The educational level of Abbot House clients is comparable to those in the national study. Thirty-nine percent of admitted guests reported having a high school degree compared to the national average of 31 percent. The findings discussed thus far are summarized in table 3.

Table 3. Length of Current Homelessness and Educational Status of Abbot House Clients Compared to the National Average

	Abbot House Guests[1] (N=444)[3] %	National Average for Shelter Users[2] (N=670) %
Length of Current Homelessness		
< 2 Months	97.4	14.0
2-3 Months	1.0	16.0
4-6 Months	1.6	16.0
> 6 Months	0.0	54.0
Education		
No High School	33.6	41.0
High School	46.8	31.0
Some College	19.6	28.0

1. Based on data from all the intake forms between September 1996 and September 1997.
2. Source: Martha R. Burt and Barbara E. Cohen, "A Sociodemographic Profile of the Service-Using Homeless: Findings from a National Survey," 17-35 in *Homelessness in the United States, Vol. 2: Data and Issues,* ed. J. Momeni (New York: Greenwood, 1989), 21-25.
3. Column percentages do not include the missing cases.

Finally, table 4 presents the percentage of admitted clients who reported some type of medical or mental health problems by age, gender, and race. As seen in table 4, only about 16 percent of the admitted guests reported an existing mental health problem. These findings are not consistent with the claims of many researchers in this area that at least 25 percent of the homeless suffer from severe mental illness.[8] Clearly, the fact that my data were based on a self-reported measure offers a partial explanation. That is, self-reports are typically more susceptible to the social desirability effect and, in this case, may result in an underestimation. However, we must also keep in mind that demonstrated mental illness translates

Chapter 6

Table 4. Percentage of Admitted Abbot Clients by Sex, Race, and Age.

	Percentage of Admitted Clients Who Reported:						
	Mental Health Problems[1] (N=444)[2]				Medical Problems (N=444)		
	Yes		No		Yes		No	
	N	%	N	%	N	%	N	%
Sex								
Male	40	15.7	214	84.3	84	33.1	170	66.9
Female	31	22.8	105	77.2	59	43.4	77	56.6
Race								
Black	13	9.3	127	90.7	39	27.9	101	72.1
White	54	23.6	175	76.4	97	42.4	132	57.6
Other	4	20.0	16	80.0	6	30.0	14	70.0
Age								
0-17	0	0.0	0	0.0	0	0.0	0	0.0
18-30	13	12.1	94	87.9	34	31.8	73	68.2
31-50	45	19.4	187	80.6	79	34.1	153	65.9
51-65	11	28.2	28	71.8	21	53.8	18	46.2
66+	2	16.7	10	83.3	9	75.0	3	25.0

1. Based on data from all the intake forms between September 1996 to September 1997.
2. Column percentages do not include the missing cases.

into eligibility for a wide range of government assistance programs, including Social Security Disability Income (SSDI). Thus, there is some doubt as to the validity of the argument that the admitted guests are savvy enough to hide their mental illness at the risk of losing their eligibility for federal benefits, which is based on a *documented* history of mental problems. In fact, my field observations from the shelter suggest that for many homeless people the connection between documented mental illness and eligibility for federal funding is common knowledge. For example, I remember a homeless woman being rather distraught about being denied SSDI benefits. As she was retelling the story to a group of other clients outside the shelter, she commented:

> I went to the Mental Health Services today. I told them I was crazy but they wouldn't believe me. I guess I wasn't crazy 'nough for 'em. Here's what I'm gonna do next time. [*She begins walking up and down the ramp to the shelter entrance with exaggerated head jerks.*]

Arguably, many street people are aware that in their dealings with human service organizations mental illness may, in fact, be an asset.

Perhaps a more plausible explanation for why Abbot House residents report a lower rate of mental illness than expected has to do with the fact than the more severe cases of mental illness are denied admission to the shelter and referred to other agencies for treatment. As stated earlier, the findings discussed above are based on a sample of a specific type of homeless people. Yet, many national studies on homelessness are not immune to this problem, causing one to surmise that there is no conclusive estimate of the actual number of homeless people who suffer from mental illness.

Admittedly, another weakness of these data is that they are based on shelter intake forms that were completed by staff and volunteers. The pertinent question posed here to the clients was usually stated, "Do you have any mental health problems?" The answer was coded verbatim and, in some cases, later modified by the social worker. The following examples of some of the less conventional answers to the question regarding mental illness provide some insight into the problems associated with this type of data gathering: "Mental Disaster," "Deaf—can lip read," "Swiss Cheese Brain," "Nerves," "Husband reports child-like mind." Clearly, these responses are a far cry from an objective psychological evaluation, but as I discuss toward the end of this chapter, this does not take away from the locally circumscribed, demographic *utility* of the cited information. For now, suffice it to say that the vagueness of the responses by no means prevents the staff from using these accounts in their everyday work, as part of the local demography of homelessness.

Having briefly emphasized the importance of interpreting the data in table 4 within the context of the organizational *practices* that make *use* of these data, let us return to their assumed manifest meaning. As a whole, it seems that whites are more likely than blacks to report a history of mental illness, women more likely than men, and the elderly more likely than the young. This suggests that the needs and the profiles of clients, even in terms of quantified official records, are varied and complex, and that no one treatment is suitable for all clients, even while the "one size fits all" approach of rules and regulations is oddly, yet organizationally, necessary.

Similarly, in regard to the physical health of most clients, table 4 suggests that whites are more likely than blacks to report a physical health problem, women more likely than men, and the elderly more likely than the young. It is also important to point out that across all the various gender, race, and age groups the rate of reported physical problems is greater than the rate of reported mental health problems. More important, where only 16 percent of all admitted clients in the sample reported a mental health problems, twice as many (32 percent) reported some form of physical illness.

In light of this finding it seems curious that the national agenda on homelessness has been less concerned about the physical health problems of street people than their psychological well-being. Although it is possible that clients find it less embarrassing to admit to having a physical ailment than a psychological one, it is also possible that the visible signs of anguish and suffering caused by a physical disorder are often mistaken by the many observers as indications of mental imbalance. At the very least, the two sets of symptoms (physical and mental) would be hard to distinguish under these circumstances, especially for survey researchers who may spend only minutes with their subjects.

Comparison of Restrictions

As discussed in chapter 5, the staff resorts to restricting access to all services and the use of any space on the property as a way of punishing those clients who do not abide by shelter policies and rules. This practice is by no means unique to the Abbot House, but it is a policy practiced by most shelters across the country. In fact, at least in one case, the restriction polices were formally challenged in court as stated in the following case briefing:

> *Tucker vs. Battitoni,* No. 6297/86 (Dutchess County)
> This action challenged a practice in about 50 percent of New York's upstate counties where persons were deemed ineligible for emergency shelter if they missed a single appointment with the welfare officer. These so-called sanctions were used to deny persons shelter for up to 90 days, even when the person appeared for an appointment the following day.

In spite of its prevalence and obvious significance, however, there is virtually no research on this aspect of life in homeless shelters. Consequently, I cannot draw comparisons between my data and the national trends in this case.

Table 5 summarizes data from current 1999 logbooks on the demographic characteristics of those who were restricted and the reasons for their restrictions. As seen in table 5, men are more likely than women to be placed on restriction, blacks slightly more likely than whites, and people between eighteen and thirty more than any other age group. Since there is no national study by which to judge these results in the context of homelessness, I turn to national data on crime to shed some light on these numbers. The probability of being placed on restriction for various demographic groups closely resembles the official data on the probability of criminal activity.[9] In other words, the demographic patterns of restriction involvement at Abbot House are similar to the national trends on criminal involvement: males, blacks, and people within the at-risk age of eighteen to thirty are more likely to commit crime. One obvious question is: Is this similarity an artifact of the shelter policies that are modeled after the national agenda of "getting tough on crime," or do they indeed reflect a tendency on the part of the stated groups to be differentially involved in law violation?

Table 6 brings us one step closer to answering this question in terms of the available official data by showing the relationship between the type of offense and demographic data. The results in table 6 suggest that gender has no effect on type

Table 5. Percentage of Restricted Clients by Sex, Race, and Age

	Ever Been Restricted[1] (N=839)[2]			
	Yes		No	
	N	%	N	%
Gender				
Male	192	29.5	459	70.5
Female	21	14.6	123	85.4
Race				
Black	123	34.5	234	65.5
White	80	30.8	180	69.2
Other	6	55.0	5	45.0
Age				
0-17	0	0.0	1	100.0
18-30	34	26.4	95	73.6
31-50	140	25.3	413	74.7
51-65	27	27.8	70	72.2
66+	2	14.3	12	85.7

1. Based on data from current 1999 logbooks, which include both sheltered and unsheltered clients who were restricted.
2. Column percentages do not include the missing cases.

of restriction offense (with the exception of mental illness and intoxication). In regard to race, it seems that more blacks are restricted for criminal activity (i.e, theft, assault, and police-reported crime) than whites. On the other hand, a higher percentage of whites were restricted for verbal abuse (threats of violence and harassment). Whites were also twice as likely to be restricted for intoxication and severe mental illness. Finally, in terms of age it appears that restrictions based on crime tend to decline with age, but cases of verbal abuse are nearly 10 percent higher for those between fifty-one and sixty-five.

Given that restricted clients are denied food and shelter at Abbot House for at least ninety days and are very likely to turn to more visible public places to fulfill those needs, understanding why people are restricted may also help us better understand some of the institutional pathways that lead to visible homelessness. Specifically, homeless people use up their resources, or in the words of Alice Baum,[10] become "institutionally disaffiliated" for a wide range of reasons. In the case of Abbot House, for example, theft (18.3 percent) and physical assault (28.6 percent) combined account for nearly half of all cases that were expelled from this last refuge for the homeless.

Table 6. Type of Restriction Offense by Sex, Race, and Age

| | Restriction Offense[1] (N=212)[2] | | | | | | | |
| | Crime | | Verbal | | Intoxication & Other Abuse | | Severe Mental Illness | |
	N	%	N	%	N	%	N	%
Gender								
Male	97	50.8	57	29.8	20	10.5	17	8.9
Female	11	52.4	6	28.6	3	14.3	1	4.8
Race								
Black	65	53.3	34	27.9	9	7.4	14	11.5
White	36	45.6	28	35.4	11	13.9	4	5.1
Other	4	66.7	0	0.0	2	33.3	0	0.0
Age								
0-17	0	0.0	0	0.0	0	0.0	0	0.0
18-30	18	52.9	10	29.4	11	4.7	51	4.7
31-50	72	52.2	39	28.3	171	2.3	10	7.2
51-65	12	44.4	10	37.0	2	7.4	31	1.1
66+	0	0.0	0	0.0	210	0.0	0	0.0

Note: Based on data from all restricted clients (both sheltered and unsheltered) in current logbooks in 1999.

1. Restriction reasons were coded from incident reports and written comments that are attached to a client's logbook page. These reasons were coded as follows: (1) Crime (physical assault, theft, and eight cases of police-reported crime, which occurred outside the shelter); (2) Verbal Abuse (threats of violence, and harassment); (3) Intoxication and Severe Mental Illness; (4) Other.

2. Column percentages do not include the missing cases.

Statistical Validity versus Local Utility

While the statistical data discussed here may help formulate insightful questions or hypotheses, they also speak to the shortcomings of data based on official documents. Arguably, such information fails to accurately capture the nuances of the clients' conditions. Indeed, when I spoke with the shelter director about the results of my preliminary analysis on the mental health status of his clients, he was quick to point out that neither he nor other staff or volunteers were qualified to diagnose mental health problems, and that my findings were unreliable.

I nodded in agreement and admitted that my data probably raised more questions than they answered. Nevertheless, one nagging question continued to trouble me: What purpose then, if any, do these data serve for the staff? In other words, while the statistical utility of the data may be dubious, is there room for local utility?

One avenue to answering this question is through examining how Abbot House's reports to its board of directors and the general public use this information. As is the case with most organizations, Abbot House does not report every piece of information it solicits from its clients. For example, a shelter handout titled "Abbot House Annual Report for Fiscal Year 1992-1993" includes such items as: (1) "total shelter nights" broken down into "single men" and "women/families" (note the absence of a separate category for single women); (2) percentage of "guests" divided into three groups "males," "females," and "children"; (3) number of "servings prepared" at the soup kitchen; (4) number of "laundry services" presented in terms of "loads washed and dried"; (5) number of case management contacts; and (6) number of volunteer hours contributed.

Admittedly, the process of aggregating and collecting these numbers and percentages fails to meet the scientific standards of quantitative research methodology and its emphasis on objectivity, validity, and reliability. No staff meetings were ever held to discuss how to operationalize variables or how to use advanced statistical techniques to better analyze the findings. However, the local practitioners of my site did follow a set of standards that was *practical* and *useful* for their needs. The very style in which these numbers are reported speaks to this fact.

Consider, for example, how women and families are placed in one group (i.e., "women/families") under the heading of "total shelter nights" in the list above. As stated earlier, the organizational ideology of the shelter is geared toward giving a priority to "serving families" to dismiss the criticism that it caters to the needs of a group of lazy men. So it follows that any data, especially as these are shared with interested parties outside the organization, is relevant in so far as it demonstrates support for this goal. Accordingly, reporting the number of single women who stayed in the shelter is not of any immediate utility. On the other hand, combining this group with families may help boost the overall percentage of "families" served.

Similarly, reporting soup kitchen activities in terms of "meals prepared" rather than the actual number of people who ate there helps better capture the scope of humanitarian services provided by the shelter. This can also be seen in the number of "laundry services," which is based on "loads washed and dried" rather than the number of people who used laundry services.

I encountered this method of data collection firsthand during my first weeks of volunteer work at the shelter. I was told to count how many people we served on a given day using the "Guest Services Logbook." I began my task earnestly and tallied the number of people served on a piece of paper. Later, I was told that the new method of data collection was to count the number of service encounters and not how many people showed up at the door on a given day. This strategy was intended to capture the number of services in cases where the same person made repeated requests on a given day.

The point here is not to question the veracity of the staff's accounts or statements, but to point out that statistical validity should not be the only criterion for evaluating the official data at this site. Instead, it is equally fruitful to examine the ways in which official records are *used* to support the organizational ideology and the local culture of the setting.[11] In this vein, official records become a narrative resource for shaping client profiles and to suggest methods of treatment. The clients, however, are not privy to the production of these records and are equally unaware as to their *use value*.

It is in this context that we can now make better sense of my intake interview encounters. It was not uncommon for clients to stare at me with skepticism, apprehension, or downright indignation when I asked them such questions as, "Are you homeless?" or "Do you have any financial needs?" In light of the self-evident truth of their presence at an emergency shelter, such questions seemed callous and inconsiderate. Eventually, I learned to preface the intake procedure with, "I know some of these questions sound stupid, but I have to ask 'em anyway—they're on the form."

I suppose my sensitivity to this problem stems from my own "homelessness" experience as an immigrant. For example, to obtain my green card (i.e., become a legal alien), I had to endure an interview at the INS (Immigration and Naturalization Service). I had opted to be accompanied by an immigration lawyer since I feared I might not fully understand the legal ramifications of some of the questions and unwittingly give the wrong answer. As soon as we entered the interview room, the INS officer asked me, "So, what are you?" I responded proudly, "I'm Iranian." He frowned at me and said, "I know that! I mean what kind of case are you?" At this time, my lawyer took over answering his questions and I remained silent except for when I was directed by my lawyer to speak.

Similarly, most clients know that they must appear cooperative by answering the questions on the intake form to receive services. However, they may not know exactly how the solicited information can be used to process their requests. At times, this gap in their knowledge may lead them to guess what the appropriate answer is. As I discuss later in chapter 8, this is most evident during their interviews with the social worker when the clients provide a list of narratives hoping that one story will "hit home," so to speak. Such seemingly senseless rambling goes on until, with the aid of the social worker, it is guided in a locally relevant direction.

It should also be noted that not every piece of information gathered from clients is immediately *useful*. In many cases staff members collect information to safeguard themselves against unforseen contingencies. Such "cover-your-ass" strategies place a premium not on the content of the information, but on the exercise of information gathering. That is, the attempt to solicit as much data as possible from a service recipient gives the appearance of professionalism—even if the data aren't of immediate use.

I have argued in this chapter that official data from the shelter can serve two purposes. On the one hand, these data ostensibly help us to draw comparisons between Abbot clients and the national profile of the homeless. Perusing the local data with this goal in mind provides a number of findings. Specifically, the analysis relatively low (16 percent) among the sheltered clients, and that physical illness seems to be more prevalent among them than mental illness.

On the other hand, I have tried to present a case for complementing issues of validity and reliability with the question of *local relevance* and *use value*. Accordingly, much in the same way that one can argue the homeless client is constructed through organizational practices and narratives, the objective data about conditions of the homeless, especially its usefulness, is equally an artifact of organizational practices and contingencies.[12] In this context, it is impossible to raise questions about the validity of the official data without considering the level and practical imperatives for data collection in the first place. In the words of Garfinkel:

> It is important to emphasize that we are not talking of "making some scientific best of whatever there is." Organizationally speaking, any collection of folder contents [client files] whatsoever, can, will, even must be used to fashion a documented representation. Thus an effort to impose a formal rationale on the collection and composition of information has the character of a vacuous exercise because the expressions which the so ordered documents will contain will have to be "decoded" to discover their real meaning in the light of the interest and interpretation which prevails at the time of their use.[13]

By extension, this argument also covers data collected under scientific aegis. If official data are collected and used for a purpose and in a given context, there is no reason to think that scientific data can somehow be bereft of a contextual validity. Some researchers may acknowledge this point and respond by stating that the goal of scientific data is to uncover the truth. However, this answer is exceedingly more difficult to accept at face value in an intellectual environment where both most consumers and producers of scientific knowledge are becoming more and more self-reflexive. The skepticism in this regard is best described by Lyotard when he states: "Scientists, instruments, and technicians are purchased not to find truth, but to augment power,"[14] or when he declares, "Knowledge . . . allows morality to become reality."[15]

Consequently, understanding how information is *used* to reproduce organizational effects is just as crucial a research task as evaluating the validity of the data. Following this line of thinking, the present chapter was not simply an attempt to supplement the qualitative text of this research with more "objective" data, but it also presented a case for the way fieldwork can provide a context for how locally produced quantitative data present narrative resources for the construction of the homeless client.

Notes

1. Jaber F. Gubrium, *Out of Control: Family Therapy and Domestic Disorder* (Newbury Park, Calif.: Sage, 1992).

2. Jamshid Momeni ed, ed., *Homelessness in the United States, Volume 2: Data and Issues* (New York: Greenwood, 1989).

3. Martha R. Burt and Barbara E. Cohen, "A Sociodemographic Profile of the Service-Using Homeless: Findings from a National Survey," in *Homelessness in the United States Volume 2: Data and Issues*, ed. J. Momeni (New York: Greenwood, 1989), 19.

4. Burt and Cohen, "A Sociodemographic Profile of the Service-Using Homeless," 25.

5. Jaber F. Gubrium and James Holstein, *What is Family?* (Mountain View, Calif.: Mayfield, 1990); Jaber F. Gubrium and James Holstein, *The New Language of Qualitative Method* (New York: Oxford University Press, 1997).

6. Burt and Cohen "A Sociodemographic Profile of the Service-Using Homeless."

7. Gwendolyn A. Dordick, *Something Left to Lose: Personal Relations and Survival among New York's Homeless* (Philadelphia: Temple University Press, 1998).

8. Christopher Jencks, *The Homeless* (Cambridge: Harvard University Press, 1994).

9. John Macionis, *Sociology* (Englewood Cliffs, N.J.: Prentice Hall, 1999), 220-22.

10. Alice Baum and Donald W. Burnes, *A Nation in Denial: The Truth about Homelessness* (Boulder, Colo.: Westview, 1993).

11. David R. Buckholdt and Jaber F. Gubrium, *Caretakers: Treating Emotionally Disturbed Children* (New York: University Press of America, 1985).

12. Harold Garfinkel, *Studies in Ethnomethodology* (Englewood Cliffs, N.J.: Prentice Hall, 1967).

13. Garfinkel, *Studies in Ethnomethodology*, 206.

14. Garfinkel, *Studies in Ethnomethodology*, 46.

15. Garfinkel, *Studies in Ethnomethodology*, 36.

Chapter 7

Staff Constructions of the Client

Recent constructionist research in the area of social problems suggests that social control agencies do more than simply service their clients; rather, in a sense, they construct the very clients they need to do their work.[1] In this vein, human service organizations provide a social context, and descriptive resources, for the production of clients. This constitutive activity, however, is constrained by organizational goals and agendas, as demonstrated in Gubrium's book *Out of Control*.

By underscoring how family therapy agencies construct the characteristics and problems of their clients differently depending on the organization's ideologies and goals, Gubrium[2] shows that the client's self is "organizationally embedded." This means that clients' presumed profiles and characteristics, as articulated by the clients themselves and their service providers, are by-products of organizational contingencies that condition how clients tell their stories and how these stories are locally interpreted.

As a whole, this line of thinking suggests that human service organizations are sites where social problems are narratively produced under the auspice of the needs and necessities of the agency. Borrowing from this approach and using interview data from Abbot House, in this chapter I look at how the staff narratively construct client identities that are consistent with their bureaucratic goals—in other words, highlighting how homelessness is constructed in relation to its service context.

Three people were interviewed here—the shelter director, the house manager, and the social worker. They form the core of the organization's administrative staff. I established different degrees and types of rapport with the respondents in the course of conducting my research as I occupied various positions in the Abbot House, ranging from volunteer to night manager. When I initiated these interviews toward the end of my project, I entered each with a good deal of background information about each respondent. Similarly, I assume that over the years each had gained some knowledge about me. Consequently, these interviews are in part framed by the mutual knowledge, and in some cases, the mutual respect we had for one another.

I did not make a conscious choice to adopt a particular kind of interviewing technique from the onset of my work. Rather, as the fieldwork progressed, interviewing seemed like a sensible and polite way of speaking with people with whom I became acquainted. As I became more methodologically grounded in my own readings, I learned that my intuitive approach was fortuitously consistent with the principles of what Holstein and Gubrium[3] call the "active interview," being especially partial to their view of its relation to ethnographic observation.

By drawing on background knowledge, active interviewers can make their research more productive, incorporating indigenous interpretive resources, perspectives, and landmarks into their inquiries. This is, of course, an implicit argument in favor of combining ethnographic observation with interviewing, not only to heighten rapport with, and understanding of, informants but to take advantage of, and reveal, the local *whats* of experience.[4]

Given the importance of this background knowledge, the following discussions begin with a brief description of how I came to know each of the three shelter employees interviewed. I then move on to the substance of the interviews, which I analyze using Gubrium's[5] notion of *horizons of meaning* to show the different ways in which the staff members construct the client. I then argue that these horizons share certain commonalities—an *institutionally preferred* gaze—as they converge on the overarching theme of the client as a failure.

Shelter Director: Clients as Undisciplined Charity Recipients

I met Tom, the shelter director, during my first week of volunteer work at Abbot House. I was somewhat intimidated by the stocky, and slightly overweight, figure of this middle-aged white man. He had a grin that seemed to be permanently glued on his face, and it was very disconcerting to me because I could never decipher if it was intended as a welcoming gesture or was a scornful sneer. After I filled out the volunteer application, I obediently followed Tom around the building as he gave me a tour and detailed my responsibilities, which were to answer the telephone, accept donations, and respond to simple client requests such as checking their mail.

During these initial contacts, Tom came across as very professional and efficient, and his demeanor with me did not change very much over the years. Later, I learned that years ago, when the shelter was first established under the supervision of a Catholic priest, Tom himself was one its first clients, and that he "lived out of his van." I also learned that Tom attended a well-known New York university as a graduate student for one semester.

I told Tom and the other staff members about my research interests from the start, but I was somewhat vague about what I was looking for since I'd never studied a shelter. This situation resulted in Tom and others attempting to help me develop a research agenda by pointing out issues that they felt would interest me. I think Tom, in particular, perhaps due to his social science background, assumed that I wanted to "discover" why people become homeless and learn how to help them. I must admit I did not find it necessary to correct him, as these were issues I was concerned with to a degree.

Of course, some of what I know about Tom came from other sources. For example, one of my closest informants, Ernest, who happened to be a talented writer, had this to say about Tom in response to my question about him: "What do I think about Tom? I think he's a shallow jerk with no personality and false expressions." Ernest's rather harsh reaction was prompted, among other things, by observing Tom's demeanor while he gave tours of the shelter facilities to members of various organizations, such as the United Way. Such groups met with him to organize fund-raising activities, or as they put it, "to put the *fun* back into fund-raising." As Tom showed these people around the shelter, with an enthusiasm that seemed disturbingly out of place, Ernest would stand to one side and jokingly whisper to me, "And to the left we have *the most* unfortunate ones."

So by the time the following interview was conducted, Tom and I were by no means strangers. That is, for better or worse, we had formed certain impressions of one another, which I suspect found their way into the interview by setting its tone and contextualizing its contents.

I conducted the interview with Tom in his office. He was very accommodating and even turned off the ringer on his telephone so that we would not be interrupted. Here is how it began.

> **Amir**: I guess we should begin with a question about what this place stands for. What does Abbot House stand for?
>
> **Tom**: Well, "stand for," that sounds pretty broad. The noble reasons why we try to be here—in the most general sense we stand for a neighbor willing to help another neighbor. People wanting to—when they see somebody in trouble, I think it's a natural instinct to want to offer a hand. And I say "natural" because I see it more in children really than some adults. I think sometimes as we grow older, maybe part of our socialization or what we learn maybe from our parents or maybe from our experiences is that, "Well, gee, we're all on our own, we're independent, you know we have to make it on our own, there's no free lunch," that sort of an attitude. Some people feel that's a virtue, the independence, and the self-made man and all of that. But I think it's more natural in children, and that's why I say it's a natural instinct for human beings maybe that when you see somebody in trouble, and if you're in a position to help, to offer a hand and to help them up.
>
> And I think that's what Abbot House. . . .That's how Abbot House got started. That was the motivation of the people that organized Abbot House and I think that's what continues us in existence all these years is that people continue to feel that way even over . . . you know we've been now since 1979 at the soup kitchen in 1980 as a shelter and so for the last sixteen or seventeen years people have been coming forward helping Abbot House as volunteers, or with their financial contributions or with their food or other in kind donations to share what they have with people that need it. Now certainly we've had trouble over the years with people who thought we weren't doing it just right or that the people we're serving don't deserve it or that if we weren't serving them that they would go away somewhere and that there are no needy people in Gainesville per se. So that we're just kind of here to make ourselves feel good and to do some kind of good works for our own benefit. In fact, one person charged that Abbot House was hurting the people that we serve because we allow them to lead this desolate life and contributing to their lethargy or whatever it is that keeps them in this situation,

the enabling part of people's response to problems. We do consider that
in a lot of our policies and in what we try to do around here.

Not surprisingly—considering that he is the director of the shelter—Tom's
construction of the client centers around the mission of the organization. This
mission, for Tom, is "people wanting to offer a hand." Consequently, he links the
client's fate with the expectations of "people [who] have been coming forward
helping Abbot House as volunteers, or with their financial contributions or with
their food or other in kind donations to share what they have with people that need
it." How the shelter responds to homelessness is as much mediated by what the
patrons of the house view as *legitimate* needs of the clients as it is by those clients'
stated needs. Tom's concern with the *patrons' demands*, as opposed to the *clients'*
needs is evident when he recounts the criticism that Abbot House hurts the people
it serves by allowing them "to lead this desolate life and contributing to their
lethargy." Thus, he sees his job as one of maintaining a balance between the clients'
needs and what his benefactors might support. As he puts it:

> We certainly do try to make guests mindful of the fact that we are a
> public charity and our guests need to, I guess, appear to be making good
> use of the charitable dollars that come our way. And that's something
> the people would be happy to support.

The goal of "making good use of the charitable dollars" is achieved by
emphasizing the kind of "progress" that resonates with the orientation of the patrons
of the shelter. Specifically, it is of utmost importance that the clients demonstrate
a willingness to help themselves. Thus, Tom rearticulates the mission of the shelter
this way, constructing client need as much in terms of clients' own neediness as in
relation to the organizational necessity of publicly avoiding "enabling."

> [W]e don't just automatically give them what they are requesting in
> many cases. We require that they try to conform to some structure in
> terms of what service do we offer at what time, and what conditions that
> we put on their receiving different services. For instance, we can't take
> anybody that's drunk. . . . We feel that it's important that they [the
> clients] know that we can only be serving people who want to be
> helping themselves to better their situation. So again we stand for the
> people wanting to help others, but at the same time, that includes the
> person wanting to help themselves I guess. And so sometimes it's a
> pretty fine line between helping somebody improve their circumstances
> and enabling somebody to continue living what we think is an unpro-
> ductive lifestyle.

The tension between "helping" and "enabling . . . an unproductive lifestyle" is
at the heart of the shelter's preoccupation with a seemingly endless list of policies
to regulate its clients. These policies, which bear Tom's influence in one form or
another, are intended to reinforce the notion of self-help and to convey to the
general public that the shelter is "making good use of the charitable dollars." Thus,

for Tom, the client is in some ways an entity to be conditioned or disciplined in such a way as to ensure the continuous flow of charitable dollars. Consider how these conditions are organized in Tom's vision of a client in the following extract from the same interview, extending the conditions from patrons' concerns to legal restrictions and the civil order of the shelter itself.

> **Amir**: Could you elaborate on some of the conditions? I think you mentioned conditions for receiving services for a person being helped.
> **Tom**: Well, right, there are some legal conditions, that are put on us. One, the housing code or the zoning code requires that all emergency shelters ask for police clearance before you allow somebody services. So we have to ask for police clearance. If they don't have a picture ID and they can't go to the police department, and the police can't establish that there are no warrants for this person through their national crime information system, then that person can't stay with us. Now, most of the time, of course, it's routine. Most of the people we're serving—homeless people—are not, I think, more criminally oriented than any other group.
>
> The other condition, as I said, is that they have to be sober. In fact if somebody comes back who is a guest, who might have been checked in when they were sober, if they come back having been drinking, we'll warn them again, saying that, "We don't give services to people if they're drinking." Now other than that the only other condition for admittance is that we have the room. Of course, that has nothing to do with the individual, but certainly if we don't have room for them, we have to turn them away through no fault of theirs. Then for our soup kitchen program, we have no other than, again, that they behave reasonably civilized. You know, it's not that everybody has to be real happy and cheerful and cracking jokes and shaking everybody's hand. Certainly not. But they have to at least not be calling people names, shouting, and getting into fights, and pushing, and shoving, these sorts of things. So they have to be acting relatively sociable. If, on the other hand, they do some of these bad behaviors, we do restrict people. And so I guess one of the other conditions to get services here is that you haven't been restricted.

Tom lists three sets of conditions for clients' eligibility for services: legal conditions (i.e, police clearance), resource limitations (e.g., availability of rooms), and compliance with behavioral codes (i.e., being "sociable" or "civilized"). What is decidedly absent in Tom's scheme is how client *needs* figure into the decision to admit him or not. While it is true that it is the social worker's responsibility to delve deeper into establishing the nuances of a client's need status *after* he has been admitted, the initial intake decision is, nevertheless, entirely based on the conditions Tom lists above and *not* on a systematic appraisal of *needs*. Oddly enough, clients' *serviceworthiness*[6] is not based on needs in the first instance, but on compliance with the institutional framework of the shelter. This is further evidenced when Tom elaborates on the "restriction policy":

The initial period is 90 days and, in that initial period, we let them think about what restriction from Abbot House means in terms of their not being able to come here for lunch and showers and laundry and being able to stay here and all that. Then, after a period of 90 days, if we see that there aren't any violations and the person seems to appreciate what they did was wrong and try to assure us that it won't happen again, then we can lift the restriction, reinstate that person, and he's eligible again. If, on the other hand, we do that and the guy violates again and gets restricted a second time, then the period of restriction is 180 days. And so, its graduated discipline until the third time and we tell them basically, you know, it's permanent more or less. There aren't too many people that are barred forever from Abbot House, but it is possible. In fact, after two/three times, a person is still doing the thing that has warranted restriction, then we figure that person hasn't learned his lesson and probably won't. And for the safety of our other guests and our staff, we need to tell that person to find his needs met elsewhere. So that's a condition. The condition being [*he chuckles as he speaks*] civilized and sociable behavior.

It is evident that "discipline" and "learning one's lesson" are intended goals of the shelter policies, but what is particularly striking is that the client's status of neediness is used as a way of implementing these goals. Tom's statement, "[W]e let them think about what restriction from Abbot House means in terms of their not being able to come here for lunch and showers and laundry and being able to stay here and all that," suggests that he uses the client's suffering from not having their basic needs met as a disciplinary measure. Again, the homeless client in this context is not, at least initially, judged in terms of the extent of his own personal needs, but rather the extent of his compliance with shelter policies. We can also see this when Tom speaks of "progress."

And then, the one other condition I guess you could say [is] that we've told people that if they're around here too long, if they're chronic in terms of if they're requesting these exceptions often, that we would say, we would try to come up with a separate agreement with that person. So that would say, "Well, if you're working every night and you have to come in and get these services, then you should be getting paid and eventually you should be saving up enough money to get your own place, then you don't need to come and get services at Abbot House." And so we put some conditions on them in terms of what progress we expect them to be making in the meantime, hopefully leading to their independence and getting into his own place.

Here the "agreement" refers to an obligation on the part of the client to make progress toward "independence" in exchange for services. Sustained dependence on the Abbot House may become grounds for termination of services.

As we can see in the example cited below, Tom sees service conditions as playing an integral role in encouraging clients to become "productive."

One example is a guy we did that with. He'd been just coming in for a shower every night, it seemed like for months. And finally we said that, "After about another three weeks, we'll expect you to be in your own place." And sure enough, we put that condition on him. Again, if we had no conditions, it would be enabling that person to work all day, get a shower, sleep on the porch or sleep in the bushes, get up, work again, have money, never have to pay rent, and we take care of all of his infra-structure needs: the bathroom, the laundry, a place to stay, a place to eat. Because we put conditions on it, then he said, "Well, I'm just gonna get my own little place." And he's got a nice little place now with his own kitchen, his own bathroom. He comes in now, he no longer has to put up with any conditions, he can take a shower at two in the morning if he wants to. He can now get out of bed whenever he wants to. Of course, other than he has to keep his job and keep paying the rent. So that's a condition I guess that all society puts on us to be productive and to maintain ourselves.

The tension between help and independence is a central theme that emerges here in conjunction with the *work* that goes into aligning clients' use of services with the implicit mission of restoring "productivity" and "independence" to their lives. "Enabling" the aforementioned client to meet his "infrastructure needs" without complying with the overall goal of independence constitutes a problem that must be resolved. Tom contends that his threat of withdrawing services from the client is what convinced the client to become independent: "He comes in now, he no longer has to put up with any conditions, he can take a shower at two in the morning if he wants to."

The response to the client and his or her needs is mediated by an organization-ally based horizon of meaning, which constitutes the client as an object of charity who must comply with a set of conditions to be considered serviceworthy. In a general sense, these conditions are the contingencies of organized charity work, which Tom, as the shelter director, links with the wishes of the donors and his responsibility to find a balance between those wishes and the client's needs:

You could say, I guess, that there might be some conditions that we would want to instill—I don't know if "conditions" is the right word—that there are some forces on us to make sure that people aren't laying around the property all day, that people aren't giving our donors a hard time, or bringing an image to Abbot House that donors would feel hard to support. And maybe that's some of where these conditions come from. We certainly are dependent as a nonprofit agency on the goodwill of the community, and we certainly don't wanna do anything like letting people walk out the door with a lot of litter that then they go and drop in front of somebody's business. Well that's going to give us some problems with the business community that we certainly need to have supporting us so that we can continue our services to all the other people who don't litter. [*He laughs*] And so we would ask them not to do things like that. . . . But generally speaking, we try to be that conduit of help that the community has to offer to the homeless person that needs it. And so we try to be as flexible as we can. We try to give

everybody the benefit of the doubt, second chances, and all of
that—certainly. So we're not really here to impose our will on anybody
or anything like that. We try to support them in whatever it is they want
to do. Now we will certainly give them our opinions in terms of what's
productive and what isn't. As I said to some of these conditions and
whatnot. It's not like we're just here to keep handing things out to
people; we do certainly put attachments to our generosity.

Tom's reference, "there are some forces on us," makes it clear that the business
of helping the homeless in the context of this charity organization is *not* simply a
matter of responding to needy people; but the very notions of *need* and the
homeless, as a category of people who are *serviceworthy,* are tentative outcomes
of a process of negotiating various "forces" that inform the *work* of human-service
providers. Oftentimes, these forces are not directly related to the presumably self-
evident condition of the homeless.

In Tom's case, his noble reasons for helping people in need are mediated by
his institutional role as someone who is accountable to donors, local businesses, and
the community as a whole. Thus, for him, the client is intricately, and unmistakably,
linked with the public relations matters that surround charity work: he must put
"attachments" on his generosity. The resulting organizational embeddedness of
need suggests that the statistics of homelessness, as far as shelters are concerned,
are as much about organizational survival and processing as they are about
homelessness in its own right.

House Manager: Clients as Friends

Now consider the house manager's perspective, which unfolded in her
interview. Again, we see the construction of homelessness in relation to its service
context. Grace is a white woman then in her forties and was hired as a house
manager after the shelter moved to a new and larger building. Although born in
Chicago, she had lived in the area for years. Her position at the Abbot House was
created in response to the rising number of service requests that accompanied the
move to larger quarters. Grace also was expected to coordinate the volunteers'
schedules and staff the front desk and the soup kitchen. On any given weekday, one
could see her short, stout body energetically moving about the shelter as she did an
endless number of chores.

My first encounter with Grace was in the context of her asking for a number
of amateur videos I had made on the topic of homelessness. She was interested in
showing them to guests at the grand opening of the new building. Her interest in my
work seemed earnest, so I agreed to show one of my videos. The one I chose for the
event contained excerpts from an interview with a homeless man nicknamed
Listerine, because he drank the mouthwash brand as a cheap substitute for liquor.
Unfortunately, not long after the interview, Listerine and a close friend were killed
in a fire they had started in an abandoned house to keep warm. The video was
dedicated to their memory.

After the screening, I was a little disappointed that instead of a meaningful discussion about the substance of the video, Tom and Grace passed collection plates, asking for donations to help "keep such tragedies from happening again." I was happy and flattered, however, that Grace thought my work was worth watching at all.

Several months later, while I was collecting data for my research project, Grace approached me about working at the shelter as a night manager. I expressed interest in the job and went on to list my prior work experiences in the field of human services. I explained that I had worked with mentally handicapped adults as a weekend counselor at a group home. To my surprise, she stated that her husband worked for the same organization. In any event, I did not have to submit a resume for the position at the shelter, and with Grace's verbal recommendation to Tom, I became a paid staff member for a brief period.

As I mentioned before, since I was somewhat vague about certain specifics of my research, Grace—perhaps more than any other staff member—pointed me in the direction of "interesting" people to interview and issues on which to focus. In fact, one of the people she introduced me to, Shorty, gradually became a mutual friend of ours. As a gesture of courtesy, I acknowledged Grace's expertise on the topic by inviting her to come to a college course I taught and give a guest lecture on the topic of homelessness.

About a year after this interview, I went back to the shelter to collect additional data from the logbooks. I asked for Grace and was told by one of the volunteers, "She's no longer with us." I probed, "So she quit?" "No, she was *fired!*" was the curt reply from the social worker. Since then, I've run into Grace at a grocery store we both go to, but I try to keep our conversations brief, maybe because I am afraid she might want to talk about the embarrassing topic of her being fired or maybe because she told me Shorty was dying from stomach cancer. I didn't know how to talk about that either.

At the time of this interview with Grace, I was no longer working at the Abbot House as a night manager. The interview took place in Grace's office, which was located in the corner of the dining area. We were interrupted several times by clients who needed the key to the pantry and various other things. The interview began in much the same way it did with Tom.

> **Amir**: Let's begin with what this place stands for as far as you're concerned and what the goal of this place should be.
> **Grace**: Well, in [local municipality], we are the only holistic homeless shelter where we provide all of the services that a homeless person might need. . . . Now we're never gonna be able to help everybody. We need to help the ones that we're capable of helping and that want help. We have to recognize that we can't solve every homeless person's problems. There are hundreds of them [that] we can't solve. And those that want help, we can help them and those that don't want help or will not acknowledge that they have difficulties in budgeting and responsibilities or whatever, I think those persons are gonna be homeless a couple of more times before they finally realize, "Whoa! I've got to fix this for the sake of my kids, or myself or a spouse, my job or whatever."

I've built a relationship with somebody who's been staying out on the porch for . . . he was living outside when I came here over a year ago. And I finally got to know him well enough by having him work with me in the kitchen that I could ask him about, "Well, what is it about living inside that troubles you?" And that kind of stuff. So he told me about problems in his past. He told me about his family; he's got a wife and kids in another city. So we started talking about how he might get some help for that. I said, "Maybe you oughta talk to somebody that's in mental health counseling. I'm not saying you're crazy; I'm just saying you've got a lot of stuff happening to you and maybe if you talked about it, it'd help." So now, *finally today,* he's supposed to go and take care of a physical problem he's got but he started talking to people at Mental Health Services. Now he's made the decision that he wants to get into housing, he's made the decision that he wants to get counseling, and now he can't wait to get in. So it's taken me the fourteen, fifteen months that I've been here to build a relationship with this person and now I can say that he's come to me and said, "I can't wait to get in my own place now." And this person has been chronically out on the porch for over a year.

As was the case with Tom, Grace begins with emphasizing the notions of *self-help* and *resource management,* but unlike Tom, who sees rules and discipline as the key remedy to the clients' problems, Grace begins to foreground the importance of forming relationships. Throughout the interview, she recounts success stories that she contends were made possible only by forming relationships with the clients. As with Tom, her own perspective combines with organizational philosophy to construct the client, which in Grace's case thematize friendship. Grace continues:

Sometimes we're gonna see immediate successes, sometimes we're not. Sometimes it takes a *long time* of relationship building. And I think that's part of working with homeless people because they are so used to being the unseen people, the people you turn away from, the people you're afraid of. And unless you can build a relationship with them or be around them a lot and they come to trust you, they're not gonna come to you, they are not gonna confide in you, they're not gonna trust you. Tammy Crawford [a client] said when Tom hired me, "What did you hire that so and so for?" because she and I had a difference of opinion over at the Food Pantry where I was working before. But, after a while, getting to know Tammy and letting her know *me,* and even though I stuck to my standards of being fairly strict, she came to realize that I wasn't really such a bad guy. I was only trying to make things work the way they should work. And now Tammy's all of a sudden my best friend and she doesn't have that same attitude. I think if I were to sit here all day and go from my office to the kitchen, the kitchen to my office, from here to the front desk, and not go out and hang out with people and meet them where they're at—like if I have a problem with something out in the porch, or somebody has a message, or maybe I need to talk to someone about being a porch monitor, or something that's come up and they're not signing in, or some other issue—I will go outside and sit out there with 'em [in] their territory and talk to 'em.

... So I think the relationship part of working with homeless people is important, too.

Grace defines the clients' needs in the context of her relationship with them so that the relationship becomes a vehicle for both understanding and fulfilling those client needs. At the same time, the way she speaks about her relationship with Tammy suggests that she perhaps forms ties with clients as a strategy for demonstrating her competence to her colleagues. However, the most remarkable aspect of Grace's approach is her sensitivity to "their territory," suggesting that she views the house as a resource she shares with clients rather than an entity she has the authority to regulate. She goes on to reflect on the potential pitfalls in her philosophy.

> I mean, you've seen that with people you work with in a relationship, and sometimes they're going to take *advantage* of you, they're just gonna want to know you for your five dollars [*referring to my informant, Ernest, who called me "Saint Amir" because I gave him five dollars to buy a six-pack*]. But if you hold them accountable. . . . Junior [*a client*], who borrowed some money from me, and I mentioned it to him and he says, "You know, I honestly forgot that I borrowed it. Can I give you five dollars before you go on vacation and I'll give you the two when you get back?" I mean, I know it's stupid for me to loan money to just *anybody*, but this is something that I was building a relationship with: he'd come to trust me and I'd come to trust him and I said, "Well, if I'm going to give it to him thinking I'm not gonna get it back, then I'm not gonna be pissed off if I don't get it back." But he did pay it back because I held him accountable to that. And it worked; it works back and forth.

Accountability for Grace happens in the context of a relationship and not through organizational discipline, as Tom would contend. She is aware of how her emphasis on relationships can become a liability and links that with what she knows of my experiences with my informants, but her faith in her horizon of pertinence remains unshaken as she forcefully argues that the risks pay off. Grace goes on to explain her approach.

> I think you have to be a certain kind of personality. Not everybody can work with homeless people. There are some people that I just—like in any situation—I can't stand and there are some people that I just adore. Any place, it could be at school, it could be at another job, it could be in the kitchen, it could be anything like that. So if you're willing to *accept* people for who they are, *right here and now*, and help them to become what they could be, I think that's a real good philosophy to hold. Like Cheri [*a client*], for example. Cheri is as crazy as the day is long. Her mental health issues are a magnitude. But every time I see her, I always say something to her. Even if it's just to say hello or goodbye or "How're you doing, Cheri? I haven't seen you for a while." She'd just washed her hair one day [*she laughs*] and you know I couldn't believe she washed her hair. I say, "Cheri, your hair really

looks nice today." Since then, she's taken the hat off [*Cheri was known for wearing a knitted hat and covering herself with a blanket even when the temperature was in the 90s*] and she's brushing her hair a little more. So those kinds of relationships are really important when you work here. Well, any kind of relationship is important with this population.

By elaborating on the nuances of her particular horizon of meaning, Grace reveals that "a certain kind of personality" that is accepting of "people . . . *right here and now*" is an integral part of how she organizes her views on the homeless problem. Using a mutual acquaintance, Cheri, she tries to establish the efficacy of her approach, narratively constructing homelessness accordingly.

At one point in the interview, however, organizational imperatives that link up with maintaining good public relations with the charity donators are brought forth, which also become matters that make her job "difficult." While at this point, we see that Grace, as a staff member, constructs need and homelessness as Tom does—as something with public pertinence—she adds biographical particulars of her own to the narrative to also construct difference.

> Because this is a college town, we have a lot of trouble getting students to work at night. [For example,] I found out Thursday night is club night, so I had a hard time getting anyone to work on Thursday night. They're all out clubbing. The faces of volunteers are changing. The folks that are in their seventies are now not wanting to volunteer so much any more because of health, travel, or whatever, and the people that are younger than that are still working or are too self-involved to volunteer. So volunteering is very difficult. It's real hard—last fall I was managing forty-nine volunteers *just* to manage the front desk area, and it wasn't enough, I still had gaps. And that doesn't count the people it takes to run the kitchen. When we moved downtown here we lost some of our soup kitchen cooks. They were afraid of this neighborhood. You know it's not really a neighborhood to be afraid of, we've got the fire department next door here on Main Street. You know *I* question the wisdom of having people hanging around out by that door [*the front entrance*] at night because it's a little intimidating. If I was some Suzy Q church person from the Northwest side of town coming down to bring some leftovers from a party, I don't think I'd wanna do it at ten o'clock at night when I saw these folks hanging around. It would be a little intimidating—it might not be a threat but she might perceive them as a threat. So, the volunteer thing is difficult.

Note that when Grace contemplates how the average "Suzy Q church person" might be "intimidated" by the "folks hanging around" the front door, she is quick to point out that such perceptions are probably erroneous: "it might not be a threat but she might perceive them as a threat." Thus, she does not accept the opinions of the donors at face value, but to effectively perform her job (i.e., recruit more volunteers, etc.), she must acknowledge them.

Nevertheless, the central narrative theme in Grace's construction of the client remains her vision of the homeless person as someone who has the potential and the need for friendship. For example, consider how she responds to the following question about what a typical homeless person is.

> **Amir**: So what would you say is a typical homeless person?
> **Grace**: I don't think there is a "typical homeless person." I think you could put it in different terms like, "What's a typical alcoholic like?" And there is no "typical" alcoholic. But the typical homeless person— we've had people at Abbot House who have had their own businesses and been wealthy and lost it all due to an injury or some other catastrophe that was beyond their control.
>
> You look at somebody like Shorty, and he's by no means typical, or some of the other folks in here. . . . So I think that as soon as we try to make somebody, make a mold that says, "This is the homeless mold and this is what you fit into," then we can't help them anymore. I think if you say, "Okay, this is a homeless person, let's talk to him about this thing, about being homeless. Okay, you're homeless because you don't have traditional housing or however you define it. Let's go from there to where you wanna be and then let's look at what steps it takes to get to where you wanna to be." And they may have dreams that are way beyond their expectations.
>
> Like that girl Vicky who was slightly retarded. She wanted to go to college! Okay, that's a nice thing, so let's start with maybe some adult education courses that she could take or something like that, see if she could handle it. Maybe she could handle it, may she couldn't. But I don't think you can squash people's aspirations. I think you could temper them a little bit but not squash them. So you know, if I were to have just taken—we'll pick on Shorty because he's a very dear friend— if I'd taken Shorty at face value, this is the guy who's done three tours in Vietnam, a lot of times he has an attitude that you just won't believe, and he smokes, and he's an alcohol abuser, even though he's recovered. . . . Someone asked me once, "Do you trust him?" I said, "Well, my gut instinct is to trust him." But if I hadn't taken the time to get to know him, and to know what his skills were—his cooking skills are unbelievable—he would have never become my friend. He never would have been able to get a job at Abbot House as a night manager, and he never would have been able to spend time with my family. We are family to each other now. His dad's gone; he has no other living relatives. And now that he has an illness [*referring to his stomach cancer*] it's kind of nice to have some people around that you can count on, that check up on you once in a while, or that you can check up on them—it's a codependency thing we have on each other: he checks up on me; I check up on him. But if I had said, "Shorty's in his homeless mode, and I have to see what I can do to fix it," rather than working with him as he was, it never would have happened. . . . Sometimes we have to have much more patience than you think you can afford. [*She chuckles*]

Grace's rejection of the notion of "a typical homeless" and the account of her friendship with Shorty add color and depth to her narrative. Added to the list of elements that constitute her horizon of meaning, we now have the notions of "family," and people "checking up" on one another. Even the presumably pathological concept of codependency is cast in a positive light to show the strength of her bond with Shorty: "it's a codependency thing we have on each other." It is also worth noting that Grace at some point speaks of homelessness as a "mode," implying that the term may describe a mental orientation as much as a housing status.

Grace goes on.

> I feel privileged that the folks out on the porch—one day they came in and called me—they call me "Mama Grace" now. And, to me, that's a privilege. That means that they have a respect for me and I appreciate that. And I'm not going to do anything that's gonna betray their trust and their respect. That doesn't mean that I'm not going to go out there and say, "This place is trashed. Clean it up." Because I will do that. But I think it's kind of cool that they call me "Mama Grace."[*She laughs*]

The contrast between Tom's notion of discipline practiced through the withdrawal of services and Grace's philosophy of building trust and respect is most striking in these comments. For Grace, being called by the affectionate name "Mama Grace" is a hard-earned "privilege." Consequently, her orientation toward the client is not solely based on a contractual agreement where, in return for conformity to rules and policies, clients become eligible for help. Instead, there is a sense of mutual obligation in Grace's account: she strives not to "betray their trust and their respect." The following best summarizes this perspective.

> It's like I said in your class [*referring to the guest lecture she gave, at the end of which she answered student questions*] when that little girl asked, "What's the best thing you can do to help a homeless person?" I answered, "Be a friend." These people don't know what friends are. Everybody's been out to use 'em or abuse 'em. Nobody has accepted them for who they are, what they are. . . . With Shorty, it was throwing his bike in my trunk and driving him halfway home. He'd get off at my house and keep on going [*to his tent in the woods near the freeway*]. And that's how our relationship started. Now he's part of the household. He was at the house one day and he called me up and says, "I got bored. I'm cleaning the house—okay?" I said, "No problem." [*She laughs*]

Social Worker: Client Relations as Professional Work

Ann, the social worker, provides yet another narrative, extending the local construction of the client in terms of the professionalism entailed. Ann is a middle-aged white woman who wears thick prescription glasses and has long hair. She greets everyone with a congenial smile, and that is how she welcomed me into the shelter the first time we met. "So, you're going to be our new volunteer," she said in a soft voice. In my attempt to appear cordial and responsive, the words "I'll try" came out of me with a nervous chuckle. It didn't take me very long to overcome my initial anxiety. Within a few weeks, I felt very much at ease at the shelter, and with Ann in particular.

Ann's political convictions were displayed on her car with an assortment of bumper stickers that promoted peace and human rights. Her office space was similarly decorated with a picture of Martin Luther King Jr., a portrait of a dark-complected Jesus, and a multitude of winged angels that appeared on postcards, presumably given to her by former clients. Combined with her ability to address people in a familiar and sympathetic tone, Ann's office was a very conducive setting for clients to "pour out their souls."

I must admit that I myself had a few soul-searching conversations with her, the most significant of which centered around why, after only several weeks, I quit my job as a night manager. Among other reasons, I attributed my decision to an unpleasant encounter with a belligerent drunk who demanded shelter at two in the morning. "I have to follow shelter policies and you're not *eligible*," was my best explanation for not letting him in, to which he replied, "You hide behind that *shit*!" Out of sheer desperation and exhaustion I yelled back, "Get the *fuck* off the property or I'll call the police." I confessed to Ann that the confrontation had forced me to accept that I was not suited for this line of work, and I expressed admiration for her ability and devotion to continue working at the shelter year after year.

The only free time Ann had for an interview was during her lunch break, so I invited her to have lunch with me at a Mexican restaurant near the shelter. When we had finished, I asked if she was ready to be interviewed. "Sure," she said, and I turned on my tape recorder. We began this way.

> **Amir**: Abbot House is called "Abbot House" for a reason. Do you think that name has any bearing on the way the place operates?
> **Ann**: I think it certainly speaks to the fact that there's a lot of religious motivation on the part of most of the people involved, both in the beginning as being a collection of people of faith—various faiths— who saw a need and organized themselves to meet the need and I still think—although it's not a hundred percent true—that a lot of the staff involved here *are* involved because they're grounded in some kind of spiritual place that leads them to want to help others. Whatever that spiritual place might be, it may or may not be organized religion even. And I think I see that in board members as well 'cause they would usually identify with some church or synagogue or something . . . a mosque or whatever. They feel like they're acting on what their faith calls them to do. I mean we don't include religion as part of our operation in the sense that we would try to proselytize people or anything like that. [*She chuckles*] I mean Tom's always said that it was enough to show by example that we were who we were in terms of collectively and individually. Sometimes I mean—I'm a Christian but sometimes my Christianity is tested by some of the individuals that I encounter that bring out the violence in me by their behavior or

whatever. [*She chuckles*]. But I guess that's when "I'm acting professionally" kicks in, when you recognize that regardless of the emotions
that might be triggered that you have to act in a professional manner.

While acknowledging that "spiritual grounding" and "faith" are significant
motivations for helping the poor, Ann highlights the complications of *practicing* her
faith in relation to the behavior of some clients "that bring out the violence" in her.
Her spiritual orientation in this context is not a concrete guideline that determines
her actions as a social worker; instead, her "Christianity" is challenged by the
circumstances of her job, and is reformulated in that context as *spiritual work*.

Similarly, her emotions are mediated by the requirements of acting in a
"professional manner."

Amir: What does that mean, "acting professionally"?
Ann: I guess identifying with the person as someone in need who is
compromised in their social abilities and that some of their behavior
comes from that place and trying to just accept that that's the place
they're at and give them respect and the dignity they deserve but at the
same time try to raise them up by giving them tools or empowering
them or motivating them or encouraging them or whatever. But if
you're going to be a professional you can't allow yourself, as the
expression would say, to "stoop down" to their level of behavior and
respond in kind. You know we have the experience of parenting or
academic or professional training to set aside emotions in the sense of
reacting out of emotions and be professionals about how we interact
with people. I mean you walk away later and shut your office door, say
a few choice words about that interaction.
   But while you're engaged in that interaction, you need to
try—there again it's about setting an example about what's appropriate
human behavior toward somebody else that you have a conflict with
and *what's not*. Now I personally come from a long background of
peace and justice activism and a commitment to nonviolence and
looking at ways of conflict resolution and so forth. I can't say that I'm
always successful at it, but in some ways it's just setting an example
about how you deal with conflict and there are ways to deal with a
conflict that are constructive. And it's always a challenge to teach some
of our clients how to deal with conflict constructively instead of
destructively, especially when the messages in the culture say something other than that.

Ann defines her professionalism in terms of "empowering" clients by
recognizing their underprivileged background and not "stoop[ing] down to their
level." Professionalism becomes a tool used to "set aside emotions" or counterbal-
ance "reacting out of emotions." It is a discursive aid for choreographing one's
emotions in relation to clients.

It must also be noted that Ann takes the notion of "acting professionally" quite
literally. Her awareness of a backstage[7] is revealed when she states, "[Y]ou walk
away later and shut your office door, say a few choice words about that interaction.

But while you're engaged in that interaction, you need to try . . . [to set] an example." She is clearly reflecting on the dynamics of an actor being viewed by an audience: she is *setting an example*. Again biographical particulars combine with an organizational role to form an orientation to homelessness.

The interview goes on.

> **Amir**: I have sat through some of your intake interviews and noticed you constantly come in contact with people who have very unusual circumstances, and you have to listen to them. How do you manage that? . . . How does that affect you?
> **Ann**: I don't know if you're trying to ask how that affects me *emotionally*?
> **Amir**: Do you let it? Do you let it affect you emotionally?
> **Ann**: I can't say. Somehow . . . I've managed in the four and a half years that I've worked this job—coming to it really green in terms of this line of work—somehow I've managed to maintain some kind of distance that allows me to be able to do it as long as I've done. And I can't say that I purposefully set out with some kind of plan of how to do that. I just feel like God let me figure it out or something so that I wouldn't go home tortured. I mean I do take it home with me and I do think about people on the weekends and so forth, but with enough distance that it's not eating me up. On the other hand, I have moments when it does get to me and I have cried. I mean Friday was a good example when I called the ambulance to come. I don't know if you noticed or not but we had to have Mr. Stanley, the eighty-three-year-old guy [*client*], transported to the hospital, and as they wheeled him out the front room on a stretcher I just burst into tears right there in the front room in front of everybody. That surprised me—in a way. I thought about it later and there was a lot of different emotions connected with it. I think part of it was the feeling of having to sort of make a decision somewhat contrary to his own wishes to call the ambulance. So it felt a little intrusive or something. He was denying that he was as sick as he was and that he was fine and he didn't need to go anywhere and I felt otherwise and made the call and he was in bad shape.

The social worker's awareness of her emotions is apparent in her talk of struggling not to "go home tortured," or not letting clients' woes eat her up. At first glance, Ann's statements may seem perfectly in synch with Arlie Hochschild's[8] notion of "the managed heart" and Hochschild's assertion that institutional settings force people to "actively try to change a preexisting emotional state,"[9] that they do so at the cost of alienating individuals from their "true feelings." However, a closer look at Ann's narrative reveals a process that involves "emotional work" rather than "emotional management." The difference is that, where the notion of management presupposes the suppression of one's "instinctive feelings" in favor of an organizational mandate, "emotional work" is more focused on how a locally circumscribed state of emotionality is constructed, maintained, and made sense of.

Ann's account of clients' troubles getting to her, despite her efforts to distance herself from them, does not center around how she must suppress her emotions to do her job better, but on how she is trying to *make sense of* her feelings in the context of her job. So she contemplates the source of her "guilt" as she considers various hypotheses in the context of the interview, and in direct relation to her occupational responsibilities:

> So I made the right call but I felt a little bit like I took away his right to choose and that was upsetting. And I also felt guilty for not having identified how sick he was twenty-four hours earlier or something and having felt like I didn't do that. And how could I do that? I'm not a medical person. . . .What do I know? And I'm so damn busy that a lot of things slip past my line of vision and I can't beat myself up over things I can't get to. But I did feel guilty that maybe I should have recognized the day or earlier that morning or something and that maybe he was in danger by us not acting.
>
> So those were some of the emotions, but part of it was just watching him go off on a stretcher with an oxygen mask and you know he was a sweet guy and I was pained by the fact that he was having to go to the hospital. And Ernest Allen [*my informant*] was one of the ones who came up to me—I mean several of the guys came up to console me—Ernest came up and he didn't know quite what to say but he said something to the effect of "My goodness, you're human after all!" or something like that and I said, "Yeah, everybody seems to think I'm some superhuman person who has no emotions, but I do." Sometimes things affect me. I have moments when I'm profoundly touched or moved by something and I guess those in a way are maybe releases or whatever.

What does Ann really feel? Clearly, not even Ann herself has a precise answer to the question. At best, she is *theorizing* her emotions. For example, at one point, she confesses guilt over not responding to Mr. Stanley's situation promptly, but she sets that against, "I'm not a medical person. . . . What do I know? And I'm so damn busy that a lot of things slip past my line of vision and I can't beat myself up over things I can't get to." She then returns to the simplest explanation: "[P]art of it was just watching him go off on a stretcher with an oxygen mask." However, as her encounter with Ernest suggests, Ann's emotional work is situationally grounded in that it occurs in a homeless shelter and in the context of interactions with clients, which in turn resonates with her emphasis on professionalism.

Another dimension of Ann's emotional work revolves around feeling drained by clients' constant demands. Note, again, how client needs are mediated by the particular narrative.

> My role can be viewed as being a one-way street. In the sense that they're [clients] there in need, asking and needing, and I'm giving. So that it's all directed in kind of one direction. . . . Of course, by the end of the day or the end of the week I usually feel like all I've done all week is give, give, give, give, give. I often . . . I have to factor a lot of quiet, private time for myself in order to recharge. I mean sometimes I

get away from work—my mind just shuts down and I can't make any decisions for awhile. You know, like say if I went to happy hour or went out to dinner or something, and they'd be like, "Well, what do you want to drink or what do you want to eat?" Sometimes it's just like, "I don't know." You know, my mind just says, "I don't want to make any decisions right now." [*Laughs*] All I've done all day is come up with answers to things, and it's just like, give me, give me some time to chill out. . . . It's like a total blank. It's like, "I don't know." [*Laughs*] "Don't ask me." But, so there's that feeling of that one-way street; it comes out of me and goes to them, information, and support, and whatever else goes on.

But this seemingly negative aspect of her work with clients is then complicated by being reconstructed as something more positive, as in the following excerpt.

But [when] Tom talks to me sometimes about other staffing roles at Abbot House, I find that I want to stay in case management. Because of the moments when it comes back to me, from that person. I feel that I have been gifted a lot of times. I mean I've put up with a lot of crap, too, and abuse, but those moments when I'm gifted by that other person, when I feel I've learned from that other person, when they've empowered me, when they've touched me with their soul, you know, the beautiful part of them that might really not have been too apparent in the beginning, or got covered up by a lot of crap and hard times and whatever. And they can walk away from me and I feel special, and I feel honored to have known them or gifted to have known them. So when it comes back that other way—which isn't something I'm seeking, usually it kind of surprises me a little bit—that I feel that I've grown as a person in having known them.

Considering her occupation as a social worker, it is not surprising that Ann is particularly apt at looking at the ameliorative and "shared" side of things. Her view of clients as emotional work does not exclude the possibility, and the potential for, "feeling special," "honored," or "gifted" as a result of the experience. In fact, as her subsequent comments indicate, she views affective involvement with her clients as the most rewarding part of her job.

Ann: I think that's part of what keeps me going. Certainly the success stories, when I feel like I've been instrumental in someone succeeding, but more than that. These, sometimes, are individuals who maybe don't succeed too well, or they do for a while and then they're back again. But they have a spirit that they shared with me and I feel privileged, honored, honored to have known them, and I'm glad to see them when I see them, so that it's a relationship like that, rather than it being—I mean, it's always going to be a little unequal. 'Cause I got the information, and I've got the experience, and they're down here needing it. I mean it's very hard to make it equal, especially when you get to the point when you're homeless. We have found that they often just sort of abdicate their responsibility. You try to get them to participate in a plan and they're beyond the point of being able to participate in a plan. They want you to lay it out for them. So it becomes my responsibility a lot of times. Now eventually they may get to a point where they take ownership for it and become responsible for it and then they succeed, but, you know, aside from all that practical information sharing, they're people and I'm people and sometimes we connect and share things that have nothing to do with the struggles of their lives, or just little beauties that they possess.

I think that's part of what made me cry when Mr. Stanley left—not that I spent that much time with him, I just thought he was really a gentle spirit, who deserved better in his final days than to be at a homeless shelter and going off to a hospital where he had no family to visit him. [*Pause*] So, you know, I don't always feel blessed on Fridays, at the end of a long hard week, but it has been a growing experience for me. Meeting so many different and often neat people. So I guess that's what I would add. I don't know how, how that relates to anything.
Amir: Oh, it does, it does.

An emotional orientation toward the client does not exclude "practical information sharing" matters. Ann is quite aware of the nature of her relationship with the clients and their dependence on her. However, again, the broader context of her understanding of the client is founded on the emotional work and the underlying professionalism that goes into client processing. At times, too, in Ann's account, the clients and their troubles are almost portrayed as the fodder or the catalyst for a spiritual journey into the world of the *other*, as the following excerpt shows.

Ann: From a spiritual standpoint, or from my years and years of involvement with peace and justice activism, I don't try to look at success as a way of evaluating my personal success in the job, you know? If I did [*laughing*] I'd be so depressed!
Amir: Right.
Ann: Because I don't feel a lot of times that my efforts toward helping people has always paid off, but I don't operate in a way of having to score myself based on how people succeed. To me, that's a cultural definition about what success entails. I try not to look at it in those terms. I look at it more in terms of being *faithful*. I don't need to be *successful*, I just need to be *faithful*. It may pay off sometimes and it may not. You know, I need to just do the job, and be out there and put out the information and the support, and the rest is up to them to some extent. . . . So part of what keeps me going are the individuals that do succeed and who write me, and who come back, who send me notes, you know, who come back a year later and say, "You made a difference." You know, that's important to keeping me going. But the other part of it is just those moments when you connect with someone and feel that you've been blessed somehow by having known them. For

however long or short a time that was.

Here she evaluates her job performance, and arguably the mission of the shelter, in the framework of "faith" and being "blessed" by simply knowing the clients. Rejecting "a cultural definition about what success entails," she recasts the value of her work in other terms: "those moments when you connect with someone and feel like you have been blessed somehow by having known them." She even jokingly suggests in the following excerpt that it would be "depressing" to use client recovery as the sole measure of "success."

> **Ann**: And it's like you can walk away and say, "You know, I still love doing this work." I mean, if I ever get to the point where I can't cry when they cart somebody off to the hospital, or I don't ever meet anybody who touches me, then I need to start looking at whether I'm burnt out, or I need to be doing something else. Because if I lose my compassion, then I don't belong in that job. 'Cause I'm not going to be of any use to them. But consciously, I don't know how I've managed to balance it all. I mean, your experience as a night manager was like, "That's getting too close; I can't handle it," you know? [*referring to my reasons for leaving the night manager position*]
> **Amir**: Right, um hm. I was losing my compassion.
> **Ann**: And, well, my mother would—she always describes me of her five, of her five children, I'm the most tender-hearted, 'cause I cry easily, things touch me easily, and my mother's always just like, "Oh, Ann." You know, I mean, they do things to try to avoid concerning me, 'cause I'm so emotional, or something. It's like I'm not afraid of emotions; I'm not afraid of tears. Tears are cool! [*laughs*] You know, it's alright, it's okay to feel deeply! I'd rather feel deeply than not feel at all.

Contrary to Hochschild's[10] argument that institutional settings force their workers to "change a preexisting emotional state,"[11] it is possible that in certain organizational settings an emotional orientation is *valued* by workers themselves as a job asset. For Ann, "compassion" and "feeling deeply" are emotional states that must be consciously sustained, almost as a sort of job requirement. Thus emotionality in this context is *not* a preexisting state, rather it is a constructed awareness that is balanced and maintained through emotional work. In the case of Ann, this work forms her horizon of meaning of clients and is best illustrated in these concluding remarks, in which she speaks of being "touched" when she needs to be:

> It's the kind of work where you could get to the point where you wouldn't want to feel—in order to protect [yourself] or whatever, that you'd have to shut off your feelings and then—I don't really know, like I said it's not been a conscious desire, I guess God's just helped me see

my way through it. And I'm touched when I need to be, but the rest of the time I can maintain a little distance and don't let it, you know, keep me awake at night. Cause if I'm too exhausted, I'm not of use to anybody.

The Institutionally Preferred Gaze: The Client as a Failure

While there are individual differences among the staff members, there is also a sense in which their narratives converge on an institutionally preferred gaze.[12] Nicholas J. Fox[13] interprets Foucault's notion of gaze this way:

> The gaze (which as the name implies, entails the making visible of a person or a population) is a technology of power, by which the object of the gaze becomes known to the observer. This knowledge, codified and organized, becomes a resource by which the observer develops both an expertise and a control over those s/he observes.[14]

Thus, as Foucault would maintain, biographical particulars are likely to be suffused with the prevailing institutional discourse, which organizes the way, in this case, the client is constructed. Specifically, the three interviewees speak in similar terms on the cause of the clients' suffering: they all view individual failure as the primary source of client problems. Arguably, this common emphasis on personal shortcomings is the unifying characteristic of the shelter as a formal organization. Consider how, in the following accounts, staff members shift between a complex, eclectic understanding of the client's position and the more intuitively informed portrayal of the client as a failure. This continually cuts across the individual staff narratives that construct the homeless, their needs, and their reasons for being who they are.

From the Narratively Complex to the Institutional

In the course of elaborating on what they thought causes homelessness, each of these respondents acknowledges the complexities of the homeless problem and the difficulties associated with giving a simple answer to the question. But this is inevitably interwoven with the prevailing institutional view that centers on clients' character flaws and their inability to function in a normal world. Take Tom's comments in this regard:

> **Amir**: You've worked here [at the Abbot House] in different capacities for about sixteen years. In your opinion, what is the cause of this [homeless] problem?
> **Tom**: The first answer is that there are a lot of different causes. And we really do have to realize that. Homelessness is a *consequence*. It isn't something that sets you in motion to end up somewhere else; it's the *effect* of something that's happened to you *before*. And besides that,

homelessness describes your physical condition. It's like saying, "Your arm got cut off." What's the reason your arm got cut off? Well, it could be a thousand different things. It describes a guy with only one arm, but just the *fact* that he has only one arm tells you nothing about how he ended up that way. And now when you look back, surely there are things that you can say [like], "They don't have enough money to go and rent an apartment. If they had enough money they wouldn't need to be homeless." Well, even that's not true for some people. Some people have money but choose not to spend it on rent. Now maybe you'd say, "If they had enough money, they'd spend it on rent and maybe whatever else they want to do." Well, you've heard of the stories of the shopping bag ladies with ten thousand dollars in uncashed social security checks. So it's really, even just to say they don't have enough money doesn't cover all of the bases. And that kind of illustrates where we're headed with this now. . . . It's psychological causes [too].

The complexity of Tom's initial formulation of the problem is reflected in his refusal to accept a single cause as the source of the problem. In drawing this complex picture, he even turns to stories of rich "shopping bag ladies" as evidence for his argument that "a lot of different causes" can account for why people become homeless. The sophistication of his prefatory remarks are further revealed in the following excerpt:

And so we've developed a list of about thirty or forty different possibilities. We've tried to subgroup them into different things. And then it gets even more complicated when we asked our case manager to start identifying a reason on that list. She came back with a little frustration that you know its not any one thing on the list, then so you have to get into that whole idea that it's a downward spiral, you know, there's a "constellation of problems." There's all sorts of different ways to describe this. Yeah, it's usually any one of these things on this list that somebody may be able to overcome and not end up on the street. And now you throw in another one and now they've got to overcome two problems. Sometimes the combination of problems makes it almost impossible to keep 'em from going on the street. Sometimes you can have three or four if they're in certain combinations, you know, then maybe they don't end up homeless still. If you have family and friends to support you, maybe that's another way to look at it, too. To see if you have one or two strengths that you can hold on to then you don't end up on the street even if you have a whole list of problems. Now if you have family and friends that are going to put up with you and have the resources themselves to rent you an apartment no matter what you do, then you may never end up homeless even though you have the whole rest of the list. So that's why one of the things on the list, of course, is "family disintegration." If you're cut off from your family and you don't have a support network, then any small thing could put you on the street. . . . [W]hen it comes to that question, "Why are people homeless?" there's all sorts of answers to that question.

"Downward spiral," "a constellation of problems," and "family disintegration" are all part of Tom's attempt to highlight the multiple reasons why people are homeless. These notions are arguably borrowed from the academic discourse on homelessness and *used* to give shape to Tom's account. It is worth noting that in the course of answering the question, the interviewee refines his own analysis and categories. "Maybe that's another way to look at it, too," he says, as if he is speaking to himself. This suggests that the interviewee is tailoring the elements of the academic discourse for the specific task at hand, not just reciting them verbatim.

Note, however, the sudden shift from the *complex* to an institutionally preferred account as Tom elaborates on his answer:

> If you really wanted to generalize it, you'd say, generally speaking, that they're low income, usually the fact they don't have disposable income to go rent a place is involved in one way or another.
>
> Again, then you always have to go back to "Well, why not?" And if you wanted to be more general than that, most of the people we see— this is hard for me to say without sounding terrible, I know that—but I think most of the people we see are very low functioning in terms of their intellectual capacity. Again, maybe they've gone to school but they were the slow kid in the class or something. So we've got a group of people among the homeless who are all the slow kids in the class for the last twenty or thirty years and they're on the street now. Now that certainly can account for quite a large percentage of the people who are on the street. Now that doesn't mean that we don't have Ph.D.s on the street, too. That might involve mental illness and other kinds of dysfunctions. . . . We're talking about people that are on the street.
>
> These're people that aren't making it in mainstream society. Now some of 'em can just say, "I *choose* not to be a rat in a maze." You know, there are homeless people that are working through that and they don't want to do what's expected of them. But then you've got people that seem to be successful and they would like to be mainstreamed and try as hard as they might, they don't make it for some reason. They can't get a job, they can't keep a job. Now that might involve some personality disorders or something else where they just can't seem to avoid conflict or they can't get to work on time or all sorts of different reasons there. So there are people who try hard, but as hard as they try, they're not successful. There are some people that I think you could say again these would be the low functioning people that are almost unemployable.

Tom marks the shift to the institutionally preferred account by stating, "this is hard for me to say without sounding terrible, I know that." He then moves on to argue that the homeless are indeed outcasts: "the slow kid in the class," "people who try hard, but as hard as they try, they're not successful" because they are "low functioning" and "unemployable." Tom elaborates on the firsthand nature of his orientation by linking it with the familiar notion of an obsolete labor force:

Certainly, our economy and our workplace has developed to where now computer literacy is almost a requirement. Certainly being able to work together in teams with other people, being able to make decisions, reading, all these things. The complexity of the jobs available have increased over the years certainly as progress has inched our way up.

One example of this that made it clear to me is that a guy who is homeless, staying at our shelter, was going around trying to get a job and I was helping him by just taking him to a couple of different places. He got back in the car once and said, "I oughta just go sit under a shade tree." I said, "Now, this doesn't sound like you," 'cause this man was working *very hard* to get a job and it sounded like he's about given up. So I said, "Oh now, why do you say that?" He says, "Well, there just aren't jobs out there anymore that I can do." This was *not* an old man necessarily. He was a strong, able-bodied young adult, but he was just saying there just doesn't seem to be the jobs. He said, "In the old days, they'd come through town, if they needed to build a road or a sidewalk, or do some kind of public works project, everybody in town could go out there and anyone who wanted to work"— and obviously it was hard physical labor, but they'd go out and they'd all dig with shovels and they'd dig a trench. Well, now they got a machine that just marches down the road digging the trench. . . . And so in some sense the developing of machinery has taken away jobs that low skilled people would be good for. So to some extent society has outgrown the abilities of some of the people, and again we're only talking about the lower one or two percent that you know maybe are not competitive anymore and because of the complexity of the world we live in they just don't fit in. I'm sure there's always been people like that. Maybe now that the numbers are growing as the threshold or the standard keeps moving up and now they're are becoming a whole class of people, a whole subgroup of the homeless in America and across the world.

This foray into a somewhat Marxist analysis of modern capitalism shows that the notion of an institutionally preferred gaze is not narratively limited to a specific discourse or a fixed set of explanations. Instead, the coherence[15] of such a gaze is locally produced and manifested through the artful accounts of the institutional agents, and it does not require rigid adherence to discursive boundaries. Although Tom's is, metaphorically speaking, all over the proverbial map as he moves from "family disintegration" to the "complexity of the jobs available," there is, nevertheless, a unifying theme in his talk: he views the client as dysfunctional, unable to compete in the job market, and essentially lacking in "intellectual capacity."

The same pattern of shifting from the complex to the institutionally preferred is also discernable in Grace's explanation of homelessness, which unfolds in the following excerpt.

> **Amir**: What do you think are generally—based on your experi-ence—the reasons for people being homeless.
> **Grace**: Well, since my husband works in the mental health field I know a lot of it is mental health. The deinstitutionalizing of mentally ill

people has been a big impact. Cost of living in this city and the wages here are not compatible. . . . So you figure first, last, security [*referring to rental payments on an apartment*], gas and water, and if you need a telephone to get a job—it's just out of somebody's reach and you would think they'd get discouraged. *I* would get discouraged. There's not affordable housing—subsidized around. . . . I don't think we'll ever have enough housing built. We have to do something. I mean if you're a doctor in this city, if you're a professor, you're going to make nice money. But the agency my husband works for, he's been working there for eleven years and after eleven years he's only making about twenty-one thousand. No wonder his wife works [*she chuckles*]; you can't live on that. So, and he's a college-educated person making that much money, what would a person who has very little education or maybe just a high school education—what are they going to earn? So it's not a one-answer question, it's a multiple.

Like Tom, Grace also initially acknowledges that the answer to the question is not simple. Although she begins with the deinstitutionalization of the mentally ill, she quickly moves on to broader economic matters and lack of affordable housing. Drawing on various descriptive resources, including her own personal life, she makes a case for "multiple" answers and does not place supreme emphasis on any one factor.

Following up on Grace's comments that "the deinstitutionalizing of mentally ill people has been a big impact," I probed further.

Amir: But you think mental illness has something to do with it?
Grace: Oh yes. Mental illness has *a lot* to do with it. And even if it's transitional mental illness, like using Amos [*a client*] for example. If you had that many tragedies in your life you'd probably be a little out of it too for a while—I mean depressed *at least*. But he can't call up his HMO to say, "Which doctor can I go to help him with my depression," because he doesn't have health insurance. He can't afford it. So what do people like that do? . . . . The trend now in mental health areas is group homes, [but] group homes are now becoming a thing of the past because *choice* is a new trend in mental health.

So you could ask somebody who is developmentally delayed, maybe they have an IQ of about fifty, "Do you like living here?" "No." "Well, where would you like to live?" "Oh, I'd like to have my own apartment." Now they may not have the first idea of how to manage an apartment, but the person working with them has to help facilitate that person's wishes to the best of their ability. So if you set somebody up in an apartment, and two months later they're clueless how to pay the bills they might be homeless then. But they had a *choice* [*she says sarcastically*].

I [also] see substance abuse, and Shorty can talk to you all day long about substance abuse, and he'll tell you flat out that he was drinking over five hundred dollars a month and that's why he couldn't pay his rent. And, so I see some of that. Crack cocaine is still heinous and it's going to be worse because the kids that are now on Ritalin, after talking to one of our guests who had been on Ritalin as a kid. . . . He was on Ritalin as a kid and when he turned eighteen and was booted out of the group home he was in he went straight to speed because he said it had the same effect as the Ritalin. So does that mean that a few years from now we're going to have a bunch of kids that are homeless because they are speed freaks? I don't know. . . . And you can't have kids that are using that kind of drugs and not have mental illness.

So you know, and basic living skills, too, when I worked with pregnant women, and I met girls who were booted out of their home when they were thirteen because a step dad came along and said, "You have two choices: either take care of your daughter or take care of me," and usually the daughter lost. So if you put a thirteen-year-old out to take care of herself, or that's pregnant and trying to raise a baby themselves, what do they know about how do they keep a house clean? They don't know. They don't have a clue. How do they keep a budget? They don't have a clue. And how do you live an orderly life? They don't have a clue. Life management skills are like *nowhere* with these folks. So I think if we could teach them, if we had a better employment system, more low income housing, and could teach them life management skills we might be able to do things a little better in this community.

Mental illness, drug use, and lack of "life management skills" are discursively linked[16] to construct the client as a down-and-outer whose personal deficiencies are exacerbated by unfortunate circumstances. The interweaving of these various explanations by Grace to create an overarching narrative suggests that reasons put forth are not inherently meaningful, but their meaning is narratively constructed in the course of locally circumscribed accounts.

Ann's response to the question is equally interlaced with discursive layers that initially acknowledge the complexity of the problem while later foregrounding the institutionally preferred explanation of the client as a failure. Here are the initial comments.

Amir: In your experience, what do you think is the reason for a person being out there [on the streets]?
Ann: There's no simple one-word answer to that. It's an extremely complex set of situations. Now I think there are some people who have a catastrophic event of some sort maybe involving a medical crisis that would lead to their homelessness. They generally find a solution out of it one way or the other, whether they recover and get back to work or they become eligible for some kind of benefit. But I'd say probably the bigger majority have gotten to that point through a set very complex circumstances, some independent and some of which feed on the other issues of lack of education or whatever. They're missing a family support network for one reason or another. I mean I feel pretty confident that if I had some reversal in my life I would not end up homeless because I have a safety net of a large family who would one way or another help out. That is glaringly missing among most of our people. Either they're estranged from their family or they don't know

where their families are, or they don't have any family, they don't have
that support network.

Again "the complex set of situations" is offered as an immediate response. In
this case the situations range from medical conditions to lack of a family "support
network," but note the familiar shift to the individual-deficiency view:

But I also think it's fundamentally a [*pause*]—like they're *handicapped*
in their ability to function in the world. And [I] think some of that
comes from their family situation. They just haven't learned certain life
skills that enable them to function in the world. So that they become
marginalized in just—some of it is educational and some is illiteracy
issues but it's much more *profound* than that.

One of the times that I had a real insight on what that was all about
was speaking to a woman who worked in speech pathology at an
elementary school. Now when I first heard that, "speech pathology,"
I'm thinking well you work with kids who stutter and have lisps and
whatever those little speech impediments are that you help 'em learn
how to talk so they could be understood. These days people who are
working in speech pathology in schools are often doing things like
teaching kids how to basically communicate. That they can go through
their family households and end up in first grade and not know how to
say, "Can you give me that?" "I would like to play with that" "Would
you pass the milk?". . . Whatever. They don't even know how to say
that. They can look at it and know they want it but they don't even
know the words to use to ask for it. So they get into school and going
to a playground and trying to share toys becomes this major conflict
because they don't know—they're just going to take it. That's what
they've learned and they don't know the words to use—I mean that just
blew me away, this woman teacher—pathologist talkin' about how ill-
prepared children are—a lot of children. Now she was in a lower
income school, who can't even go to first grade and go to the teacher
and articulate what it is they need.

Now how do you function in a world where you can't do that?
How do you go to an employer and tell them you want a job if you
don't know how to say that? So it's like a disability, a handicap, a
dysfunction, whatever would be the correct label to put on it . . . things
that you and I take for granted and understand in our second nature and
all that kind of stuff. They are very, very compromised individuals. And
by the time you get to be an adult how can you teach somebody those
skills? It's very difficult if they haven't learned it already. Whatever
their unsupportive family situations were, or maybe even in the case
where the parents did the best they could, somehow they missed
learning some of those things that enable 'em to function. And I think
that leads into how some of them become chronically homeless.
Because it's probably less threatening to live in that unstructured
homeless environment where it's sort of acceptable and *okay* to be
unable to function than to be in society. I mean it must tremendous—it
must be like someone who can't hear trying to function in a hearing
world. It must be *tremendously* stressful to be in the functioning society

when you don't know how to function. When you don't know how to articulate yourself; you don't have the language to ask simple questions even. So that this [the street] becomes safer somehow.

In her discursive shift from "complex situations" to personal failure, Ann links a narrative of family troubles with the notion of the dysfunctional individual who eventually becomes a homeless client. Failure to "communicate" in proper English adds another layer to the story of the client who is unable to function in the real world. "So it's like a disability, a handicap, a dysfunction, whatever would be the correct label to put on it," she says in desperation. Denoting our presumably common middle-class heritage ("things that you and I take for granted and understand in our second nature") she sympathizes with "the compromised individuals" and their desire to retreat into the "safer" world of the streets, thus completing the portrait of the client as a failure and an outcast.

What is remarkable about the three cases analyzed above is the intricacy of the narrative quilt that articulates the staff's understanding of the client. Each staff member *makes use of* a wide range of narrative resources to eventually construct a shared gaze on the client as a failure whose return to "functional society" is at best only an unlikelihood.

Notes

1. Jaber F. Gubrium, *Out of Control: Family Therapy and Domestic Disorder* (Newbury Park, Calif.: Sage, 1992); James A. Holstein, "Producing People: Descriptive Practice in Human Service Work," *Current Research on Occupations and Professions* 6 (1992): 23-39; Donileen R. Loseke, "Creating Clients: Social Problems Work in a Shelter for Battered Women," in *Perspectives on Social Problems*, vol. 1, ed. J. Holstein and G. Miller (Greenwich, Conn.: JAI Press, 1989), 173-93.

2. Gubrium, *Out of Control.*

3. Jaber F. Gubrium and James Holstein "Biographical Work and New Ethnography." in *The Narrative Study of Lives*, vol. 3, ed. Amia Lieblich and Ruthelen Josselon (Newbury Park, Calif.: Sage,1995), 45-58.

4. Gubrium and Holstein, "Biographical Work and New Ethnography," 45.

5. Jaber F. Gubrium, *Speaking of Life: Horizons of Meaning for Nursing Home Residents* (Hawthorne, N.Y.: Aldine de Gruyter, 1993).

6. Donileen R. Loseke, *The Battered Woman and Shelters* (Albany: State University of New York Press, 1992); William J. Spencer, "Homeless in River City: Client Work in Human Service Encounters," in *Perspectives on Social Problems*, vol. 6, ed. J. Holstein and G. Miller(Greenwich, Conn.: JAI Press, 1994), 29-46.

7. Erving Goffman, *The Presentation of Self in Everyday Life* (Garden City, N.Y.: Doubleday, 1959).

8. Arlie Russell Hochschild, *The Managed Heart* (Berkeley: University of California Press, 1983).

9. Hochschild, *The Managed Heart*, 219.

10. Hochschild, *The Managed Heart.*

11. Hochschild, *The Managed Heart*, 219.

12. Michel Foucault, *The Birth of the Clinic* (New York: Vintage, 1975); Michel Foucault, *The History of Sexuality* (New York: Vintage, 1978); Michel Foucault, *Power/Knowledge* (New York: Pantheon, 1980).

13. Nicholas J. Fox, *Postmodernism, Sociology, and Health* (Buckingham, United Kingdom: Open University Press, 1993).

14. Fox, *Postmodernism, Sociology*, 24.

15. Jaber F. Gubrium and James A. Holstein, "Narrative Practice and the Coherence of Personal Stories," *Sociological Quarterly* 39 (1998): 163-87.

16. Gubrium and Holstein, "Narrative Practice and the Coherence of Personal Stories."

Chapter 8

Narrative Practice and the Interactive Dynamics of Client Work

The social construction of the client in the context of human service organizations has recently been the focus of much research attention. Donileen Loseke,[1] Holstein;[2] and Gubrium[3] all have examined the *production* of clients in various institutional settings within an overarching project that can be summarized as follows:

> [H]uman service workers are as much people *producers* as people *processors*, and this task constitutes a significant aspect of their work. Consequently, analysis of human service work and occupations must consider how workers constitute their clients in order to understand the contingencies affecting service delivery.[4]

This attention to the "work" of human service organizations marks an important analytical shift in the study of social problems to the consideration of "descriptive practice"[5] instead of concrete societal conditions. However, this emphasis on the active constitutive practices of the institutional agents may lead to the false conclusion that service recipients themselves are only passively involved in the production of their own identities as clients.

Noting this gap, Spencer[6] develops the notion of *client work* "to refer to clients' descriptions of themselves and their situations in encounters with human service agents."[7] Accordingly, he focuses on the various themes clients use to craft a locally sensible identity that helps them to become "serviceworthy," or in his words: "clients constructed their narratives as rhetorical devices which could accountably cast themselves in ways which would guarantee their reception of services."[8]

Spencer's analysis, however, suffers from the analytic opposite of the problem he critiques. By focusing on the client's descriptive practices, Spencer loses sight of how institutional agents help develop *client talk*. For the most part, institutional agents in his analysis are reduced to mere solicitors of information, a shortcoming that he acknowledges.

> Subsequent work is required to further explore the interactive dynamic of social problems work in human service encounters. Cursory examination of the present data suggests that the ways social workers solicited, and responded to, clients' narratives were crucial in shaping their form and content.[9]

Fortunately, Gubrium and Holstein's[10] more recent work with the concept of *narrative practice* paves the way for striking a balance between clients' self-descriptions and the institutional agents' role in shaping these descriptions. Specifically, Gubrium and Holstein develop the concept of *narrative editing* as a process through which the storyteller "constantly monitors, manages, modifies, and revises the emergent story."[11] At the same time, the authors put forth the concept of *formal narrative control* (or the explicit, external efforts to direct a person's narrative) as the analytical counterpart of *narrative editing*. Thus the two concepts combined have the potential for capturing "the interactive dynamics of social problems work" to which Spencer[12] alludes.

Borrowing from Spencer's insights and building on Gubrium and Holstein's[13] analytic bracketing of narrative practice, in this chapter I aim to empirically present the ways in which institutional agents, or the shelter staff in this case, actively guide clients' narratives through the following editing styles in response to clients' presentations: *incredulous, confrontational, collaborative,* and *dismissive*. I argue that these editing types are among some of the descriptive tools used by the staff to manage their limited resources and ensure that clients speak in organizationally relevant terms.

The Waiting

First, however, let us consider the social context within which this client presentation occurs, one that involves considerable waiting. After clients have been admitted into the shelter as *guests*, they are required to make an appointment with the social worker to further assess their needs and to formulate short-term plans. While the specifics of the information solicited from clients may vary from one intake to another, in general, the social worker first verifies clients' identities by checking their driver's licenses or other forms of identification and then moves on to establish their needs using self-reports or official documents from other human service organizations.

The informational goal of these meetings with the social worker is twofold. First, the social worker must determine if the client's stay at the shelter should be extended. Extensions are usually granted if the client can show proof of a job offer, for example, in which case he is permitted to stay at the house until he receives his first paycheck. The second purpose of the mandatory meetings with the social worker is to determine if the client should be referred to other agencies for additional services. For example, the social worker may refer clients to a local agency that provides clothing to the needy.

These meetings are given special importance by the fact that a client's failure to show up can be grounds for his expulsion from the shelter. On any given weekday, one can see clients nervously waiting for their appointments in the parking lot. Some solicit information from other clients about what to expect, while others are given unsolicited advice such as, "Honey, you better tell her *that*." Still a few others solemnly wait just outside the shelter entrance in a cloud of cigarette smoke.

This scene was reminiscent of Scheherazade's predicament in the *One Thousand and One Nights,* in which a young woman has to please her captor with a different story every night to delay her execution. The clients' survival also depends on the merit of their tales. Using various discursive resources, they must assemble stories of being homeless to meet the institutional demands of the local setting. Like their fellow street panhandlers, the clients have to convey institutionally believable stories to be eligible for charity.

For clients, the narrative goal of these meetings is to provide a serviceworthy chronicle[14] of their situations. Consequently, accounts of medical disability, sudden and unexpected financial misfortune, and family crises rank high among institutionally acceptable stories. However, the particulars of the clients' narratives are altered, shaped, or in some cases ignored by the social worker in the interactive context of the intake interview.

I recorded these intake interviews by positioning myself in the social worker's office with the client's permission. Ann, the social worker, explained to the client that the purpose of my presence was to conduct research on "why people become homeless" and ensured the client that everything would remain confidential. I would then leave my tape recorder on Ann's desk and sit in the corner of the room, silently listening and occasionally nodding in sympathy.

Patently Directive Editing

Client Cathy is a Tennessean in her late forties. She came to the shelter after she was discharged from the Crisis Stabilization Unit (CSU), where she had been held for several days under the Baker Act. (In the state of Florida the Baker Act allows for the involuntary commitment of those who are allegedly a danger to themselves and the community.) In her leather boots, plaid shirt, and tight jeans, she seemed remarkably fit for her age. Her Southern accent was complemented by her elegant and self-assured manner. As she sat in the office waiting for Ann she caught a glimpse of Tom, the shelter director, in the other room, and got his attention by telling him firmly: "Tell Ann I am here waiting." Tom gave her a side glance and simply replied, "Okay."

Later, when Ann came into the office, Cathy and I were introduced. Cathy asked me several questions about my national origin and nodded in approval, telling me she had had pleasant dealings with Middle Eastern people in the past. When told that my research findings would be presented in an anonymous format, she interjected, "I don't think there's any such thing as anonymous since they put the man on the moon." Nevertheless, she agreed to my presence there and the interview began.

Social Worker: What is your social security number?

Cathy: Unless it's on my driver's license, which I'll give you and let you look. They looked at the police station. I don't know 'cause it's my truck and other personal belongings that I don't know where they are. They're in storage or wherever they towed my truck . . .

Social Worker: Um-hmm.

Cathy: which, hopefully . . .

Social Worker: The number they wrote down here for your driver's license is not . . . doesn't have as many digits as a social security number.

Cathy: Well if it's not in there, but at one time I thought it was.

Social Worker: Maybe they miswrote it.

Cathy: Um, it's in my billfold amongst other things, but that's in the truck wherever they took it. I'm sure it's accruing interest. That's what my attorney is supposed to be working on. And I got to see him, that's why he told me he'd be in touch. He knows how to find me at the Abbot House. Or most likely, anyplace else in [local municipality], since your town isn't that big.

Social Worker: Um-hmm.

Cathy: I don't think they put it [the driver's license number] on the library card. . . . I don't think there's any other numbers punched in on it. That was in Tennessee. Now you look and see . . . [*She hands Ann a card.*]

Social Worker: There's some other kind of number [*on the card*], but it's not your social security number.

Cathy: You see those numbers are all related to . . . [*She pauses as she watches the social worker examine the card.*]

Social Worker: That's not enough; it needs to be nine digits. That's not enough digits.

Cathy: That was all I had to show the police.

Social Worker: Um-hmm.

Cathy: For identification till I can get everything else straightened out or he can . . . [*There is a pause as the social worker examines Cathy's intake form.*]

Social Worker: Under emergency contacts, they listed two cousins. Where are they?

Cathy: Manchester, Tennessee, which is Coffee County.

Social Worker: Is your mother also in Manchester?

Cathy: No, she's is in Bell Buckle. The reason I listed them is because she's older. She's in Bell Buckle, Tennessee.

Social Worker: "Bell Buckle?"

Cathy: "Bell Buckle," two words.

Social Worker: That's unique.

Cathy: Yeah, it's supposedly the only town in the country with that name of Bell.

Social Worker: I guess so.

Cathy: It's in Bedford County. The counties join.

Social Worker: Well, I picked up bits and pieces, here and there, indirectly of your—

Cathy: Of this erratic life of mine.

Social Worker: Yeah, truck being held, and attorney and all. But, tell, tell, give me . . .

The interview begins with a simple question: "What is your social security number?" The client attempts to respond by linking her answer with the story of being Baker Acted and having her belongings taken away, but the social worker adamantly keeps to the task at hand. Ignoring the potential relevance of "they towed my truck," Ann continues to examine various documents in search of a nine-digit number. The client then exerts her authorship over the unfolding narrative by stating, "That's all I had to show to the police," thus questioning the necessity of the search for the nine-digit number by invoking the authority of another agency (i.e., the police). Having exhausted the search, the social worker turns her attention to the next administrative matter of establishing contact names. Finally, she is ready to hear the client's story and directs her to begin, which proceeds as follows.

> **Cathy**: Well, I moved down last March to Florida to the Mary and Robert Thompson Farm, supposedly to work the horses, bringing my horses . . .
> **Social Worker**: Moved from Tennessee?
> **Cathy**: Right.
> **Social Worker**: Uh-huh.
> **Cathy**: After several moves I lost my farm in 1989. So I've lived out of boxes or more or less, actually no life of living, it's just, sort of, been trying to get another life after that point. And so, things were so ridiculous, it seemed that we could not get things going there [in Tennessee]. This [invitation to come to the farm in Florida] was a deal offered to live, to work the horses, my horses to work with their horses, so and so on. But things didn't mesh together. Communication either was absolutely zero or . . .
> **Social Worker**: What does that mean, "work with horses?"
> **Cathy**: Train. Breed. You know, there's so much activity with livestock.
> **Social Worker**: Uh-huh.
> **Cathy**: So my background with working horses had been since nineteen. . . . Well I've ridden horses all my life, but started working with and going for the show ring and so forth since around 1958. I didn't get to it till after I graduated from high school in 1960. So all the span of my life has been working with Tennessee walking horses, which in our area is rather big and have even shipped overseas.

After an excursion into her background in horse training, invited by Ann's question ("What does that mean 'work with horses?'"), Cathy returns to her problems on the Florida farm that eventually led to her involuntary commitment. As the following excerpt indicates, the farm owners' lack of financial resources coupled with their poor management skills made it difficult for Cathy to continue working with them, but she could not leave the farm for "lack of finances," as she puts it.

Cathy: Their finances and their schedule and so forth was just off the schedule of what was presented to me in Tennessee. Plus, it's just like a bad marriage. The two people didn't connect very well.
Social Worker: Um-hmm.
Cathy: Our goals, apparently, are not the same at all.
Social Worker: Um-hmm.
Cathy: So it didn't mesh together.
Social Worker: Uh-huh.
Cathy: And I have not been able to find another place . . . lack of finances.

Up to this point, Cathy's story for the most part goes on unimpeded. Aside from the minimal "um-hmm's," Cathy's narrative is not interrupted or edited by the social worker. But note how her account is questioned as she tries to describe the conditions under which she was Baker Acted and the subsequent events.

Cathy: However, I haven't the foggiest idea why they [*the farm owners*] had to go to the extremes that they did. 'Cause I had been trying to find something that would work out for me. And I did not want anything of theirs or was not saying I needed wages for anything. Nothing, you know, just a clean, clear divorce is all I wanted.
Social Worker: Um-hmm.
Cathy: Is the easiest way I can put it in terminology. But now I'm not so sure I feel that way 'cause I don't like being handcuffed and taken some place.
Social Worker: Well, what happened?
Cathy: Nothing happened. I was feeding horses, watching horses that day at the farm on a normal schedule. We're supposed to get hay. They left saying they were going to get a new puppy. They come back and that afternoon the law picked me up and took me to the Crisis Stabilization Unit in handcuffs as if I had been violent. I did refuse to go at first. I didn't know who he was and I couldn't believe it. I said "Why?" And all Rodney [*the farm owner*] would [do is to] look and say, "You need help," and I say . . .
Social Worker: When did this happen? You came to stay here Thursday, so?
Cathy: Wednesday, a week ago.
Social Worker: Wednesday, the twenty-second?
Cathy: Right. So, I was taken to the Crisis Stabilization Unit. They said it was a "Baker Act." And I am trying to find out . . .
Social Worker: I mean, generally, in order to do that, you'd have to present a danger to others or to yourself.
Cathy: That's what they said.
Social Worker: What did they base it on?
Cathy: I do not know. They went to a judge and got the papers drawn up. They're saying that because I was living with animals . . . I have no idea how they presented it to the judge. None whatsoever. So I was under observation for a week and one day before they released me.
Social Worker: Now wait a minute. So it was the week before.
Cathy: This will be two weeks this Wednesday. I've been here since . . .

Social Worker: Okay.

As the social worker probes deeper into Cathy's narrative, she brushes aside the substance of the story to get at dates. For example, while Cathy is painting the scene of her confrontation with her accusers, who tell her, "You need help," the social worker shifts the focus away from the exchange to, "When did this happen?" which narratively prompts an institutionally useful story. Interestingly, Cathy is never invited to return to specifics of this encounter, which is arguably a climactic point in her narrative, from her perspective.

At the same time, the social worker also begins to inquire about the "basis" for Cathy being Baker Acted. Note that she is not interested in the client's reasoning but asks, "What did they base it on?" This type of inquiry is not simply a way of clarifying the contours of the clients' narrative, but it actively edits the substance of the unfolding story into organizationally relevant themes. In this case, dates and the professional assessment of CSU staff are deemed more important than the drama of Cathy being hauled away in handcuffs as she demands to know why.

Cathy goes on to describe her stay at the Crisis Stabilization Unit.

> **Cathy**: And I'm trying . . . of course, I was asking for an attorney immediately, before I was even taken from the farm, but *no*, I had *no rights* whatsoever. So I didn't say anything else. All I asked for was an attorney. And I couldn't see one. I finally got the numbers to call and none of 'em would take it 'cause I had no money, except this one [attorney]. But I didn't get to see him or really make contact with him until I got here.
> **Social Worker**: Well, when they discharged you, then, from CSU, did they have any recommended follow up or anything?
> **Cathy**: One doctor talked to me ten minutes, and then in a few minutes, somebody just sliced their wrists, and he said "That's important, I'll have to go. I'll see you later." Didn't see him again for three or four days. Then another doctor saw me on Monday. Nobody would give me any answers because it's the weekend. You can't get anything done; you're just stuck. If you don't get out on Friday, then you *have to* stay Saturday and Sunday. Monday after, a doctor saw me about ten minutes that morning, said my mother was in town. I understand from the conversation the next day, she told me, which I didn't know that day, that she'd requested to see me. They flew down from Tennessee.
> **Social Worker**: Um-hmm.
> **Cathy**: They were refused the right to see me. He talked to me about 10 minutes that afternoon. Told me he thought I was paranoid and delusional. And I said, "Perhaps I am, but I don't know anybody who's not a little paranoid by the time they reach fifty years old" [*Ann laughs*] . . . particularly in the horse business. But anyway, they couldn't give me any good clear reasons why he [*the doctor*] kept wanting to put me on medication and I asked him why. I said, "You raised holy-hell with me because I wanted aspirin." I had to sign papers I could not even see, 'cause I didn't have my reading glasses, couldn't be furnished any reading glasses. And all I wanted was a lawyer 'cause I didn't want to

sign anything. So they kept trying to get me to take it. Couldn't tell what kind of medication, just wanted [to give me] medication and wanted me to stay for treatment. I said "For what? " you know.

Social Worker: Um-hmm.

Cathy: Because two people got mad at me and wanted me locked up out here. So the next day I saw a doctor. Wait a minute, I cannot remember his name. But I'm sure his name would be down on some of the papers. I asked him where he was from and he told me he was from Cuba, but he lived here for a good long while. Alfredo or Al. I want to say Alfonso, Alfredo, something like that. It started with an "A," I'm pretty sure. And he talked to me the longest of any one particular person there.

Social Worker: Um-hmm.

Cathy: Told me he did not think that, uh, there was anything basically wrong, other than, you know, regular. He didn't find any paranoid or any. What he wrote down, I don't know. He called my mother, talked to her over the phone, handed the phone to me, and that's when I found out she had been down the day before, requested to see me. So, he spent probably twenty or thiry minutes at least with me, maybe forty-five. The longest of any one particular person, other than some of the nurses. You have to get your . . . the therapy session I sat in on a time or two, but, you know, it was clear they did not want to . . .

Social Worker: But when they discharged you . . .

Cathy: They knew mine was legal . . .

Social Worker: But when they discharged you, they didn't recommend a follow up or like . . .

Cathy: No, they kept holding me, saying that I didn't have anyplace to go. Well, I said, "When I get out, I'm certainly telling the homeless where to come." 'Cause all they have to do is come out here and say they don't have any place to go [*she chuckles*] and you all will feed them three meals a day.

While the client is busy painting a picture of injustice, the social worker once again is less interested in the client's assessment of her plight and more eager to learn what recommendations, if any, were made by a fellow human service organization. This patently directive inquiry is a form of editing in that it relatively passively guides the narrative in the direction of official nuances that may or may not support the client's story.

Cathy's reference to not being able to see her mother when she first arrived from Tennessee, and her interrupted allusion, "They knew mine was legal . . . ," are of no immediate practical interest to the social worker. On the other hand, knowing about follow ups is useful in that it provides Ann with an official assessment of the client's mental health status and could serve as a guide for future action in regard to the client.

As Cathy goes on to talk about her lawyer, the social worker continues to comment on the client's narrative in search of officially collaborated evidence that would explain what "really" happened.

Social Worker: How did you pick him [*the lawyer*] or how did that come about?

Cathy: The *only* one of all of the ones I called, from out there or here, that would even *talk* to me.

Social Worker: Um-hmm.

Cathy: Because I had no money.

Social Worker: Uh-huh.

Cathy: And because I was there [at the CSU]. And he seems very nice.

Social Worker: Yeah, I'm not familiar with him, so.

Cathy: He [*her lawyer*] doesn't seem to have a problem because I'm female. He doesn't seem to have . . . you know, I mean he realizes that a person shouldn't be locked up against their will without some kind of. . . . You know, I had no knowledge that you could go just sign papers. Somebody could just get mad at you, according to the way I understand it. Let's just say, for instance, we work here. We decided that we didn't like your politics or the way you handle things, or we decided to oust you or make your voice incredible, you know, unreliable or whatever, to the public. What a way to do it. Go sign some papers and put you in like that.

Social Worker: But the judge would still . . .

Cathy: And it's on your. . . .

Social Worker: But the judge would still have to make a ruling that there was justification. They don't just cavalierly sign those orders. So, had there been some kind of verbal exchange or something that they would, that they could have put down as evidence?

Cathy: I'm sure they could have put down whatever they wanted. I had not one idea that they were doing this. Nor did I have any kind of legal representation. And whether they took a paper and got how many people to sign something or took letters or anything else, I have no idea what was presented to the judge.

Social Worker: Um-hmm

Cathy: I'm still saying I did not have my day in court in all. There was nothing represented . . . you know, you can make *anybody's* life sound pretty bizarre if you really want to stretch it. And the *interesting* thing they were saying [was] that because I had lived with animals [I was mentally incompetent]. I was living the same life-style in Tennessee when they [*the farm owners*] liked me so well. And these people lived there from November until March, until we moved back down here. She leaves her farm and comes up there. And it's perfectly fine—that life style . . . until February 1995. [*Pause*] I find that a little ridiculous. I find it to be something else besides just saying that . . .

Social Worker: But you can't recall any kind of incident that maybe they blew out of proportion that, they might have presented . . .

Cathy: No. We haven't agreed on things. But it's in discussions.

Social Worker: Um-hmm.

Cathy: Nothing specific. I mean, I've seen him get mad. He'd get violent and he threw his fits, make a hole in the wall. I just hang a lamp up over where it was. [*They both chuckle.*]

Cathy: Can have spells wherever they want and you can call that mature, you know? So, nothing as far as . . . I knew I was at their place.

> There was a lot of things I didn't like from the first time I arrived, but I was in a *situation*. It's like you go in a motel room, you might not like everything, but you know it's not yours. You're not going to go in there and redecorate it.

All in all, the social worker's line of questioning is perfectly reasonable institutionally. She is interested in verifying the client's account by soliciting information about "evidence." Specifically, Ann wants to know what the judge's ruling was based on (i.e., what was the judge's reasoning?). By contrast, the client's own reasoning about her life is given secondary importance and considered doubtful, as she is reminded, "They don't just cavalierly sign those orders."

This patently directive editing of the client's narrative was not just a way of verifying her story, but it in effect guided her narrative composition. What the client otherwise freely narratively composes, in other words, is directed so that it fits with intake-pertinent information. The social worker's interjection about "evidence," for example, held Cathy reasonably accountable to tell her story in light of the assumed justifications for her involuntary commitment. In this sense, patently directive editing mediates the telling of the story of homelessness: it requires the client to narratively both acknowledge and rebut the official details of her story.

The client in turn is actively involved. In Cathy's case, her responses to Ann's editing cues were more than passive acknowledgments. For example, when she is asked to account for the evidence against her, she indignantly retorts, "I'm sure they could have put down whatever they wanted." So the interactive dynamic of the story in this case can be understood in the context of the tension between the social worker's *editing cues* and the client's *resistance* to these demands.

At the same time, another context for the interactive dynamics of the construction of the client is the broader institutional setting. Cathy's story is being told at a homeless shelter to a social worker. The site of the client's narrative and her audience are *not* incidental nuances. In particular, the shelter's institutionally preferred gaze on the client as a failure (as discussed in the previous chapter) informs what the social worker will or will not listen to, or what she considers to be a relevant part of the story of homelessness. Thus, it is no accident that Cathy's narrative of being unfairly treated by the farm owners, the court, and the CSU staff is approached with skepticism. As far as the shelter is concerned, it is far more believable for Cathy to be a "loony" (as Ann referred to her after the interview) than for various agencies to have mistreated her.

Confrontational Editing

Now, consider the form of editing that presented itself in Tim's intake, in which the intake worker took a more active, even confrontational role in shaping the client's narrative. I spotted Tim, a white man in his fifties, outside the shelter on a weekday afternoon. He was wearing a checkerboard coat and a brown felt hat. Like most clients waiting for their first intake interview, he appeared anxious. I approached him with my tape recorder. I introduced myself as "Amir," shook hands with him, and asked if I could chat with him a little while he was waiting. He nodded, "Sure, go ahead."

Noticing that he was searching his coat pockets for matches to light the cigarette he had just finished rolling, I offered a light. As he cupped his hands around his cigarette in anticipation, I noticed the yellow burn calluses on the tips of his right index and middle fingers. I knew this was caused by letting unfiltered cigarettes burn to the very end, even as the glow slowly cooked the fingertips.

Standing in the parking lot smoking cigarettes, I briefly told him about my research project and reminded him he did not have to talk to me. He nodded as he listened, but before I was done with my introduction, he pulled his mouth open with his finger and mumbled, "I have syphilis. I'm here to get shots at the hospital." I shuddered as I stared at the sores in his open mouth and immediately thought of washing my hands as soon as possible. Nevertheless, I went on with the interview.

> **Amir**: So you're gonna stay here for awhile?
> **Tim**: Uh-huh, if I can, if they let me stay for another week, you know, till Monday,
> **Amir**: Uh-huh.
> **Tim**: You know, next Monday. Then my check will be here.
> **Amir**: Right.
> **Tim**: Then I got to go, then I go to my own doctor. Another town, another state, you know. I go to my own doctor. I buy a car and I go, you know.
> **Amir**: Right. You're not from around here though, are you?
> **Tim**: From Jacksonville.
> **Amir**: You're from Jacksonville?
> **Tim**: Uh-huh.
> **Amir**: So you're trying to go back to Jacksonville after awhile?
> **Tim**: Ten weeks.
> **Amir**: Yeah. You're staying in the shelter for now, right?
> **Tim**: Um-hmm.
> **Amir**: How are things in Jacksonville?
> **Tim**: So-so.
> **Amir**: So-so?
> **Tim**: If you got a car, you got a job, you got money, you know, okay. As long as you got money.
> **Amir**: Right. So you've been traveling for a long time, just go from—
> **Tim**: Like the wind.
> **Amir**: Um-hmm.
> **Tim**: I'm the wind, man.
> **Amir**: Um-hmm.
> **Tim**: On the run.
> **Amir**: From what?
> **Tim**: I'm a gangster. The goddamn hoodlums.
> **Amir**: Um.
> **Tim**: You know. The goddamn hoodlums. I'm not a hoodlum, I'm the insurance man. You know you work for the store. You sell suits and ties. You sell car insurance, you know. You got to sell life insurance. I

got, I lost my job. No more business, you know. You got to have business, if you ain't got no business, you ain't got no job.

Amir: Um-hmm.

Tim: They hire too many people. Gotta let you go. Next guy says, "I ain't got no work." They say, "Hey man, fuck him, I'm screwing his wife. Ha. Ha. Ha. Fuck him, I'm screwing his wife." So someone's got my wife, see? I'm a straight apple.

Amir: So you're married?

Tim: Yeah, I got a wife. I got a wife; she's from Texas.

Amir: Got any kids?

Tim: No, no kids.

Amir: Uh-hum. [*Pause*]

Tim: I wonder whose hammer that is? [*Pointing to a hammer that was left in the parking lot*]. Let me go get some water. I'll get some water. I'll be right back. [*He glances in the direction of the water fountain, but does not leave.*] You married and got kids?

Amir: Yeah, I got one.

Tim: You got one?

Amir: Yeah.

Tim: I ain't got none. They got a joke over here. They got a joke here in America. It goes like this. I'll put the goddamn man. The man's got a good-looking wife. We gonna fuck the wife; we gonna put the man in the penitentiary. I'll figure out a way. We'll put him in there, change his name, then we'll put him in the crazy house. Okay? Then we'll give him shots to make him crazy. Pretty soon, you're "yi-yi-yi-yi-yi, ooo, baby, ah, ah, babeee, ah."[*He babbles.*] Forty years, eighty years, a hundred years like that. They do it over here, ooh, *c'est la vie*, *viva la France*, I'm in the shit. Huh? It's nothing. It's nothing. Everyone does, you know? It's a whole room and I ain't done nothin' wrong. I got a little ol' wife. Then you go see the women in the family. In my family I've got women, nice looking women, Yankee girls, you know.

Using an unstructured interview format that had proved effective with other clients, I had hoped to build this interview around themes of the client's choosing, but Tim's initial coherence in response to my broad questions about his plans slowly degenerates into babbling. Picking up on the last sensible part of his commentary, I tried to keep the interview going, but I slowly lost hope for any form of a coherent narrative as Tim's train of thought rapidly leaped from one topic to another. By the end of our "little chat," which ended only because he was called inside to see Ann, Tim was informing me how the doctors at the hospital had conspired to inject him with "Negro blood" to make him "act like a monkey," and how the "Arabs" were "taking over the country."

I followed Tim inside to Ann's office. As usual, Ann asked for his permission to have me present during the interview. He approved and the intake interview began with Tim telling the social worker how he had been trying to get treatment for his syphilis.

Tim: And, uh, but anyway, I, uh, I'm gonna go back over there. The doctor told me to go back over there and he wrote me a referral slip to go back over there, you know.

Social Worker: Who wrote you a referral?

Tim: Uh, the doctor at the hospital just down the street.

Social Worker: What hospital?

Tim: Al-ka-alchua.

Social Worker: Uh-huh.

Tim: He wrote me another referral to go back over there. So I go over there tomorrow afternoon and see if I can get some more shots.

Social Worker: Do you have that referral? Could I see it?

Tim: Yes, uh-huh. [*There is a pause while Ann copies something from the slip.*]

Social Worker: Do you have Medicaid?

Tim: Right.

Social Worker: Is that who's paying for all these visits?

Tim: Right, uh-huh.

Social Worker: I was going to say, you're really making the rounds.

Tim: Right, uh-huh. And so, I need to stay, uh, my check won't be in till Saturday or Monday, Saturday at the earliest and Monday probably, you know. So, uh, I, if I can, I need to stay here probably till about Monday. Next Monday then?

Social Worker: And then your plan is to?

Tim: Go back to Jacksonville.

Social Worker: Hitch, hitch or something up to Jacksonville?

Tim: Right. Hitch up to Jacksonville and get my check. And I got to go shopping. And uh, and uh, if I have some money where I can do what I want to, buy my own food, you know. Come and go as I want to. And I may get myself a little ol' cheap car.

Social Worker: Um-hmm.

Tim: You know, where I can get around, you know.

Initially, Tim is fairly coherent about expressing his needs. In contrast with the outside babbling, he methodically presents his documents and describes his plans. Ann, in response, takes note of the documents and advises him about various shelter services that could assist him with his goal of returning to Jacksonville and getting a used a car. But as the social worker tries to close the interview, Tim's narrative becomes fragmented once more.

Social Worker: All right. Can you think of anything else?

Tim: I think that's probably got it.

Social Worker: Okay.

Tim: That's got me fixed up. Not unless you got any million-dollar checks.

Social Worker: Um, let me check my drawers here. [*They both laugh.*]

Tim: Okay. Remember when we were talking about, you know, what was it World War, World War I and II veterans, supposed to have some allies in Burma, you know. Uh, Burma, and uh, Algiers, all different kinds of places, you know, where they, and they, you know, army people, military people are funny, you know, about money. Where it's at, who gets it and everything, you know.

Social Worker: Um-hmm.

Tim: Who's acceptable, you know. They may not like someone because he may be a tuffy. May not be any good. They say, "No, you ain't gonna get no money. We don't like you." And so you'll never get no money.

Social Worker: What money is that?

Tim: There used to be . . . in other words, you get, you at least get a million dollars, you know, to put in the bank.

Social Worker: From who? I'm confused.

Tim: From Uncle Sam.

Social Worker: Why would Uncle Sam give you a million dollars?

Tim: To make sure you're up on your feet.

Social Worker: That you're what?

Tim: Up and on your feet.

Social Worker: I don't think they'd give, ever give you as much as a million.

Tim: Yeah, well, whatever, at least enough to get you up on your feet.

Social Worker: Yeah?

Tim: Yeah, uh, oh well. Well so much for all that.

Social Worker: So what are you saying? You didn't get your money when you got out of the service?

Tim: No. Uh, I didn't get no million if I supposed to get one. I didn't get one.

Social Worker: I don't think they give you guys a million or everybody would join the military.

Tim: I wish they would. They owe me one after they didn't, you know, if that's what's going on. And, uh, I need me a million.

Social Worker: Well, think about it, Tim. If they gave you a million dollars when you got discharged from the service, then everyone would join the service.

Tim: Right, uh-huh.

Social Worker: And they're not, so I don't . . . there may be some kind of separation pay.

Tim: Uh-huh.

Social Worker: But it's not as much as a million bucks.

Tim: Uh-huh. [*Pause*] Well, that should do me, hon.

Social Worker: Okay.

Tim: Thanks much.

Social Worker: Okay, all right, well as long as you keep cooperating and so forth while you're here, we'll have you through the weekend.

Tim: Okay, well, I thank you so much, dear.

Social Worker: All right.

Tim: See you later.

Ann does not indulge Tim in his narrative excursion. At first, she tries to make sense of his comments by explicitly stating, "I'm confused." Tim tries to elaborate on his story, but Ann *confronts* him by questioning the logic of his narrative: "Well, think about it, Tim, if they gave you a million dollars when you got discharged from the service, then everyone would join the service." Consequently, the social worker stops the client's attempts to add color to an unlikely story by explicitly challenging him. Sensing the forcefulness of the challenge, and perhaps fearing the potential consequences to insisting on the validity of his story, the client admits defeat as he is reminded that the continuance of his stay at the Abbot House is contingent on his cooperation.

Note that unlike my attempts to indulge the client in his flight of fancy, Ann's confrontational editing abruptly puts an end to Tim's story. Where my research agenda set the context for my patient attention to the client's chaotic narrative, the social worker's practical interests required that she put an end to the "nonsense." Thus confrontational editing, as a style of narrative control, issues a direct challenge to the client to get his story straight, so to speak.

Collaborative Editing

Collaborative editing is a third way that staff shape the client's presentation at intake. To illustrate, consider Connie and Ray, who were admitted to the shelter as an "unmarried couple." Ray, a white man in his late twenties, appeared articulate and self-confident. He spoke in the soft, friendly voice that puts most women at ease and makes some men feel self-conscious about their masculinity. His mate, Connie, a white woman in her mid twenties, on the other hand, did not speak much at all unless she was directed to do so by a subtle gesture from Ray. Her short, plump figure was attached to Ray's in an appendage-like fashion, like a small child who sought safety in an unfamiliar setting by latching on to her parents. After the usual waiting and the introductions, the interview began.

> **Social Worker:** Well, let's see, Ray and Connie.
> **Ray:** Yes.
> **Social Worker:** My name is Ann if you hadn't already figured that out. Sorry you had to wait a little bit. [*Looks through her papers for a few seconds.*] That signature doesn't look like it says Ray Williams. Is that your signature?
> **Ray:** I was writing in Korean in the army, picked up the signature then.
> **Connie:** He used to write like that all the time. Everytime he signed something, he'd write like that.
> **Ray:** It used to be a lot worse.
> **Social Worker:** So when were you in the service?
> **Ray:** '87 to '92.
> **Social Worker:** And you served in Korea at one point?
> **Ray:** Yeah, for about six weeks until I caught something called "Chinese Food Poisoning Sickness," some word like that. So they sent me home. So I was very sick; that's how they shipped me. I've been here [back in the United States] since then and it's never bothered me. So I don't know what they were talking about. Maybe they just wanted to get rid of me. I don't know.
> **Social Worker:** Well, it is a very real syndrome.

Ray: Oh, okay. They called it "Chinese something something."
Social Worker: Yeah, "Chinese Restaurant Syndrome" or something like that. Because . . . I don't know if they do so much anymore . . . but they used to use a lot of MSG in their cooking. My mother used to use a lot of it years ago and as the truth came out about it, she realized it was the source of some of her depression and headaches and she stopped using it. That made a difference.
Connie: He had a lot of headaches.
[*The social worker goes back to writing notes.*]

The social worker does not begin by questioning the reasonability of Ray's insistence on signing his name in Korean; instead, she just uses it as a narrative link[15] to probe the client's background in the military. As Ray explains how he was sent back home because of "Chinese Food Poisoning," Ann collaborates on his account by saying: "Well, it is a very real syndrome," and she goes on to provide the client with the appropriate medical jargon: the "Chinese Restaurant Syndrome," a label that is actually used in some of the medical literature as a synonym for *MSG symptom complex*.

The social worker makes the client's narrative even more credible by comparing it to her own mother's problems with "depression and headaches," at which point Connie also elects to confirm Ray's account by saying: "He had a lot of headaches." Through this act of collaborative editing, Ray's account smoothly moves from his Korean signature to the validation of his medical status.

The same pattern can be discerned regarding other parts of Ray's story as the interview moves ahead.

Social Worker: You have no income at the present time?
Ray: No, I've got a VA [Veteran's Administration] check but I've owed it to all my friends and stuff.
Social Worker: So that's a VA disability check?
Ray: Yeah.
Social Worker: How much is that?
Ray: $260. We've been living with a family; we wrote them dated checks for the end of this month when it comes in and we stayed in a motel in [a nearby town] and we wrote them a check and dated it for the end of the month. So we only have a little bit left.
Social Worker: What is your VA disability based on?
Ray: Stress.
Social Worker: Stress?
Ray: The thought of being shot at did not excite me.
Social Worker: But that continues to be a problem even though you're not in a military situation?
Ray: Hum. Um, as long as they're giving it to me I'm really not going to complain.
Social Worker: Yeah, yeah. Are you taking any medication or anything for it?
Ray: No.
Social Worker: Okay.

Ray: They said in the paper that in Washington they're talking about getting rid of it [*the VA disability benefits*]. They've been trying to get rid of us since '92. But you know, I'm not gonna complain. [*He chuckles.*]
[*There is a pause as Ann staples some papers together and examines the clients' intake form.*]
Social Worker: So I take it you guys are a couple?

Once again, the social worker neither disbelieves nor confronts the clients' narrative, but she *collaboratively edits* his narrative to sustain the coherence and meaning of his story.[16] Instead of confronting Ray about why he continues to receive disability benefits for a condition that admittedly has no bearing on his present health status, Ann follows with, "Yeah, yeah. Are you taking any medication or anything for it?" The clients' self-incriminatory comments are silenced with a long pause, and then a new subject is broached: "So I take it you guys are a couple?"

Connie's story of illness is similarly helped along.

Social Worker: They wrote down, Connie, under medical problems that your heart races when you get hot. What is that all about?
Connie: When out in the sun too much, it's like someone is sticking a knife in my back.
Social Worker: Have you got medical treatment for that?
Ray: She's applied for SSI; they are going to give her something tomorrow. The lawyer said her appeal is going to go in in February. They're going to give her something to fix it. They told her pretty much, "When it happens again, then you come in and give your paperwork and then you go to HRS with the paperwork."
Social Worker: What's the diagnosis? Do you know? Have they given it a name?
Connie: I have no idea what caused it. When I'm out in the sun for a period of time riding my bike or something, then it hits me.
Ray: Or when she's trying to go up a hill on her bike.
Social Worker: Your SSI claim is based solely on that or are there other issues?
Connie: Oh, it's just based on . . . I have a little bit of asthma every now and then, but I'm getting that taken care of so there's no problem with that. It's going be based on me having a situation where I can't go out and get a job. Like most other people, they can just go out and . . . wham . . . they got a job! When I go out to get a job that gets in my way. I mean I tried, tried, and tried to get a job.
Ray: She never graduated from high school.
Social Worker: So you have a learning disability, is that part of it?
Ray: She was born two months early . . . seven months.
Connie: I was born premature.
Ray: She lived in an incubator. . . . I'm not trying to sound like a doctor but it sounds like that Attention Deficit Disorder. She can read a book and ten minutes later she won't remember having put it down.
Social Worker: I don't know if Attention Deficit Disorder will cause you to not recall something, but it may be a related condition.
Connie: I think my family has something similar to that and that's the reason why.
Ray: Her mom did about every kind of drug there was when she was pregnant with her. She shot up. She smoked this and that and probably a few things we've never even heard of.

> **Connie**: My mom did this and that when she was pregnant with me. She didn't want to feed me, she didn't change my diaper. . . .
> **Ray**: Okay, we're talking about your *mental health*.
> **Social Worker**: Well, what a mother does when she's pregnant can certainly affect the mental functioning of her child. Though it sounds like the attorney is basing the claim on a combination of all those issues. Although February is long way off to wait for that funding.
> **Connie**: I hope something comes through. [*Pause*]

Exposure to the sun, learning disability, asthma, premature birth, and parental negligence are all marshaled within a few short sentences to establish Connie's neediness. Sensing that Connie's litany is losing focus as she recounts how infrequently her diaper was changed, Ray monitors the story by reminding her, "Okay, we're talking about your *mental health*." However, Ann counters Ray's intrusion with, "Well, what a mother does when she's pregnant can certainly affect the mental functioning of her child," thus reestablishing the coherence of Connie's story. In the context of the same statement, the social worker manages to edit the evolving narrative back to matters of local relevance: "Though it sounds like the attorney is basing the claim on a combination of all those issues. Although February is long way off to wait for that funding," in response to which Connie bemoans their predicament with, "I hope something comes through."

Dismissive Editing

A fourth form of editing is "dismissive," which involves the direct rejection of the client's claims regarding their serviceworthiness. This is illustrated in the following intake with Paula, a black woman in her late twenties, who came to the shelter several times during my volunteer shift to make an appointment with Ann. She was not a shelter guest, but she insisted on seeing Ann about "getting help," refusing to be any more specific. She addressed me and the other volunteers in a formal standard English tone that was unintentionally punctuated with an African American dialect.

She was eventually given an interview, which began with her foregrounding of her criminal record in the context of not being eligible for government-subsidized housing, causing the social worker to probe:

> **Social Worker**: How old are the charges?
> **Paula**: About maybe a year or two.
> **Social Worker**: What's the nature of them?
> **Paula**: They said I was trying to obtain . . . they didn't even have, what you call it, they couldn't even define what the charge was. Because I was trying get my son some medicine for his tooth and they were saying I was trying to obtain a prescription for drugs. And I'm not a drug addict, ever have been . . .
> **Social Worker**: But I mean, you were convicted of something?
> **Paula**: That's what they say.

Social Worker: How come *they* say that and *you* seem a little puzzled?
Paula: Yeah, because they're saying I was trying to "obtain" it . . . a prescription for drugs . . . I did it for his toothache, and they said it was, what you call it, a drug.
Social Worker: But you were unable to fight that? Public defender or somebody?
Paula: I wasn't able to do it. Sure wasn't.
Social Worker: And what type of sentence did you receive?
Paula: It was probation.
Social Worker: Uh-huh.
[*There is a pause for about five seconds as Ann waits for the client to go on.*]
Social Worker: Well, that probably is going to be somewhat of an obstacle. I can't make that go away.
Paula: I can't either, you know. I just deal with it.

Ann's skeptical editing of the client's narrative is initially similar to the style discussed earlier in connection with Cathy, the client who was Baker Acted. She is even somewhat confrontational when she asks, "How come *they* say that and *you* seem a little puzzled?" However, the social worker's approach quickly shifts into a dismissive mode signaled by the statement: "I can't make that go away." But the client is not ready to accept that response. She counters, "I can't either, you know. I just deal with it," and goes on to expand on her narrative. The client states that she and her two children were forced to leave her husband due to "domestic problems" caused by a "divorce situation." Paula states that she is currently living with "a friend" under a temporary arrangement.

After listening to the client's remarks for a few minutes, Ann lists the various public housing agencies that could help Paula, but she points out that she is "guaranteed a long wait." She then asks the client:

> **Social Worker**: What was the response at the privately owned ones . . . Reagan Homes?
> **Paula**: Well, they, they was puttin' me up on, uh . . . What is it, . . . the preference list?
> **Social Worker**: They put you on the *preference list*?
> **Paula**: Yeah.
> **Social Worker**: On what *basis*?
> **Paula**: Because I was *homeless*, ma'am.
> **Social Worker**: But who *documented* that? They don't take *your* word for that.
> **Paula**: They don't? [*She chuckles.*] 'Cause I went to HRS.
> **Social Worker**: Then I'm a little puzzled what more I can do for you today.
> **Paula**: I was coming to see could I get any help from you guys. Like if I'm tryin' to find a place to get in till my situation gets better. Or even I can hear from Kennedy or Gardinie Homes.
> **Social Worker**: I'm not sure what you're asking. Be more specific.
> **Paula**: Like maybe rental assistance or something like that.

Social Worker: Oh, okay. The only rent money we have available is for people living in the shelters. It is not available to someone who's not living in a shelter. So maybe I misunderstood . . . I thought you were trying to get my assistance to get on a preference list, as an emergency. It sounds like you already *accomplished* that through HRS. [*Pause*] You mean you actually got an HRS caseworker to write you a letter to that effect? I'd be interested in seeing that; they usually don't help with that.
Paula: I hope I still have it.
[*She searches for the letter in her purse, finds it, and hands it to the social worker.*]

Paula's resourcefulness surprises Ann, who reacts by demanding to know how she "documented" her condition. Ann's assertion, "They don't take *your* word for that," signifies her displeasure with this breach of bureaucratic procedure and confirms that the client's "word," or story, is believable only if verified within the formal boundaries of an institutional setting.

It is worth noting that the client is ironically a victim of her own resourcefulness: her talent for soliciting help from various agencies casts doubt on her neediness. Paula's strategy of making the rounds also worked against her since it may have triggered an interorganizational dispute over the processing of homeless clients, as indicated by the social worker's statement, "You mean you actually got an HRS caseworker to write you a letter to that effect? I'd be interested in seeing that; they usually don't help with that."

Subsequently, the client's request is quickly dismissed because it supposedly does not fit the procedural parameters of the organization. Once again, Ann lists other agencies that might be of use to the client and reminds Paula that she is not qualified for emergency services because she is not literally without a place to stay, but Paula makes a final appeal:

Paula: Ms. Allen? [*Refers to the social worker by her last name.*] You know, no one knows what's like to be in a place where they're not family and those people are just reaching out, because . . . I'm pretty sure God has a lot to do with it, you understand?
Social Worker: Uh-huh.
Paula: It seems that sometimes people look at you and they think you aren't in *need*, but if they only knew, you know, understand me? Because a lot of times you keep the best for the outside, you know?
Social Worker: Uh-huh.
Paula: And you go on, you know, and you try to make it like that.
Social Worker: Uh-huh.
Paula: But if people only knew what you feel and what your situation really is. You know, it's like you cry for help and you wonder: do God hear you, do other people. You reach out, and reach out, and reach out.
Social Worker: Well, unfortunately, a lot of times agencies' hands are tied because of limited funding or the rules that they have.
Paula: Yeah.

Social Worker: I mean the rules on our rent program are prescribed by the federal government. If I don't follow the rules, they may decide next year they're not gonna give us the money.
Paula: Uh-huh.
Social Worker: So, there're consequences, if I don't follow the rules.
Paula: Right, right.
Social Worker: So we don't always have the freedom to help out of compassion because we have guidelines that we have to follow.
Paula: Right. I'm just speaking up about, you understand, in general about society.
Social Worker: Oh, sure. [*There is a short pause.*] Well, these are the places with food pantries [*pointing to a map that shows the locations of other charity organizations*].

The client's plea for sympathy and expression of need is dismissed and countered with the need to "follow the rules." The social worker's statement, "So we don't always have the freedom to help out of compassion because we have guidelines that we have to follow," is very telling in this regard because it shows how the recurring tension between help and procedure can be used by the staff as a way of dismissing clients. Ann's final comments do not question, confront, or collaborate the client's story by addressing the specifics of her plea for help; instead, she categorically dismisses her by invoking the limitations of her compassion.

Arguably, given the limited resources of the shelter, dismissing service requests is an integral part of client processing. Dismissive editing enables human service workers to turn down these requests whenever it is either difficult or infeasible to assess the legitimacy of the client's needs. Much in the same way that city dwellers reject the appeals of pesky panhandlers by just stating, "Sorry, I don't have any money," charity workers dismiss unworthy clients by invoking the official limitations of their compassion.

The goal of narrative editing[17] at Abbot House is to ensure the clients' stories remain locally relevant. Given the potential for some clients to literally babble through an interview, as in Tim's case, the social worker must enter client narratives to keep them on track, so to speak, but she does not accomplish this task in a unified and consistent manner. Instead, she has at her disposal a repertoire of editing styles, which she artfully uses to guide the telling of homeless stories, depending on her assessment of the individual storyteller.

Kollock, Blumstein, and Schwartz[18] have empirically demonstrated that "power" affects the interactive dynamics of conversations between couples, with the more "powerful" person being more likely to interrupt his or her partner. Similarly, it can be argued that editing strategies are selected based on the local relevancies of a given situation. For example, the social worker may be more likely to collaboratively edit the story of one client as opposed to another, based on their perceived social status.

This opens the possibility of a new understanding of discrimination in institutional settings. Given the assumption that institutional agents are often placed in a position to discriminate between client narratives, assessing their credibility based on their substance and composition, it can be argued that the storytellers themselves are subjected to discrimination to the extent that the descriptive resources of their accounts are linked with less legitimate sources. Thus, a black client's narrative of homelessness that centers on the theme of racism may be confrontationally, or dismissively edited by a white authority figure.

On the other hand, as we saw in the analysis above, clients do not passively follow editing cues they receive from their service workers. On the contrary, they often resist theses cues, at least initially, by pursuing what *they* think are relevant parts of their stories. This is not to say that there are no consequences for those who refuse to be responsive to institutional editing guidelines; in fact, a client's insistence in pursuing an officially sanctioned narrative task may be the quintessential act of disobedience and is punished accordingly. Rather, my point is that client processing, discriminatory or otherwise, is best understood in the context of what Spencer[19] refers to as "the interactive dynamics of client work."

As a whole, as Gubrium and Holstein[20] have suggested, it is clear that the social construction of clients, particularly in the context of human service organizations, is intricately linked with how their stories are edited with the help of their service providers. Arguably, the client would not *be* a client, in the strict sense of the word, if he or she was free to narrate his or her experiences in terms of his or her choosing, unaffected by measures of formal narrative control.

Notes

1. Donileen R. Loseke, "Creating Clients: Social Problems Work in a Shelter for Battered Women," in *Perspectives on Social Problems*, vol. 1, ed. J. Holstein and G. Miller (Greenwich, Conn.: JAI Press, 1989), 173-93.

2. James A. Holstein, "Producing People: Descriptive Practice in Human Service Work," *Current Research on Occupations and Professions* 6 (1992): 23-39.

3. Jaber F. Gubrium, *Out of Control: Family Therapy and Domestic Disorder* (Newbury Park, Calif.: Sage, 1992).

4. Holstein, "Producing People," 24.

5. Holstein, "Producing People," 23-39.

6. William J. Spencer, "Homeless in River City: Client Work in Human Service Encounters," in *Perspectives on Social Problems*, vol.6, ed. J. Holstein and G. Miller (Greenwich, Conn.: JAI Press, 1994), 29-46.

7. Spencer, "Homeless in River City," 29.

8. Spencer, "Homeless in River City," 39.

9. Spencer, "Homeless in River City," 42.

10. Jaber F. Gubrium and James A. Holstein, "Narrative Practice and the Coherence of Personal Stories," *Sociological Quarterly* 39 (1998): 163-87; Jaber F. Gubrium and James Holstein, *Institutional Selves: Troubled Identities in a Postmodern World* (New York: Oxford University Press, 2000); James A. Holstein and Jaber Gubrium, *The Self We Live By: Narrative Identity in a Postmodern World* (New York: Oxford University Press, 2000).

11. Gubrium and Holstein, "Narrative Practice," 164.

12. Spencer, "Homeless in River City," 29-46.

13. Gubrium and Holstein. "Narrative Practice," 163-87.

14. Spencer, "Homeless in River City."

15. Jaber F. Gubrium and James Holstein, *The New Language of Qualitative Method* (New York: Oxford University Press, 1997); Gubrium and Holstein, "Narrative Practice."

16. Gubrium and Holstein, "Narrative Practice."

17. Peter Kollock, Philip Blumstein, and Pepper Schwartz, "Sex and Power in Interaction: Conversational Privileges and Duties," *American Sociological Review* 50 (1985): 34-46.

18. Spencer, "Homeless in River City."

19. Gubrium and Holstein, "Narrative Practice."

Chapter 9

Client Constructions of the Shelter
and Homelessness

Not all client narratives, of course, are told to social workers; clients construct homelessness on any number of occasions besides intake. When these narratives are opened to view, it is clear that the meaning of being homeless or being sheltered in a facility like the Abbot House involves additional perspectives.

Looking at client narratives in this context provides contrast between stories told to a social worker for the purpose of receiving services versus stories told to a researcher, presumably for the sake of knowledge. Admittedly, the theoretical boundary between these two realms of meaning making (research practice versus organizational practice) was often crossed in the course of my fieldwork, since these interviews were conducted while I worked at the shelter as either a night manager or a volunteer.

On many occasions, in spite of the fact that I explicitly reminded the respondents that their willingness to talk with me had no bearing on their status as service recipients in the shelter, they went on asking me for help regardless. At various points during, before, or after an interview, they asked if I knew anyone who could offer them jobs or help pay their overdue utility bills. In a few cases, I was even asked if I could let informants stay at my place for a few days until they got back on their feet. Typically, I politely brushed aside these requests and pressed on with the interview.

The open-ended format of our talks and my minimal editing arguably allowed for clients to tell their stories in relation to themes of their own choosing. In other words, "organizational relevance" was not foregrounded in these interviews. Rather, following Gubrium's notion of "horizons of meaning,"[1] I examine how clients make sense of their lives in relation to the topic of homelessness. Namely, Abbot House narratives are autobiographically embedded: shelter experiences are conveyed in relation to biographical particulars.

By giving primacy to how the homeless narratively give coherence to their own experiences, this chapter challenges the conventional ethnographic genre[2] that textually privileges the researcher's conceptualization of the problem over the native's narrative practices. Such research compartmentalizes the substance of homeless stories into "research-relevant" themes (e.g., "survival strategies" or "daily routines"), thus narratively butchering the respondents' accounts into snapshots of how "they" live. Instead, following Gubrium and Holstein,[3] I have opted for an approach that aims to preserve the coherence of the clients' stories and at the same time understand how that coherence is narratively accomplished. When compared with shelter-contingent narrative, this further highlights the constructed quality of being homeless.

Overall, I conducted about twenty formal interviews in or around Abbot House, which were not part of the shelter's client processing. They were tape-recorded in various settings ranging from my campus office to the parking lot of the shelter. Most began with the simple directive: "Tell me about yourself." Early in the course of my work, I also solicited help from one of my informants, Dave, to gain access to and establish rapport with people who may have otherwise been reluctant to participate in my research. In their minds, I was a stranger who could have been a police informant or a narc, but it wasn't long before I became a familiar face.

I have selected six of these interviews for the purpose of analysis because they are representative, both substantively and demographically, of the wide range of people and stories of being homeless I encountered in the field.

"Starting Everything New"

The first story is Tony's. Leaning against the wall by the shelter's front entrance with a cigarette in his mouth, Tony seemed like the poster child for a "stop runaway youth" campaign. At nineteen, his pale face had the curious look of someone a lot older. His facial expressions were void of the vivacity one expects from people his age. His face was paved with a cold, indifferent gaze. This portrait of a lost youth came to life as he began to speak in a monotonous voice that still cracked enough to give away his true age. As I walked by Tony that afternoon, he asked if I knew anyone who could give him a ride to the interstate so he could hitchhike two hundred miles south. Although he was given a bed at the shelter for that night, he had decided to stay on the road till he got to his uncle's house. Since I frequently used the opportunity to drive people to the interstate as a chance to collect data, I offered him a lift without hesitation. Along the way, I began the interview.

>**Amir**: Tell me like, you know, what happened from the beginning and why you had to leave and what you do and what your plans are and all that business.
>**Tony**: Well, in the beginning, uh, most of my time up there in Michigan is just work and lose a job here and there and work again, lose a job, and nothing seemed to work out for me. And relationships were, were all going sour on me.
>   Uh, I was hanging out with my friends about three weeks before I left and, uh, we're all up at the party store, getting some pop and some chips and stuff for a party and, uh, we walk outside and we stand outside talking to one of our friends for a minute, and, uh, a group of black people walked up and wanted my friend's coat and my coat. And we fought with them for a few minutes, physically. And then one of them pulled out a gun and pointed to me. I gave him up my coat and then they pointed at my friend. And he refused to give it and they shot him in the chest.

I stayed low for awhile. I went to court. I put the people in jail and then I got another job and I worked there for like three days and then they fired me and when it just came down to it, it was time to leave. So I started heading south. I got into, uh, Covington, Kentucky, and I stayed there for like a night and tried to see how things would work out the next day, getting a job and everything and I had a lot of offers for positions, just I didn't have no residency [permanent housing], so I couldn't get a job. So I just went over to the truck stop on I-75 and just headed south. With a trucker, pulled into Palatka a couple of days ago. Stayed there. Now I'm heading south to my uncle's place.

Amir: So you didn't leave with the intention of going to your uncle's place?

Tony: No. I didn't find out my uncles were down here till I got to Palatka. So, my intentions were to just come down and start everything new and do everything that I can to start a whole new life and try to live it to the fullest.

Ironically, for Tony being homeless marks the start of everything new. Leaving the economic hardships and personal tragedies of Michigan behind, he has embarked on a journey into another world of uncertainty. Consequently, Tony places his status of being without a home in the context of searching for a new future, the latter of which is an image that resonates in the popular imagination. The interview goes on.

Amir: But as far as like staying up in Michigan with your family, that's not going to work for you?

Tony: No. No. It wouldn't work.

Amir: Why not?

Tony: Uh, my family's too much into themselves, more than anybody else. So, it's kind of like, well, maybe I'll stay and maybe I won't, maybe I will. And then Monday, I just thought about it and I just left. Didn't feel like staying.

Amir: How old are you?

Tony: I'm nineteen.

Amir: So you finished high school?

Tony: No, I dropped out, ninth grade. I tried going back a few times. I just couldn't do it. So, it don't matter to me. I'll get my GED when I get settled. Probably get my business license like I want.

Amir: What kind of business?

Tony: Uh, entrepreneur, small business for teenagers . . .

Amir: Oh.

Tony: Teenagers, college students, high school students, and, uh, junior high students. Something to keep them off the streets to get rid of some of the gangs and the trouble.

Amir: You were never in a gang, were you?

Tony: Yeah, I was.

Amir: Oh, you were in a gang.

Tony: Yeah, I was in a gang for like three years. A gang called "Deuce," up in Michigan. We got into a lot of real stupid things, but none of it broke the law. I even used to do drugs. I know what the drug

experience is like. And, uh, almost everything . . . I've tried everything
at least once. I haven't . . . I've been clean for over a month now.
Amir: So was it because of your gang involvement you're leaving?
'Cause things were getting too . . .
Tony: Well, it's not that my gang involvement's getting too rough or
the people are getting out of hand. It's just that there's nothing up in
Michigan anymore. Everything's gone. The jobs are all heading out of
state. I know of almost 14,000 people that lost jobs because of a factory
closing. My father and my grandfather was one, two of them.

At this point, Tony's story appears to be yet another example of how
unemployment and poverty cause homelessness, and that may well be part of the
case. However, if we were to set aside the conventional social science discourse on
the topic, listen to the substance of his story, and pay attention to the method of its
production, we may also notice that the recurrent theme of starting everything new
is the contextual reference point giving coherence to the story, even serving to
explain his homelessness and current poverty. Tony's contention that he's going to
finish high school and his aspiration for starting a business both point to this very
theme. Thus, homelessness in Tony's account is not the proverbial end of the road,
but the beginning.

Tony goes on.

Amir: So you didn't even plan to stay there [at the shelter]. You
just . . .
Tony: For a few days, yeah.
Amir: So, what happened?
Tony: Uh, when I talked to my mom on the phone, she said she
contacted my uncle and my uncle wanted me to come to where he is,
since I'm not . . . I haven't gotten a place to stay anywhere in the state.
And she told me she had his phone number and his address for me. I
jumped to it and took it down as fast as I could . . . . I kind of just, once
I get down to Newport [*where his uncle lives*], the main thing that I've
been wanting to do ever since I was a kid was to see the ocean. That's
one of the neat things I'd like—
Amir: You've never seen the ocean.
Tony: I've never seen the ocean once. And that's one of things I'm
going to do.

Tony's search for a better future is not entirely instrumental; his conventional
goals are intertwined with simpler desires, such as seeing the beach for the first
time in his life. Again, this is *more* than just the story of someone who is buffeted
about in a turbulent economy. To understand Tony's story we must pay attention
to how he narratively links his story of being currently down-and-out with his hopes
for the future.

For Tony, the shelter is nothing more than a temporary rest stop on his way to
what he hopes is a better life. It's in the context of going to his uncle's place (a
relative whom he later confesses he has never met), getting a job, and even seeing
the beach that Tony's story of homelessness and his presence at the shelter take

form. The fact that Tony left his home in Michigan suggests that the term "homeless" may be somewhat of a misnomer for his situation, even though his presence in and about the shelter would figure him in the statistics. "Homeward bound" may better reflect his search for a new home and "everything new."

"A Different Skin Color"

The second interview centers on Mr. Washington, who is a short black man in his forties. When I met him, I was still an Abbot staff member and on several occasions we had brief chats about the weather and his favorite football team. Once, he even challenged me to an arm-wrestling match, which I turned down mostly because I was afraid he would beat me in front of other clients, and not for any fear that I might seem unprofessional. After I turned him down, as if to rub my nose in the challenge, he got down in front of the counter and did twenty push-ups on his thumbs. This amused other clients and inspired them to brag about their own physical fitness.

Mr. Washington was married to a white woman, also in her forties. They had six children between the ages of five and fourteen, who stayed with them in the shelter. The eight members of the Washington family were housed in 9A, a room, approximately ten by ten feet, that was larger than the others. In the corner of the room their stacked belongings formed a precarious-looking mountain of stuff (i.e., clothes, appliances, cookware, toys, etc.).

The Washington family's stay at the Abbot House was extended for six months for various reasons, including the fact that they could not find a subsidized housing arrangement in a safe neighborhood. During these months, the children went to school from the shelter every morning, while their mother, Angela, had to compete with other clients for the use of the bathrooms as she hurriedly got them ready. When they returned to the shelter from school, Angela found it particularly challenging to keep all six children in Room 9A. She was often reprimanded by the staff for letting them "wander around the house and disturb other clients." In fact, the situation with the children was informally cited to me as one of the reasons why the Washington family was finally expelled from the shelter, despite the fact that they were still searching for suitable housing.

I approached Mr. Washington for an interview a few months after I had left my job at the shelter. We sat in my car with the windows rolled down and began the interview. Mr. Washington explained to me that he and his family became homeless after their Section 8 Housing contract was terminated by their landlord, supposedly because he and his wife refused to pay $1,400 for repairs to their apartment. According to Mr. Washington, most of the repair costs were either overestimated or falsified, and he simply refused to pay. About the same time, he began writing worthless checks to support his family, for which he was later arrested and imprisoned for several days.

His family was admitted to the shelter while he was in jail. Following his release, he did not immediately join them at the shelter, but instead slept in the back porch and in the parking lot for a few weeks, fearing that the interracial nature of his marriage might adversely affect his family's residential status.

> **Amir**: Why did you have to sleep on the porch for two and a half months before they let you in?
>
> **Washington**: Well, at that point, their mind was . . . the way I saw things, I didn't want to jeopardize my family, number one. I had already saw the way things was running. And by me being black or whatever, I felt like I was, you know, jeopardizing [them] if I went on the inside. And a lot of things, you know, taking place on that level, and I wasn't ready to deal with it. I [thought] maybe my whole family will probably be jeopardized. Them two and a half months was a condition, in fact. It was to condition myself so that I could deal with just about anything that come my way, to keep them from suffering any.
>
> **Amir**: Did they know you were married to her, during the two and a half months?
>
> **Washington**: No, no, not at that point. No, they didn't. They found out just shortly before I went on the inside that I was married to her.
>
> **Amir**: And once they found out, they let you in?
>
> **Washington**: Well, no, I actually went in, I actually went in, during the time that a white lady that was staying on the inside there had . . . I had bought my wife an earring and so she went to the staff and said that my wife had went in her room and stole the earring. And so I had to go in and write a little thing saying that I had bought them. You know, which I had purchased them. And then she went back and she changed her story, saying, well my son or my daughter or something had went in the bathroom and that she had left them in the bathroom. And I told them, I said, "Well, you know it's either one or the other. She either went in the room and stole 'em or my daughter went in the bathroom and took 'em out the bathroom or I bought them. You all pick it. *I'm* saying *I* bought 'em." So I went and got the guy that I bought them from and he come in and verified that he sold them to me. And from that, the woman called HRS [Department of Health and Human Services] and said that my wife was abusing my kids and everything. The HRS and the police came out here. And the police wanted to . . . like HRS wanted to strip my kids down and everything and check 'em out. So that from that point on, that's the night I came on the inside, because I felt like my kids was in jeopardy, and I felt like I had to make a move at that point. I felt like, well, you know, it's not going to be like that. She is in there by herself, but if we both go in, then it's a different story.
>
> **Amir**: Um-hmm.
>
> **Washington**: So that, that, that's the day that I went inside. It was behind that accusation there, while the police was in here, I went on the inside. And I dealt with the police and I told 'em that there wasn't nobody fixing to go in there and dress down one of my kids without me or her being present with each one, you know, she with the girls and I'm with the guys. Because at that point my kids was crying and afraid and everything and it wasn't just no way, nobody was going to walk into those rooms, no police officer, nobody else, was going to walk in those rooms and intimidate them in that way. So I went on the inside, so I

could be able to do that. And since I went on the inside, that's why I just stayed in there. So I come off the porch at that point. I felt like that, that threatened me more than any racial thing that they could throw at me.

Amir: Threatened?

Washington: By the fact that HRS was being pulled into. They already are in a homeless shelter or whatever and HRS was just fixing to come and, you know, take them down. I felt like it was time for them to deal with both the parents, rather than just one.

Amir: Um-hmm.

Washington: So I felt like it overrode the racial things. I was probably going to have to go through being on the inside. Which I went through quite a lot of it . . . [like] when they throw some sort of racial cracks, a joke or whatever, you know.

Amir: Like what?

Washington: Well, you know, it's some of them. Like for number one: "The reason why I am this color is 'cause I'm full of shit."

Mr. Washington's racial awareness is the organizing theme that gives narrative coherence and shape to his experiences with poverty and his stay at the shelter. He makes sense of his relationship with the staff and their perceptions of him in the context of his racial identity, which in this particular setting he sees as a liability, as something that could "jeopardize" the status of his family. As he comments at one point:

> Maybe, I said, maybe they think if she had a white man, she would probably be one less client that they would have in there. Maybe, [they have] some form of resentment to me. I can't say that everything is dealing with a black or white, but it's definitely dealing with a wrong or right. You know, I mean in my eyes people are people. And I think every person should be treated like a person. I don't, I don't . . . I was never prejudiced against no race at all. But I have actually . . . you know, we have been together for seventeen years, and I have actually really dealt with a lot of racism. I have learned to see it in areas that people wouldn't believe it exists. A lot of people will say, "No, that's not happening." Well they haven't seen it in the true colors that it comes in. But I see it. It's there.

Washington fears that his identity as a black man may be used as a convenient explanation for his family's poverty. His assertion that "wrong or right" transcends the dichotomy between "black or white" highlights the moral implications of the racial prejudice that he has experienced in his seventeen-year marriage; and the proclamation, "I have learned to see it in areas that people wouldn't believe it exists," both helps establish his expertise and points to his anticipation of being disbelieved. Consequently, he follows with, "But I see it. It's there," which is sadly reminiscent of a testimonial about a close encounter with an unidentified flying object.

He goes on to elaborate on his treatment in the shelter, further linking his and his family's status as homeless with racism.

> **Washington**: For awhile there, I was like the only black member in house, and for about the first three months I was constantly escorted toward the door because I didn't belong there, because they failed to ask me, was I resident there, before they wanted to put me out. I mean I couldn't even sit down and enjoy a meal without a volunteer coming up to me and telling me I got to go out the door because they're not feeding outside guests. . . . Instead of them coming to me and asking me, was I an in-house resident or whatever, they just come to me and tell me to get out. I got to go. I mean I'm sitting down and trying to eat my food. Man, I even had one come and snatch my plate from me. I'm sitting down here and trying to eat. He snatched my plate and told me I got to get out. And I got to communicate with him, "Why don't you go in there and check your paperwork?" "No, you don't belongs in here; I know you are not in-house." "Well, why don't you go in there and check your paperwork. My name is Leonard Washington and see if I belongs in here or not." "No, no, no, you're not telling me this. I know you don't belong. I never saw you in here before. You got to go out." And then I had two or three other in-house guests that told him, well, yeah I did belongs in here.
>
> **Amir**: Why do you think they treated you like that?
>
> **Washington**: Well, I think, personally, that, I mean, you know, I think it was a color thing 'cause at the very same night that this incident here takin' place, this white guy was sitting down eating and he was an outsider. He wasn't on in-house and he was not disturbed and he was sitting down eating. And when I came to sit down and eat there, *I* was addressed. I look at it this away, sitting in the front [by the front desk in the main lobby] a lot of the times, I see 'em, with every black male that comes through there, they're immediately either told that they can't come in or asked if they're in-house. And also, I look at the same things, such as the white ones, I noticed how they can just walk right past the front desk and walk right on in the back and remove anything from back. You know, just like, that's where they belong. They never question about, do they live inside or are they an outsider or they could go in there and fix food or whatever. I don't see 'em doing the same, taking the same measures such as guarding 'em out from going back there as they would a black person. I'm not saying that all the staff is racist, but I am saying that, I feel like they, in their minds, they feel like the average black man is not an in-house guest. . . .
>
> I have had about twenty different volunteers to literally put their hands on me to push me out the door. And I just didn't present myself in no violent fashion. Until last week or so, I had one who just kept going so far. It's like just keep pushing and pushing and pushing till I made the statement, "If you put your hands on me one more time, I'm going to lay your ass out on this here concrete here." And all of the sudden I go into a meeting with Ann [the social worker] that day and that was mentioned to me, but the other twenty times or so there's nothing done. I mean it's continually happening. And no sooner than I

started standing up to shield it from happening, then all of the sudden it's like I'm a problem or I threatened somebody, but failing to understand I done stop before then at least ten times trying to communicate this same problem. I don't appreciate nobody putting their hands on me. They have anything to say to me, say it. Keep your hands off of me. . . . I don't think that's their job.

With me, I know myself to be a nonviolent person. And so when I start feeling the need to revenge with violence, I can understand a person that has that type of a nature, and not being as patient as I would have been. And it's getting to me. It makes me feel like busting up one of 'em up side of the head, just to let 'em see, "Hey, it's flesh and blood here, this *is* real. I have feelings and I'm capable of putting my hands right back on you, such as you was me."

The selective enforcement of the shelter policies is the source of Mr. Washington's rage. He links his frustration with the potential for violent retaliation as a way of being heard and seen, or as a way of confirming the concrete reality of his existence: "Hey, it's flesh and blood here, this *is* real." The repeated negative encounters with the volunteers have helped solidify his belief that race is a key factor in the way clients are processed at the Abbot House.

The interview continues:

Amir: So what do you think it takes to get help here?
Washington: Well, [*chuckles, pauses*] I'm going to make this statement and it is going to be not speculations, but things that I have been through in trying to get help here. It definitely takes a different color of skin than mine; of course mine is black. So, I don't know whether to call it racial or not. . . . I have been denied medical vouchers such as for prescriptions. You know, I was like sick one time and I had a prescription and it cost like $35 to fill and I went to Ann [*the social worker*] and I asked her. I told her I didn't just want no handout, but if she filled it for me that day, 'cause I had my prescription and I'll pay her when I got my pay. . . . And she told me that the Abbot House didn't provide vouchers for medication. Well, [there] used to be a girl here, a white girl with her little baby. And her baby got sick and needed a prescription filled and Ann wrote her out a voucher, but the girl didn't take the voucher to the drugstore. I took it down on my bike, and I took it to Value Drug Store. And got the meditation with it. . . . So, to me, she flat out lied about not having no type of forms for that. She wasn't aware that I was the one that took that voucher either.

Bus tokens. I had a job. I had to be there at three o'clock, I waited for her to come back from lunch, 'cause she had told me that she would give me bus tokens for interviews or whatever. And when she got back from lunch, she told me she didn't have but two tokens and they were for emergency use.

[She told me to] walk to my interview, that she had walked farther. And I walked and I got there something like about twenty minutes later than when I should have gotten there and the lady that was working at the same place, she said, "If you had got there twenty minutes earlier. If you have been right there at three o'clock, you had the job. They were waiting on you, you had it." So I felt like I missed the job all behind her not wanting to release the two tokens. . . . She was more concerned about making a point out of it to me, she said, "Walk." She kind of laughed, "What's wrong with that? I walked farther."

Also, Tom [the shelter director] said that he had money for people that had been here a little bit of time that was trying to get away from here. They had, they had a fund to help pay your first and your deposit on your rent or your lights. . . . He told me that they had funds and to ask Ann about it. Well, I asked Ann about it and Ann denied that they, that they had that type of a fund. But then she turned around and helped four families which was white, with the same forms. They hadn't even been here as long as we had been here. You know, and all four of them is out of here now. . . . We was in communication. One of them, she even paid two debts that stopped him from getting into a place. He had his first and last, but he couldn't pay the debt, you know to wipe his slate clean. So she paid that. He showed me the voucher for it. And, and I feel like they got the forms, but they hold them for certain people. I just feel like my skin color don't qualify me to be one of them people.

Unlike other clients, such as Tony, who use the shelter for brief periods and move on, Mr. Washington's long stay at the house makes him far more dependent on the shelter and its resources. At the same time, his six-month stay puts him in the position to be more familiar with the various services for which clients may be eligible. For such a client, who feels he has been the victim of discrimination, this combination of dependency and familiarity with the organizational policies produces a harsh critic. The shelter is eager to be rid of these malcontents. In Mr. Washington and his family's case, their eviction from Abbot House ignited an atmosphere of jubilation. In fact, when I inquired about their whereabouts during my next volunteer shift, I heard one staff member say, "They're gone, yay!"

"This Is Not My Normal Reality"

The third interview was with Dean. I met Dean, a white male in his mid twenties, during one of my graveyard shifts. I was being flooded with client requests and was especially annoyed with the people who wanted wake-up calls ranging from 4:00 to 6:30 a.m. Dean, dressed in jeans and a plaid shirt, silently watched me struggle from his chair in the main lobby. After everyone had gone to bed about 11:00 o'clock or so, he came up to the front desk and without any introductions in a calm voice advised, "You know they're playing you like a three-dollar fiddle?"

I didn't know what to say at first. Although I was impressed by his candidness, I felt that my authority was questioned. I considered my various options for a few seconds and decided to put on my researcher's hat. So I responded with, "Really? I'd be interested in knowing why you think that." He seemed a little surprised that

I was not offended by his comment, but he went on, "These guys will take advantage of anybody who's too nice to them. You have to be firm." He added that as a former police officer he was quite skilled at dealing with "these people." In turn, I disclosed that I found it difficult to juggle my roles as a researcher, a staff member, and a compassionate person and asked if he would be interested in telling me more about himself in a research interview. We began the interview the next morning at the end of my shift.

Amir: How did you end up in this place?
Dean: Well, I, uh, was visiting—I came up here to visit some friends of mine. After I got into town I realized that the friends I came to visit had since moved. So I figured, "Well, what the hell. I'll just hang around here for the night and party and go home the next day." I left this party I was at and walked over to the university. I was just gonna walk around and get some air. And I was wearing this pair of boots that are hard on my feet and I stumbled on this rock in these boots, and the University Police thought that I was drunk and walking—you know, public intoxication. So they stopped me and they were going to arrest me for public intoxication. I tried to explain to them, "I'm not drunk." And when they ran my record, this warrant came up that'd been issued in '93. The warrant was for the failure to comply with a court order, which was given because, when I was arrested in '93 for a speeding violation, the court gave me twenty-five hours of community service, but at the time I didn't live here and so I asked if they could transfer the service hours to where I lived in Jackson County, and they said, "Not a problem." So I did them [community service hours] down there back in '93, and I paid for it back here and whatnot.

But somewhere along the lines the paperwork got lost, and so the court system up here had no record that I ever did anything. So the judge automatically issued the warrant. So it's been sitting up here in this county for two years. I stepped into the county, I ran into a policeman, and they arrested me. And I spent the night in jail, got out the next morning. When I got out, I realized that the person that I'd come up here with had just disappeared with not only my transportation—his car, I mean it was his car— but you know, he had the clothes I had with me and my wallet, the whole nine yards. So my first concern was getting the court thing straightened out. . . . I went to [local county] Court Services, and explained the situation to them, and they said if I can get a hold of the reverend that I did my community service with, have him call to the Court Services and they write it down and everything'll be straightened out. So I went and got all that taken care of, meanwhile I was staying here. I went and got all that taken care of and then, um, I just found out Wednesday—I was supposed to go home yesterday—I found out that they're not going to release me from my bond until the fifth when I see the judge. And basically I have to go in front of her and show her the same slip that I've been showing everybody else, and then she'll say, "Case dismissed." But until then, I'm kind of stuck here in town and I have no money and I have no place to live or anything like that. So I'm staying here. And that's how I ended up here. I'd prefer not being here. I would much rather be home in my nice comfortable house.

In Dean's narrative, his experience with homelessness is presented as an inconvenient mishap, a rupture in the stream of his otherwise conventional life. Consequently, in Dean's story, his current status (i.e., a client at a homeless shelter) is not the result of a gradual process of being cast out of society, or falling through the cracks, instead he tells us he "ended up" at the shelter through an unexpected chain of events: a bizarre mix of accidents and miscommunications.

He goes on to explain that a "nice comfortable house" awaits him in a very near future and that he is kept from home due to bureaucratic errors. Thus, for Dean, the idea of "home" is not a distant, inaccessible reality, but something immediately available and easily envisioned, a point that narratively separates him from other clients. He reflects on the difference between his world and the world of other homeless clients in this "ironic" tale.

> **Amir**: You said that you would get violent [when you got drunk]. Did you hurt people or something?
> **Dean**: Yeah, I was very nasty at one time and, ironically enough, I put a former guest of this place in the hospital. It was an older gentleman and it was back in '89. . . . I was here in town. I had decided I was gonna go for a walk after I was drinking to a point, and then the people who were with me figured the best thing for them to do was to allow me to go but follow me so I don't get myself in too much trouble. So I left the party and was walking up Campus Avenue. And this older gentleman—you could tell he was a homeless person, you know, he was tattered and I had seen him panhandling on the street from time to time— was walking toward me. And normally when you have two people walking on a collision course on the street somebody usually moves to one side. Well, he moved over and just before we were about to pass each other I leaned over a little bit and he bumped up against me. And that was an excuse for me to turn around and start to *beat* on this person. And before my friends realized what was going on, he was laying on the ground with blood all over his face and everything and they pulled me off and I was fighting with them.
> The next morning I woke up, didn't even realize what had happened the night before. And my friend, Dave, woke me up and Dave's eyes was all puffy and whatnot, and I was like, "What happened?" And he's like, "You happened last night. Not only you beat *me* up but you put some guy in the hospital." And so I called over Bethesda Hospital and it turned out the guy . . . was staying here [at Abbot House]. I don't know what he was doing out that night but, um, I broke his jaw, his nose, and cracked three of his ribs in just a matter of less than a minute.
> **Amir**: Were you charged with anything?
> **Dean**: No, I have a rather wealthy father and he managed to smooth things out. See, at the time, we were getting along and I had plenty of money, and I had lots of credit cards . . . and I had three cars, and I was just some little rich college boy. But anyway, I ended up paying for the

guy's medical bills and ended up paying him a thousand dollars and whatnot. But sometimes the irony of things just really overwhelm me. I guess the attitude that I had that night was, "This person is *scum*, he has no place to *live*, he doesn't *do* anything, he has *no* job, he has *no* money. I mean look at the way he's dressed. He lives in a homeless shelter." And I basically assaulted the man for that purpose, and now six years later I'm in that very same homeless shelter, and I'm a resident. I'm not just visiting, I'm staying here. So, in a way that's kind of a little ironic.

Dean's admission of assaulting a homeless man serves as another marker of what sets him apart from others. His confessional account contains narrative linkages to his membership in a world of affluence and privilege, where the homeless are regarded as "scum." The fact that he finds himself in the same homeless shelter as his victim becomes an ironic twist of fate worthy of self-reflection. In this sense, Dean's narrative is less about how he became homeless than about how he is atypical.

We turn to the meaning of homelessness as the interview proceeds.

> **Amir**: So you consider yourself homeless now?
> **Dean**: I don't know. I don't know if I would consider myself homeless. I would consider myself without a place to stay. Because I'm not homeless, I have a home. It happens to be four and half hours away and the courts will not let me go to it. So to me this is kind of like a free hotel. Because I can't afford to pay for a hotel and I don't have anybody here in town anymore that I can stay with.
> **Amir**: What's the difference between not having a place to stay and being homeless?
> **Dean**: Well, I suppose the difference for *me* is that I know on Tuesday I can get on the bus and in a few hours be sleeping in my own bed and opening a closet that has my clothes in it, and my things are all around me and I have a roof over my head, and the electricity is on and you know. I know that this is my home, this is where I live. Where I find that on Tuesday there is a lot of people around here that aren't going to be able to say that. They're *homeless*. You know, eventually they will get a place that they can call their own and sleep in their own bed, but until then they. . . . I don't know, I think in some ways I feel very sad for the people around here 'cause I know that come Tuesday afternoon, you know, when I get on that bus, life for me goes back to normal—this is abnormal for me—life for me goes back to normal. I'm gonna go home and I'm gonna take a shower and get dressed and sit down at my desk and look through my mail, and feed my cat, and maybe go to the pool and lay out by the pool for a while, make a few phone calls, and then Wednesday go back to work. But the people who live here, this *is* their reality, this is their normal, this is what they do everyday. And in a way I guess to me it's saddening, that they don't have the opportunities that I have.

By narratively foregrounding the immediate accessibility of a home and all its comforts (e.g., shower, phone, pet, etc.) Dean elaborates on the theme of how homelessness is "their reality" and not his. In fact, he expresses sorrow for them: "And in a way I guess to me it's saddening, that they don't have the opportunities that I have." Dean's narrative construction of homelessness does not take the fact that he's a resident at a homeless shelter as prima facie evidence that he is indeed homeless. On the contrary, he constructs his presence at the shelter as a brief stay at a "free hotel."

Admittedly, other researchers may be interested in the factual dimensions of Dean's narrative. For example, Snow and Anderson[4] might have conducted an informal investigation and concluded that Dean was using "fictive storytelling" as a way of escaping the stigma of homelessness. Aside from the practical, as well as ethical, complications, such an approach would offer very little in the way of understanding how clients' constructions of homelessness contextualize their dealings with the shelter. In Dean's case, understanding how he sets himself apart from other clients provides a meaningful context for how he comes to see the shelter as a "free hotel," or as he later puts it a "treatment center."

Dean proceeds to elaborate:

> **Amir**: This is *not* you're reality, you're saying?
> **Dean**: No, this is my reality, but it's not my normal reality. This is not the norm for me. You know, when I say, "This is not the normal for me," I'm sure at one time this is not the norm for everybody. But when I say, "This is not the normal for me," this is a *temporary* situation. When I say "temporary," I mean temporary as far as a week. This is going to last for a week, approximately. And in that time it's gonna be over and done with, and I'm gonna be going back to doing what I did before I came here.
> **Amir**: Which is what?
> **Dean**: Taking care of my house and my cat, and going to work, and coming home and getting a paycheck. You know, and trying to restore my car and whatnot. So, this is kind of like—like I said, this is a homeless shelter but I don't really look at it that way. I keep thinking this is like a treatment center. I'm stuck here for a week to "dry out" or whatever, and I'm gonna go back to whatever I did before.
>   And the whole time I was thinking, "I'm here, I'll make the best of it. At the end of the twenty days, I'll go back home, sleep back home, feed my cat, maybe relax by the pool, go back to work, maybe that night go out and have a drink—if I'm in the mood.

Dean emphasizes the transitory nature of his experience with homelessness by drawing a distinction between what he calls "normal reality" versus "a temporary situation." He goes on to establish the contours of his normal reality by listing its features (i.e., the comforts of home). Homelessness in his case is narratively conveyed as a "temporary" state that will soon be resolved when Dean returns "home" where he can "relax by the pool, go back to work, . . . and have a drink," if he's "in the mood."

"We're Not Gonna Get Very Far"

My fifth interview is with Al and his wife, Frannie. They were both in their mid twenties. As a white couple sleeping on the back porch or under a bench in the back lot, they were more conspicuous than other clients, who were mostly black men. Al had a small build and, had it not been for his facial hair, he could easily pass for a teenager. He always wore a baseball hat, which he used to cover his face by simply pulling the visor down. His wife, Frannie, was shorter than Al and somewhat overweight.

When I approached them for the interview, they were both sitting outside the shelter on a bench that also served as their bed. Al was nervously handling a rather large pocket knife, which he conspicuously displayed on the table for the other outside clients to see. His wife seemed more relaxed. With a warm smile, Frannie accepted my request for an interview, while Al simply acknowledged my presence with a side glance from under the rim of his baseball hat.

> **Amir**: Basically you could start [your story] anywhere you like. You know, things about why you're homeless and what you thought about the time you spent here and why you're back out here again and things like that.
>
> **Frannie**: Well, why we're homeless is, um. . . . We originally were, when we first came down to Gainesville we were living with my best friend's family and the trailer got a little bit too crowded. So, me and my husband had to come here [to the shelter]. And that wasn't too bad. Yeah, you know, it really wasn't that bad to stay here [as inside guests]. I mean, what I really didn't like was being questioned why me and my husband—since we were supposed to be homeless—were able to have a TV and a VCR that we had kept in our room and that, basically, [was] the stuff came down from Pennsylvania with us. [After leaving the shelter], I was working at Food Lion and that. And I lost my job there because I had to go up north, up to New York to take care of my sister 'cause she had to get an operation done. And my boss wouldn't hold my job for me. So I basically had to quit my job 'cause I wouldn't have a job to come back to if I had left anyway. And we were renting this one house up on 81st. And that was a verbal agreement for $300 a month and the lady that we were renting it from, Rose something, she went and gave the house back without consulting us to see if we wanted to rent to own it. And so we moved from that house to a house down on, where was it, 42nd Terrace? [*She asks her husband and he nods in agreement.*] Well that house was in such bad shape it was condemned.
>
> **Amir**: Um-hmm.
>
> **Frannie**: And now from what I understand there's already somebody else living in the house that's condemned. . . . So we are like basically back out here till he could find a job, and get back on our feet again. But, anything you want to add in? Did I forget anything? [*She asks her husband, and he responds in the negative by shaking his head without looking at her.*]

Frannie tells the culturally familiar story of homelessness caused by unemployment and lack of stable affordable housing. Her employment was terminated because she had to respond to a family crisis (i.e., her sister needing an operation). These events are narratively linked with the couple's financial demise and provide an explanation for why they are at Abbot House. Later, her husband, Al, joins in to elaborate on their situation.

> **Amir**: What does it take to get help?
> **Al**: To have a child.
> **Frannie**: No, not really, 'cause even when you have a child, you can't get on housing.
> **Al**: With an infant, you can.
> **Frannie**: No.
> **Al**: I've seen more of that than I've seen of anything else.
> **Frannie**: Yeah, but there's a lady who was here back when we were staying inside—that girl with the long brown hair— she had a three-week-old son. They refused her for housing.
> **Al**: I remember her.
> **Frannie**: I mean, I don't really know how to get help around here any more.
> **Al**: Neither do I. They're not—no consideration at all. Even when somebody's trying to look for a job, all they want is experience. And you can't get experience unless you have some kind of training, or something. A guy like me, we're not gonna get very far. I'm not gonna get anywhere.
> **Amir**: Why not?
> **Al**: I don't have the training and the experience that most employers want. Now I'm not going to lie to you, I have a record up in Pennsylvania.
> **Amir**: Um-hm.
> **Al**: But it, it's, you know, it's minor. Something I was, I did when I was younger. You know. But they seem to hold that over your head for the rest of your life. I didn't kill nobody or nothing like that. I just wasn't that . . . but I guess that people like me . . .
> **Amir**: What'd you do?
> **Al**: Uh [*pause*]. It's a long story.
> **Frannie**: It's smoking . . .
> **Al**: Yeah, but . . .
> **Frannie**: He was smoke bombing mailboxes.
> **Al**: That was—well, that was dropped. Uh, the major one that stuck was the, uh, I was accused of "contributing to the delinquency of minors." At the time, I did not know that bottle of rum was in the back of my Volks, my father's car. And I stopped over at a friend's house and there was my brother and two other girls in the back of the car. My brother and his friend went back to the car, got the bottle out, without me knowing it. I didn't know it was there. And the two girls that were under age eighteen got all drunk. And the next day, I had two cops at my door, saying, "You're under arrest for contributing to the delinquency of minors." And my own friend that was supposed to back me on this turned me in. I got accused of it, 'cause I had no witnesses state

I did not know and they cannot appeal this.

Amir: Right.

Al: So, I cannot go into the military or anything like that. That's going to stick with me for the rest of my life. And every time I go for a job that's somewhat decent, they do a search on me. And it always turns up: not hiring.

The tone of desperation in the couple's story is accentuated as they jointly reason through having an infant as a viable method for becoming serviceworthy. In fact, I was later told by the couple that Frannie was indeed carrying a child a few months earlier, but her pregnancy was terminated due to a miscarriage. In particular, Al's account paints a convincing portrait of a man with no hope for the future: "A guy like me—we're not gonna get very far. I'm not gonna get anywhere." His legal problems coupled with his lack of job training and experience are the narrative linkages that help shape his story of a man with no way out. Unlike Dean, who saw his situation as a temporary nuisance, Al sees his condition as something much more permanent. In his words: "That's going to stick with me for the rest of my life. And every time I go for a job that's somewhat decent, they do a search on me. And it always turns up: not hiring."

The interview goes on.

Amir: Are you scared out here?

Al: I'm scared to death of being homeless. I don't like it.

Amir: What about sleeping on the back porch?

Al: I sleep on the back porch. What scares me the most is the fact, you know I'm not racist or anything. But it scares the hell out of me, the fact that there is more colored people . . . and there's like three white people on that porch.

Amir: Do they harass you?

Al: No, they don't harass. You know, I just, it's the fact that there's. . . . I don't know how to say it without sounding racist. It just scares me, you know, because of her. I don't want her to be exposed to this.

Frannie: Hmm.

Al: You know, I don't know what to say. I just . . .

Amir: You ever had a situation back there recently?

Frannie: [*laughs*] In the lunchroom today.

Amir: Really?

Al: In the lunchroom today.

Amir: What happened?

Al: There's this gentleman that, uh, he's out there.

Frannie: Oh he's been harassing me since me and Al first got here.

Al: He's, you know, I don't want to be . . . he, he is gay. I'll say that much he is. And there was an incident last week, I think it was Wednesday, in the shower room, where he just looked at me over the shower stall. And ever since then, I have been watching him like a hawk because I don't like the way he looks at her. I don't like the way he looks at me. And, today in the lunchroom, I was watching him when he went by. And then he started giving me all kinds of hard time. You know, cursing me out. Well he didn't curse, but in his own, their own

language, their jiving or something. And, we just had words. He
threatened me, saying that he's goin' around the back porch and we'll
settle it then. . . . Like a pack of hungry wolves, out there.

Not surprisingly, Al's views of the shelter are similarly pessimistic. Finding
himself where his racial identity has become a liability he voices his fears: "I'm
scared to death of being homeless." While, at first, he links his worries with the
vulnerability of his wife as a white woman (i.e., "It just scares me, you know,
because of her. I don't want her to be exposed to this."), as his story continues, he
confesses that he is equally concerned about his own safety: "I have been watching
him like a hawk because I don't like the way he looks at her. I don't like the way
he looks at me."

But Al's pessimism is somewhat balanced by his wife's cautious hope and
optimism.

> I don't know, there's, there's guys out there that will look out for
> everybody. There's about six, seven of them. I mean really cool guys,
> real nice guys. But then, you always got one or two that are gonna be
> troublemakers, or think they're a, you know, Mr. Billy Bad Butt and all
> tough and everything. There's about two guys out there that are like
> that. But everybody else, you know, they're, they're cool about it. We
> joke around and stuff. I mean it's like, everybody realizes that we're all
> in the same boat. I don't know, it's kind of like, you know, looking out
> for each other. I keep telling him and telling him over and over again,
> I wouldn't care if we're dirt, you know, dirt poor living in a shack with
> 20,000 kids running around me and we don't have two pennies to rub
> together and we've got to scrounge for every penny we get. As long as
> at night I'm laying next to the guy I love than to be married to some-
> body who's got money that they don't even know what to do with and
> can give me everything I want and need on a silver platter and have to
> go to bed with him at night and not love him. And that's basically it.
> When I married him, he had no money. While we're married, we have
> no money, but to me that does not matter. The money is not the biggest
> part of it to me.

Where Al's sense of his homelessness experience is one of despair and
hopelessness, his wife Frannie, manages to retain a relatively positive outlook on
their predicament. While acknowledging Al's concerns about their safety, she
points out the more benevolent side of street life. Furthermore, by drawing on
romantic notions she narratively redefines their current circumstance as one of
togetherness rather than neediness.

"How're They Able to Do That? *I Can't*"

When I first started interviewing clients at Abbot House, I asked my informant,
Dave, if he knew anyone who was interested in talking about his or her experiences
at the shelter and homelessness in general. The last interview analyzed here was

practically scheduled and conducted by Dave. Although I was present during the interview, I felt that given his rapport with the subject and his interest in my project, Dave was better suited for conducting the interview.

The interviewee, Sam, a white male in his forties, had been receiving various services at the shelter for many years, although at the time of the interview he was living in his own apartment and could be seen around the shelter only occasionally during the soup kitchen hours. As we walked across the campus to my department's conference room, where I planned to record the interview, I couldn't help noticing that with his graying hair and reading glasses, Sam looked like an English professor, and Dave and I could have probably passed for his students.

In the conference room, Dave and Sam began their preparations.

> **Sam**: I guess you're gonna ask me how long I've been homeless.
> **Dave**: Yeah.
> **Sam**: Various questions like that.
> **Dave**: Yeah.
> **Sam**: So, you're not gonna take any notes? [*He asks Dave.*]
> **Dave**: No. No.
> **Sam**: Why not actually have a little bit of format, just to prompt people to get them talking about, you know, various things?
> **Dave**: Generally, we've just done a stream-of-conscious thing. [*He turns to me.*] Do you like that, Amir?
> **Amir**: Yeah, I think that works. [*I turn to Sam.*] But, you know, you're not limited to what we ask you. You can go in a direction you want to talk about, whatever you think is relevant.

This interview format was somewhat new to me. By letting Dave take the lead, my hope was to directly introduce "native" concerns into the data collection process, but I soon realized that the so-called native concerns are informed by a cultural literacy not very far removed from my own. As Dave and Sam engaged in this semirehearsal, it became evident to me that my "natives" were not only aware of standard interview protocol but insisted on using it. So with the start of the interview, their speech became more organized and their tones more formal.

> **Dave**: What do you think is the biggest problem facing homeless people today and stuff?
> **Sam**: Oh, mostly the social attitude of people. It seems like we're getting a society that doesn't like . . . I guess they're mostly fed up with the whole homeless issue and the poor people that are out there and stuff.
> **Dave**: Yeah, I've noticed that. It seems like it's been going on for such a long time, they've been talking about it and it's been such a big issue that people seem tired of it now, upset about it.
> **Sam**: One of the things that they see is—they think of some guy sitting on the corner with his bottle of wine, you know, being a real scuzz bag. And in truth there are quite a few dyed-in-the-wool derelicts out there, but there are also a lot of people out on the streets that just because of circumstance have ended up on the street-loss of a job.

The interview begins with echoes of run-of-the-mill assumptions about the homeless. Dave and Sam manage to touch on the entire gamut of issues commonly associated with homelessness in the span of several sentences: from media representations of the problem to the various theories on why people become homeless (structural versus individual). These academic and popular theories of homelessness were soon permeated by Sam's personal history and insight.

> A homeless man will get a job as long as he's able to *endure* emotionally and spiritually at this job, you know. But having money, having a place to live, having food and all that—we think that takes precedence, it *doesn't*. What takes precedence is a person's ability to feel good about what they're doing, or about *who they are*. You know, there are some people who can take a menial job and feel like they are working, but how long can they hold on with just that concept, "Okay, well, I'm working, I'm working." Especially if it's the very job they hate getting up and going to every morning, you know. And that's what the poor people end up with. The jobs that you see at the labor pools are jobs they—*at any price, at any wage*—couldn't get somebody in their own little company to do. They go to little Joe Blow, who's way at the end of the line, and say, "Joe, would you clean up this septic system for us?" He looks at his boss and says, "Man, I *quit* before I do *that*." "Fine, we got guys out here desperate for work." You know the labor pool is able to make money for that reason—"Well, labor pool, we'll pay you eight dollars an hour for every man that you send us, per hour, per man." And they send you out to these really nasty jobs that they couldn't get anybody within their own company to do it, *at any price*.
>
> The thing that society doesn't realize is that they need us. They need the poor because if we are able to stand out there and call our own wage—"I won't work unless you give me X amount of dollars"—then who're they gonna get to do these sloppy little nasty jobs? They'll have no one to do that. It's funny, but society is set up so that the man who's out there breaking his nuts, actually sweating hard at a job, pushing that big, heavy wheelbarrow, working, you know, *working*, goes home tired at the end of the day, he's the one getting the minimum wage. While this other man sitting in the air-conditioned office with his feet propped up, who goes home refreshed every night, and actually has time to go stop by the gym and work out, he's making the big bucks. Society is just set up that way—the man who works the *hardest* makes the *least*.

Sam's story of homelessness is intricately tied to his awareness of "society's" double standards. First and foremost, Sam challenges common perceptions about work and its relationship to poverty. Specifically, he rebels against the idea that material well-being is the first priority in the lives of the homeless: "But having money, having a place to live, having food and all that—we think that takes precedence, it *doesn't*. What takes precedence is a person's ability to feel good about what they're doing, or about *who they are*."

By theorizing about his experiences as a homeless man, Sam's narrative supports the notion that "participants are ethnographers in their own right."[5] Sam is not a "cultural dope."[6] On the contrary, he is actively engaged in constructing and theorizing about his own homeless experience, as indicated in the functionalist statement: "The thing that society doesn't realize is that they need us." The contention that "society" exploits the poor is further evidenced in this declaration: "Society is just set up that way—the man who works the *hardest* makes the *least*."

According to Sam's native theorizing, the term "society" represents a malign version of Mead's *generalized other*, in relation to which the homeless *self* tries to makes sense of his world; it represents a culturally distant *other* whose value contradictions and misplaced priorities make exploitation of the poor possible. Sam, speaking as an outsider, goes on to theorize about his strained relationship with this sense of the generalized other.

> I was on the streets for fifteen years off and on. You know, I'd keep a job for a while and end up on the street again; it was a continuous cycle for me. Uh, society has a way of presuming that everyone within that society are all—have all the same abilities. I ended up on the street because for some reason it's just not my makeup to be able to handle, uh, all these different things at one time. Like someone can hold a budget, take care of this, take care of that, uh, things have to come to me slowly, gradually. I can't keep my head full of a whole bunch of different jobs I've gotta do today; my mind just isn't capable of holding that, capable of assimilating all this information. So I have to take everything very piecemeal, like, "Okay, this is the project I'm gonna take care of, I stay with it till I complete it." Where some people they're able to whistle, dance, and juggle all at the same time. Well, I'm not able to. I can either whistle, I can either dance, or I can either juggle. And do any one of them with a certain amount of efficiency. I look at other people and I am *awed* at people who have really busy schedules—I'm almost at awe with them. I say, "How're they able to do that? *I can't.*" I wish I could because it would make me more progressive. I'd make a lot more money; I'd do a lot better.

Here, awe and envy act as "narrative footings" that give coherence to Sam's story of being an outsider.[7] He is both amazed and bewildered by the pace of modern life and openly confesses his inability to be like the *other*: "I'm almost at awe with them. I say, 'How're they able to do that? *I can't.*'" Sam's horizon of meaning in a sense echos the themes of a postmodern critique of advanced capitalism (i.e., displacement, inherent contradictions of capitalism, and alienation), thus casting homelessness as a form of rebellion against society, as indicated below.

> And there are certain benefits to being poor or homeless. I did, at one time, think that people who had jobs were jerks. "You stupid sucker, you get up everyday and drag yourself to work for a boss who doesn't appreciate you, doing something you don't like doing and then drag your butt home." Saw my dad do it, saw my grandfather do it. You know, I asked my dad, "You like your job?" "Well, it pays the bills." You know, not everybody can get up in the morning and get excited about their jobs, "Wow, I'm going to work today." You know, it doesn't happen.

Clearly, Sam's horizon of meaning is as much informed by rebellion as it is by the realization of his shortcomings. His former contempt for the average working person and his monotonous routines foregrounds Sam's refusal to settle for a life that is void of "excitement." Sam's preoccupation with leading a vivacious and adventurous life is also evident in the following:

> **Sam**: There is a certain romantic adventure to the whole thing. That's one of the things I wanted to do really bad, "I've got to jump a train." I wasn't happy till I jumped a train. But the train was going nowhere. You know what I mean?
> **Dave**: Yeah.
> **Sam**: Nothing advanced in my life. Sure, I've seen a lot of things and stuff. And I thought about this the other night, "If I could change my life, would I?" Uh, now that I'm forty-two years old and I'm in a situation where I've got to slow down, my body just won't let me do the things I did when I was sixteen, seventeen, eighteen, twenty years old, you know, running around and everything. Geez, the stories that I can tell, but that's all they are. The adventures that I've had make great stories, but that's all they mount up to. I can sit down and tell you *fantastic* stories about working down on the oil rigs in the Gulf, climbing halfway down the Grand Canyon to place a few pennies there—which I believe are there *today*—I put them there in 1972, if they haven't corroded away by now. And I did all this because that was my whole thing, I believed that life is made up of adventures. I really was against the idea of sitting down on a regular job, doing the same thing everyday. I wanted to see the world, I wanted to have adventures, I wanted to go places. And one of the greatest things that people used to joke about—friends of mine—you know, a train would go by in the distance and you hear "woo-woo." And they say, "Plug Sam's ears. Plug Sam's ears." And I would hear it, and I'm serious, I'd be sitting out there talking in the woods with my buddies, and we'd be around the camp fire and I'd hear "woo-woo." I jumped up and ran knowing that as long as I was alive, I'm alive. "Well, you left your shoes." "I'll get new shoes. I'm alive." "Well, you left your backpack." "I'll get a new backpack, I'm alive." All I wanted to do was to get on that train and get to wherever it was going, not caring where it was going, but just wanted that adventure of being somewhere else, of seeing something different. And a lot of my life, I look at it now and I say, "Geez, I really had some real adventures."
> **Dave**: So you did find some value in it—in being homeless.
> **Sam**: Yeah, exactly. I enjoyed it, I really did. But I never thought I was gonna live to be forty-two. You know, we think when we're young, we think we're immortal.

The juxtaposition of a life full of stories versus a life without "adventures" serves as another illustration of *difference* in this narrative of homelessness. Once again, Sam vacillates between the "value" of being homeless and the advantages of membership in mainstream society. Anchoring his homelessness in his aging body and his life course in general, he signals his defeat and willingness to accept "society's" conventions.

> Yeah, the thing is, you can tell the kid, "Don't touch that stove, it's hot"—I'm the voice of experience telling him that, *"Don't touch that stove*, it's hot." The dumb kid touches that stove, he even sneaks behind my back to touch it. . . . And it's like that with society. . . . What I think about now is when I turn sixty what kind of burden am I going to be on society? I've got to accomplish something now. I'm a late starter.

We can see here that within the framework of his sense of difference, Sam evaluates the consequences of belonging to either group—homeless versus society. Placing his experiences with homelessness in the broader context of his life course, he foresees the need for reconciling differences and *becoming* like *others*: "What I think about now is when I turn sixty what kind of burden am I going to be on society? I've got to accomplish something now. I'm a late starter." It should not come as a surprise then, given Sam's overall horizon of meaning, that he has a fairly pessimistic outlook on Abbot House and its staff. As indicated below, Sam's understanding of the shelter is organized along the same lines as his general narrative of homelessness. He views the shelter as a place where the clients are taught to be "selfish" and the staff are paid to be "good."

> **Sam:** When you go to Salvation Army—someplace like this—they bring a box of clothes out and they say, "Here's some clothes," and I know on the bottom of this box there's a couple of good pairs of socks. And you happen to need them and you got fifty people diving for this box. Well, you tend to set your "niceness" aside. You tend to say, "I'd better get mine." And you jump in with the crowd. And these places almost—they do unconsciously—but they *teach* people how to be very *selfish*. "There is only enough for the first five people in line." Well, you're gonna push, you're gonna shove, you're gonna to do everything to be one of those first five people in line. . . . Right now we go down to the Abbot House and I can set a box of cookies out there and say, "One cookie for everybody," and have enough cookies for everybody, but I guarantee people're gonna grab five or six cookies.
> **Dave:** What do you think the Abbot House or the Salvation Army does to encourage that?
> **Sam:** Well, just the way they're structured. Just the fact that the first fifty people in line get fed. If you don't push your way to the front of the line, if you don't get into that feeding frenzy attitude, you might miss your meal. So you got to get up there and grab what you can. Uh, one of the problems with places like the Abbot House is that they need to get people working these places who would be doing what they're doing now regardless of whether they're gonna get paid or not. What it all boils down to is that if you have to pay a man to be a good man, if you have to pay someone to be concerned about society, to be concerned about the homeless, to be a good man, that is *not* a good man. Because anybody'll be the way you want 'em to be as long as you're paying them to do so.

Sam ended the interview by telling Dave and me that he thinks of the shelter as a "depressing place" that he tries to avoid as much as possible.

Conclusion

The notion of *horizons of meaning*,[8] as used in this chapter, has two implications for understanding homelessness. First, this concept helps illustrate the variation among the clients' narratives of homelessness. Specifically, we can see that both homelessness and the shelter itself have different meanings for individual clients. In the case of Tony, the young boy from Michigan, leaving home presented new opportunities and the shelter was just a rest spot along the young man's path to something better. For Mr. Washington, on the other hand, race prejudice was the meaning-making frame within which his homelessness was conveyed. Yet, Dean, the former police officer, rejected the very idea that he was homeless, vehemently arguing, "This is not my normal reality." By contrast, Al and Frannie, the couple living outside the shelter, for the most part had surrendered themselves to their predicament. Finally, Sam presented a structurally informed perspective on his life, which was appropriately complex and ambivalent.

Thus, the first implication of applying the concept of horizons of meaning to this group was to show that their stories are not uniformly dictated by their seemingly similar circumstances. Instead, they each have a somewhat different interpretation of being a homeless client. In other words, looking at the clients' horizons of meaning enables us to make sense of the homeless experience in a larger context of the client's life narrative, as opposed as to a biographically isolated event in a person's life course.

The second advantage of using horizons of meaning here is that it shifts the focus away from the ethnomethodologically impossible task of validating clients' accounts against an "objective" reference point. Rather, the goal is to examine the nuances of their narratives and understand the method of their production. In Gubrium's words, the horizons-of-meaning approach enables us to "be faithful to folk experience."[9] Accordingly, the interest here was not so much whether Sam, Dean, or any other client was telling "the truth," but how they made sense of, and communicated, the substance of their world.

Notes

1. Jaber F. Gubrium, *Speaking of Life: Horizons of Meaning for Nursing Home Residents* (Hawthorne, N.Y.: Aldine de Gruyter, 1993).

2. Eliot Liebow, *Tell Them Who I Am: The Lives of Homeless Women* (New York: Free Press, 1993); David A. Snow and Leon Anderson, *Down on Their Luck: A Study of Homeless Street People* (Berkeley, Calif.: University of California Press, 1993).

3. Jaber F. Gubrium and James A. Holstein, "Narrative Practice and the Coherence of Personal Stories," *Sociological Quarterly* 39 (1998): 163-87.

4. David A. Snow and Leon Anderson, "Identity Work among the Homeless: The Verbal Construction and Avowal of Personal Identities," *American Journal of Sociology* 92 (1987): 1336-71.

5. Jaber F. Gubrium and James Holstein, "Biographical Work and New Ethnography," in *The Narrative Study of Lives*, vol. 3, ed. Amia Lieblich and Ruthelen Joseselon (Newbury Park, Calif.: Sage, 1995), 45-58.

6. Harold Garfinkel, *Studies in Ethnomethodology* (Englewood Cliffs, N.J.: Prentice Hall, 1967).

7. Gubrium and Holstein, "Narrative Practice."

8. Gubrium, *Speaking of Life*.

9. Jaber F. Gubrium, *Analyzing Field Reality* (Newbury Park, Calif.: Sage, 1988).

Conclusion

The Lessons of Narrativity

When I first started studying homelessness, I was overwhelmed by the wealth of research on the topic. "Where should I begin, and what can I say that has not already been said?" I asked myself repeatedly. However, as I became more involved in my fieldwork, I realized that it was equally important to ask: How does the existing body of knowledge lend itself to the everyday practices that constitute the reality of homelessness in and around Abbot House?

My field observations pointed to the fact that the shelter clients and their service providers artfully, and purposefully, produced the category of homelessness using a wide range of descriptive resources. These observations were consistent with what Gubrium and Holstein[1] refer to as "interpretive practice." As they put it: "In the course of their everyday life, individuals adroitly construct selves using locally available and meaningful materials shaped to the specifications and demands of the interpretive task at hand."[2]

In fact, this description became the blueprint for my project, shifting my analytical focus from an attempt to augment the academic discourse on the profile of "the homeless" to investigating how this academic discourse is *used* and reproduced in everyday life. In an ethnomethodological sense, this project brackets[3] the taken-for-granted aspects of homelessness to understand the methods of its production. As a point of illustration, consider how homelessness is rhetorically constructed in the following excerpt from a television program aired on the Public Broadcasting System in 1994.

> I think there is an overriding point to realize here, and that is unlike the conversation of ten years ago we are arguing here about how sick the homeless are, not whether they are just like you and me. And we are not talking about some Hollywood couple who were in a fine house with a picket fence and suddenly the world fell apart and they were on the street and we should all shudder because we could all be in that condition. What we are talking about now is the nuances of data. We should realize that the political discourse ought to catch up. That is to say, we ought to realize that homeless people have vast needs and they are not just like the rest of us.

In this passage, Douglas Besharov, a panel member on this program, which incidentally was titled "The Think Tank," does not just describe the condition in question but actively sets a new "discourse" for its study as he calls for the political discourse to "catch up." Similarly, another research endeavor constructs the problem in this way:

> Only when policy makers and their constituents accept the truth—that somewhere between 65 and 85 percent of the homeless population suffer from serious chronic alcoholism, addiction to drugs, severe chronic psychiatric disorders, or some combination of the three—will our society be able to develop programs and services that have any real potential for helping these most unfortunate Americans break the degrading cycle of homelessness.[4]

Rather than accepting such positions as taken-for-granted starting points for analysis, this research has attempted to show how these and other related accounts construct a statistical profile used by homeless clients and service providers to establish serviceworthiness.[5] That is, the social significance of homelessness is constructed through academic and literary texts as well as through everyday practices of human service organizations.

In terms of the textual construction of homelessness, the overarching theme is that while the factual nature of current information on the characteristics of the homeless population is of great importance to policy makers and practitioners, equal importance must be placed on the way in which this information is *used* to construct a profile of the problem population for various practical purposes. Thus, objective validity can be considered alongside "practical validity," as Garfinkel[6] would suggest. The academic discourse on homelessness cannot be judged solely in terms of how accurately it portrays the "truth" about the condition of being without a permanent residence; its significance in everyday life is tested in terms of its everyday utility: the more useful the findings, the greater their practical validity.

Studying homelessness in relation to practical experience also implies sensitivity to how that experience is conditioned and articulated in various settings. For the purpose of this project, the setting is Abbot House. Its practitioners, the clients and the staff, in the course of their interactions constitute the reality of being homeless. This constitutive activity was perused from three standpoints. First, I showed how the staff, through various policies and discourses, narratively articulate their image of a serviceworthy client, giving support to the notion that the client profiles are organizationally embedded.[7] Second, the interactive dynamics of client work was foregrounded to suggest that the production of a homeless client at this site is not a unidimensional enterprise, and that clients are actively involved in the process through narrative practice.[8] Finally, clients' accounts of being homeless were analyzed to show how they view the shelter based on the particulars of their own life course and positions in society, or what Gubrium[9] would refer to as their "horizons of meaning."

The attention to the place of homelessness in the context of a client's life course can form the basis for a future longitudinal study where potential shifts in the meaning of being homeless can be studied over a period of time. In particular, this may enable researchers and interested practitioners to devise prevention and treatment programs that meet the demands of specific subsets of the homeless population.

Notes

1. Jaber F. Gubrium and James Holstein, "Individual Agency, the Ordinary, and Postmodern Life," *The Sociological Quarterly* 36 (1994): 555-70.

2. Gubrium and Holstein, "Individual Agency," 557.

3. Harold Garfinkel, *Studies in Ethnomethodology* (Englewood Cliffs, N.J.: Prentice Hall, 1967).

4. Alice Baum and Donald W. Burnes, *A Nation in Denial: The Truth about Homelessness* (Boulder, Colo.: Westview, 1993), 29.

5. William J. Spencer, "Homeless in River City: Client Work in Human Service Encounters," in *Perspectives on Social Problems*, vol. 6, ed. J. Holstein and G. Miller (Greenwich, Conn.: JAI Press, 1994), 29-46.

6. Garfinkel, *Studies in Ethnomethodology*.

7. Jaber F. Gubrium, *Out of Control: Family Therapy and Domestic Disorder* (Newbury Park, Calif.: Sage, 1992); Jaber F. Gubrium and James Holstein, "Analyzing Interpretive Practice," in *Handbook of Qualitative Research*, 2d, ed. N. Denzin and Y. S. Lincoln(Thousand Oaks, Calif.: Sage, 2000), 487-508.

8. Jaber F. Gubrium and James A. Holstein, "Narrative Practice and the Coherence of Personal Stories," *Sociological Quarterly* 39 (1998): 163-87.

9. Jaber F. Gubrium, *Speaking of Life: Horizons of Meaning for Nursing Home Residents* (Hawthorne, N.Y.: Aldine de Gruyter, 1993).

Selected Bibliography

Adler, Patricia A., and Peter Adler. *Membership Roles in Field Research*. Newbury Park, Calif.: Sage, 1987.

Anderson, Nels. *The Hobo: The Sociology of Homeless Men*. Chicago: University of Chicago Press, 1923.

———. *The Milk and Honey Route: A Handbook for Hobos*. New York: Vanguard, 1931.

Atkinson, Paul. *Understanding Ethnographic Texts*. Newbury Park, Calif.: Sage, 1992.

Axelson, Leland J., and P. W. Dail. "The Changing Character of Homelessness in the United States." *Family Relations* 37 (1998): 463-69.

Baum, Alice S., and Donald W. Burnes. *A Nation in Denial: The Truth about Homelessness*. Boulder, Colo.: Westview, 1993.

Becker, Howard S. *Outsiders: Studies in the Sociology of Deviance*. New York: Free Press, 1963.

Bernard, Thomas J. *The Cycle of Juvenile Justice*. New York: Oxford University Press, 1992.

Beson, Paul. *Anthropology and Literature*. Urbana: University of Illinois Press, 1993.

Blasi, Gary L. "Social Policy and Social Science Research on Homelessness." *Journal of Social Issues* 46. no. 4 (1990): 207-19.

Blumer, Herbert. "Social Problems as Collective Behavior." *Social Problems* 18 (1971): 298-306.

Breakey, William R., and Pamela J. Fischer. "Homelessness: The Extent of the Problem." *Journal of Social Issues* 46, no. 4 (1990): 31-47.

Bruns, Robert A. *Knights of the Road: A Hobo History*. New York: Methuen, 1980.

Buckholdt, David R., and Jaber F. Gubrium. *Caretakers: Treating Emotionally Disturbed Children*. New York: University Press of America, 1985.

Bunis, William K. , A. Yank, and D. Snow. "The Cultural Patterns of Sympathy toward the Homeless and Other Victims of Misfortune." *Social Problems* 43, no. 4 (1996): 387-402.

Burt, Martha R. 1995. "Critical Factors in Counting the Homeless: An Invited Commentary." *American' Journal of Orthopsychiatry* 65, no. 3 (1995): 334-39.

Burt, Martha R., and Barbara E. Cohen. "A Sociodemographic Profile of the Service-Using Homeless: Findings from a National Survey." In *Homelessness in the United State*. Vol. 2, *Data and Issues*. Ed. J. Momeni. New York: Greenwood, 1989.

Census Bureau. "Census Bureau Releases 1990 Decennial Counts for Persons Enumerated in Emergency Shelters and Observed on the Streets" (press release). U.S. Department of Commerce News. Cited in R. B. Sraw, "Looking behind the Numbers in Counting the Homeless: An Invited Commentary." *American Journal of Orthopsychiatry* 65, no. 3 (1991): 330-33.

Clifford, James. "Introduction: Partial Truths." In *Writing Culture: The Poetics and Politics of Ethnography*. Ed. J. Clifford and G. E. Marcus. Berkeley: University of California Press, 1986.

Clifford, James, and George E. Marcus, eds. *Writing Culture: The Poetics and Politics of Ethnography*. Berkeley: University of California Press, 1986.

Conrad, Peter, and J. W. Schneider. *Deviance and Medicalization*. St. Louis: Mosby, 1980.

Currie, P. L. "Crimes without Criminals: Witchcraft and Its Control in Renaissance Europe." *Law Society Review* 3 (1968): 7-32.

Denzin, Norman K. *Images of Postmodern Society*. London: Sage, 1991.

Deutsch, Albert. *The Mentally Ill in America: A History of Their Care and Treatment from Colonial Times*. New York: Columbia University Press, 1945.

Dordick, Gwendolyn A. *Something Left to Lose: Personal Relations and Survival among New York's Homeless*. Philadelphia: Temple University Press, 1998.

Dreier, Peter, and John Atlas. 1989. "Grassroots Strategies for Housing Crisis: A National Agenda." *Social Policy* 19, no 3 (1989): 25-38.

Dreyfus, Hubert L., and Paul Rabinow. *Michele Foucault: Beyond Structuralism and Hermeneutics*. Chicago: The University of Chicago Press, 1982.

Durham, Mary L. "The Impact of Deinstitutionalization on the Current Treatment of the Mentally Ill." *International Journal of Law and Psychiatry* 12 (1989): 117-31.

Ellis, Carolyn, and Michael G. Flaherty. *Investigating Subjectivity: Research on Lived Experience*. Newbury Park, Calif.: Sage, 1992.

Erickson, Kai T. *Wayward Puritans*. New York: Wiley, 1966.

Fagan, Ronald W. "Homelessness in America: Causes, Consequences and Solutions." *Journal of Interdisciplinary Studies* 7, no. 1-2 (1995): 101-18.

French, Laurence. "Victimization of the Mentally Ill: An Unintended Consequence of Deinstitutionalization." *Social Work* (Nov-Dec 1987), 502-5.

Foucault, Michel. *The Archaeology of Knowledge*. New York: Pantheon, 1972.

———. *The Birth of the Clinic*. New York: Vintage, 1975.

———. *The History of Sexuality*. New York: Vintage, 1978.

———. *Discipline & Punish: The Birth of the Prison*. New York: Vintage, 1979.

———. *Power/Knowledge*. New York: Pantheon, 1980.

Fox, Nicholas J. *Postmodernism, Sociology, and Health*. Buckingham, United Kingdom: Open University Press, 1993.

Fuller, Torrey E. "Thirty Years of Shame: The Scandalous Neglect of the Mentally Ill Homeless." *Policy Review* (Spring 1989), 10-15.

Garfinkel, Harold. *Studies in Ethnomethodology.* Englewood Cliffs, N.J.: Prentice Hall, 1967.

Giamo, Benedict. *On the Bowery: Confronting Homelessness in American Society.* Iowa City, Iowa: University of Iowa Press, 1989.

Goffman, Erving. *The Presentation of Self in Everyday Life.* Garden City, N.Y.: Doubleday, 1959.

Grob, Gerald N. *Mental Illness and American Society, 1875-1940.* Princeton, N.J.: Princeton University Press, 1983.

Gronfein, William. 1985. "Psychotropic Drugs and the Origins of Deinstitutionalization." *Social Problems* 32 (1985): 425-36.

Gubrium, Jaber F. *Analyzing Field Reality.* Newbury Park, Calif.: Sage, 1988.

———. *Out of Control: Family Therapy and Domestic Disorder.* Newbury Park, Calif.: Sage, 1992.

———. *Speaking of Life: Horizons of Meaning for Nursing Home Residents.* Hawthorne, N.Y.: Aldine de Gruyter, 1993.

Gubrium, Jaber F., and James Holstein. *What Is Family?* Mountain View, Calif.: Mayfield, 1990.

———. "Individual Agency, the Ordinary, and Postmodern Life." *The Sociological Quarterly* 36 (1994): 555-70.

———. "Biographical Work and New Ethnography." In *The Narrative Study of Lives,* vol. 3. Ed. Amia Lieblich and Ruthelen Josselon. Newbury Park, Calif.: Sage, 1995.

———. *The New Language of Qualitative Method.* New York: Oxford University Press, 1997.

———. "Narrative Practice and the Coherence of Personal Stories." *Sociological Quarterly* 39 (1998): 163-87.

———. *Institutional Selves: Troubled Identities in a Postmodern World.* New York: Oxford University Press, 2000.

———. "Analyzing Interpretive Practice." In *Handbook of Qualitative Research,* 2d. Ed. N. Denzin and Y. S. Lincoln. Thousand Oaks, Calif.: Sage, 2000.

Heritage, John. *Garfinkel and Ethnomethodology.* Cambridge: Polity, 1984.

Hesse, Hermann. *Hermann Hesse: Poems Selected and Translated by James Wright.* New York: Noonday, 1970.

Hoch, Charles, and R. A. Slayton. *New Homeless and Old: Community and the Skid Row Hotel.* Philadelphia: Temple University Press, 1989.

Hochschild, Arlie Russell. *The Managed Heart.* Berkeley: University of California Press, 1983.

Holstein, James. "Producing People: Descriptive Practice in Human Service Work." *Current Research on Occupations and Professions* 6 (1992): 23-39.

Holstein, James, and Miller, Gale. "Social Constructionism and Social Work." In *Constructionist Controversies.* Ed. G. Miller and J. Holstein. Hawthorne, N.Y.: Aldine De Gruyter, 1993.

Holstein, James A., and Jaber Gubrium. "Phenomenology, Ethnomethodology, and Interpretive Practice." In *Handbook of Qualitative Research*. Ed. N. Denzin and Y. S. Lincoln. Thousand Oaks, Calif.: Sage, 1994.

———. *The Active Interview*. Thousand Oaks, Calif.: Sage, 1995.

———. *The Self We Live By: Narrative Identity in a Postmodern World*. New York: Oxford University Press, 2000.

Hopper, Kim. "Definitional Quandaries and Other Hazards in Counting the Homeless: An Invited Commentary." *American Journal of Orthopsychiatry* 65, no. 3 (1995): 340-46.

Hooks, Bell. *Black Looks: Race and Representation*. Boston, Mass.: South End Press, 1992.

Horwitz, Richard P. "Just Stories of Ethnographic Authority." In *When They Read What We Write: The Politics of Ethnography*. Ed. C. Bretell. London: Bergin & Garvey, 1993.

Jahiel, Rene I. "The Situation of Homelessness." In *The Homeless in Contemporary Society*. Ed. R. D. Bingham, R. E. Green, S. B. White. Newbury Park, Calif.: Sage, 1985.

Jahiel, Rene I. "The Definition and Significance of Homelessness in the United States." In *Homelessness: A Prevention-oriented Approach*. Ed. R. I. Jahiel. Baltimore, Md.: The Johns Hopkins University Press, 1992.

Jencks, Christopher. *The Homeless*. Cambridge: Harvard University Press, 1994.

Kitsuse, John I. "Societal Reaction to Deviant Behavior: Problems of Theory and Method." *Social Problems* 9 (1962): 247-56.

Koegel, Paul. "Understanding Homelessness: An Ethnographic Approach." In *Homelessness: A Prevention-oriented Approach*. Ed. R. I. Jahiel. Baltimore, Md.: The Johns Hopkins University Press, 1992.

Koegel, Paul, and M. Audrey Barnum. "Problems in the Assessment of Mental Illness among the Homeless." In *Homelessness: A National Perspective*. Ed. M. Robertson and M. Greenblatt. New York: Plenum, 1992.

Kollock, Peter, Philip Blumstein, and Pepper Schwartz. "Sex and Power in Interaction: Conversational Privileges and Duties." *American Sociological Review* 50 (1985): 34-46.

Kuhn, Thomas S. *The Structure of Scientific Revolutions*. Chicago: University of Chicago Press, 1962.

Lee, Barrett A., D. W. Lewis, and S. H. Jones. "Are the Homeless to Blame? A Test of Two Theories." *The Sociological Quarterly* 33, no. 4 (1992): 535-52.

Liebow, Eliot. *Tell Them Who I Am: The Lives of Homeless Women*. New York: Free Press, 1993.

Levingston, Leon Ray. *Hobo-Camp-Fire-Tales*. Cambridge Springs, Pa.: A-No.1, 1991.

London, Jack. *The Road*. New York: Macmillan, 1907.

———. *The People of the Abyss*. New York: Archer House, 1963.

Loseke, Donileen R. "Creating Clients: Social Problems Work in a Shelter for Battered Women." In *Perspectives on Social Problems*, vol. 1. Ed. J. Holstein and G. Miller. Greenwich, Conn.: JAI Press, 1989.

———. *The Battered Woman and Shelters*. Albany: State University of New York Press, 1992.

———. "Writing Rights: The 'Homeless Mentally Ill' and Involuntary Hospitalization." In *Images of Issues: Typifying Contemporary Social Problems*. Ed. J. Best. Hawthorne, N.Y.: Aldine De Gruyter, 1995.

Lyotard, Jean-Francios. *The Postmodern Condition*. Minneapolis: University of Minnesota Press, 1979.

Macionis, John. *Sociology*. Englewood Cliffs, N.J.: Prentice Hall, 1999.

Marvasti, Amir. "'Homelessness' as Narrative Redemption." In *Perspectives on Social Problems*, vol. 10. Ed. J. Holstein and G. Miller. Greenwich, Conn.: JAI, 1998.

McChesney, Kay Y. "Family Homelessness: A Systematic Problem." *Journal of Social Issues* 46, no. 4 (1990): 191-205.

Mechanic, David, and Rochefort, David A. "Deinstitutionalization: An Appraisal of Reform." *Annual Review of Sociology* 16 (1990): 301-27.

Momeni, Jamshid, ed. *Homelessness in the United States*. Vol. 2, *Data and Issues*. New York: Greenwood, 1989.

Orwell, George. *Down and Out in Paris and London*. San Diego: Harcourt Brace, 1933.

Reinarman, Craig, and Harry Gene Levine. "Crack in Context: Politics and Media in the Making of a Drug Scare." *Contemporary Drug Problems* 16 (1989): 535-77.

Ronai, Carol R. "Multiple Reflections of Child Sex Abuse: An Argument for a Layered Account." *Journal of Contemporary Ethnography* 23 (1995): 395-426.

Rosenau, Pauline. *Post-Modernism and the Social Sciences: Insights, Inroads, and Intrusions*. Princeton, N.J.: Princeton University Press, 1992.

Rothman, David J. *The Discovery of Asylum*. Boston: Little, Brown, 1971.

Ruddick, Susan M. *Young and Homeless in Hollywood: Mapping Social Identities*. New York: Routledge, 1996.

Said, Edward W. *Orientalism*. New York: Pantheon, 1978.

Salo, Matt T., and Pamela C. Campanelli. "Ethnographic Methods in the Development of Census Procedures for Enumerating the Homeless." *Urban Anthropology* 20, no. 2 (1991): 127-39.

Schutt, Russell K., and Gerald Garrett. *Responding to the Homeless: Policy and Practice*. New York: Plenum Press, 1992.

———. "The Homeless Alcoholic: Past and Present." In *Homelessness: A National Perspective*. Ed. M Robertson and M. Greenblatt. New York: Plenum, 1992.

Scull, A. *Decarceration: Community Treatment and the Deviant—A Radical View*. New Brunswick, N.J.: Rutgers University Press, 1984.

Shinn, Marybeth, and Beth C. Weitzman. "Research on Homelessness: An Introduction." *Journal of Social Issues* 46, no. 4 (1990): 1-11.

Shlay, Anne B., and P. H. Rossi." Social Science Research and Contemporary Studies of Homelessness." *Annual Review of Sociology* 18 (1992): 129-60.

Snow, David A., and Leon Anderson. "Identity Work among the Homeless: The Verbal Construction and Avowal of Personal Identities." *American Journal of Sociology* 92 (1987): 1336-71.

————. *Down on Their Luck: A Study of Homeless Street People*. Berkeley, Calif.: University of California Press, 1993.

Solenberger, Alice W. *One Thousand Homeless Men: A Study of Original Records*. New York: Charities Publication, 1911.

Sosin, Michael, Irving Piliavin, and Herb Westerfelt. "Toward a Longitudinal Analysis of Homelessness." *Journal of Social Issues* 46, no. 4 (1990): 157-74.

Spencer, J. William. "Homeless in River City: Client Work in Human Service Encounters." In *Perspectives on Social Problems*, vol. 6. Ed. J. Holstein and G. Miller. Greenwich, Conn.: JAI Press, 1994.

Sraw, Roger B. "Looking Behind the Numbers in Counting the Homeless: An Invited Commentary." *American Journal of Orthopsychiatry* 65, no. 3 (1995): 330-33.

Sutton, John R. "The Political Economy of Madness: The Expansion of Asylum in Progressive America." *American Sociological Review* 56 (1991): 665-78.

Tierney, Brian. *Medieval Poor Law: A Sketch of Canonical Theory and Its Application in England*. Berkeley: University of California Press, 1959.

Torrey, Fuller E. *Nowhere to Go: The Tragic Odyssey of the Homeless Mentally Ill*. New York: Harper and Row, 1988.

Wagner, David. *Checkerboard Square: Culture and Resistance in a Homeless Community*. Boulder, Colo.: Westview, 1993.

Wegner, Eldon L. "Deinstitutionalization and Community-based Treatment for the Chronic Mentally Ill." *Research in Community and Mental Health* 6 (1990): 295-324.

Wright, James D. *Address Unknown: The Homeless in America*. Hawthorne, N.Y.: Aldine de Gruyter, 1989.

————. "Poor People, Poor Health: The Health Status of the Homeless." *Journal of Social Issues* 46 (1990): 49-64.

————. "Housing Dynamics of the Homeless: Implications for a Count." *American Journal of Orthopsychiatry* 65, no. 3 (1995): 320-29.

Wright, Talmadge. *Out of Place: Homeless Mobilizations, Subcities, and Contested Landscapes*. Albany: State University of New York Press, 1997.

Index

About the Author

Amir Marvasti is a visiting assistant professor of sociology at Penn State Altoona. His research interests include deviance, race and ethnicity, and social psychology. His work has been published in *Qualitative Inquiry* and *Journal of Contemporary Ethnography*. He is currently working on a book on the immigration experiences of Middle Eastern Americans. He holds a Ph.D. and an M.A. in sociology from the University of Florida in Gainesville, Florida, as well as a B.S. in psychology from the same institution.